D1519804

Explaining Consumer Choice

Also by Gordon R. Foxall

CONSUMER BEHAVIOUR: A PRACTICAL GUIDE

MARKETING BEHAVIOUR

STRATEGIC MARKETING MANAGEMENT

CONSUMER CHOICE

INNOVATION: MARKETING AND STRATEGY

ADVERTISING POLICY AND PRACTICE (*with John Driver*)

MARKETING IN THE SERVICE INDUSTRIES

CONSUMER PSYCHOLOGY FOR MARKETING (*with Ronald Goldsmith and Stephen Brown*)

CONSUMERS IN CONTEXT: THE BPM RESEARCH PROGRAM

MARKETING PSYCHOLOGY: THE PARADIGM IN THE WINGS

CONSUMER BEHAVIOUR ANALYSIS: CRITICAL PERSPECTIVES IN BUSINESS AND MANAGEMENT

CONTEXT AND COGNITION: INTERPRETING COMPLEX BEHAVIOR

UNDERSTANDING CONSUMER CHOICE

Explaining Consumer Choice

Gordon R. Foxall

© Gordon R. Foxall 2007

All rights reserved. No reproduction, copy or transmission of this publication may be made without written permission.

No paragraph of this publication may be reproduced, copied or transmitted save with written permission or in accordance with the provisions of the Copyright, Designs and Patents Act 1988, or under the terms of any licence permitting limited copying issued by the Copyright Licensing Agency, 90 Tottenham Court Road, London W1T 4LP.

Any person who does any unauthorized act in relation to this publication may be liable to criminal prosecution and civil claims for damages.

The author has asserted his right to be identified as the author of this work in accordance with the Copyright, Designs and Patents Act 1988.

First published 2007 by
PALGRAVE MACMILLAN
Houndmills, Basingstoke, Hampshire RG21 6XS and
175 Fifth Avenue, New York, N. Y. 10010
Companies and representatives throughout the world

PALGRAVE MACMILLAN is the global academic imprint of the Palgrave Macmillan division of St. Martin's Press, LLC and of Palgrave Macmillan Ltd. Macmillan® is a registered trademark in the United States, United Kingdom and other countries. Palgrave is a registered trademark in the European Union and other countries.

ISBN-13: 978–1–4039–9862–0   hardback
ISBN-10: 1–4039–9862–0   hardback

This book is printed on paper suitable for recycling and made from fully managed and sustained forest sources. Logging, pulping and manufacturing processes are expected to conform to the environmental regulations of the country of origin.

A catalogue record for this book is available from the British Library.

A catalogue record for this book is available from the Library of Congress.

10   9   8   7   6   5   4   3   2   1
16   15   14   13   12   11   10   09   08   07

Printed and bound in Great Britain by
Antony Rowe Ltd, Chippenham and Eastbourne

UNIVERSITY OF
TORONTO AT
MISSISSAUGA
LIBRARY

*To Victoria James, Jorge Oliveira-Castro, Teresa Schrezenmaier,
Valdimar Sigurdsson, and Mirella Yani-de-Soriano*

Contents

List of Figures, Tables and Exhibits

Figures

Tables

Exhibits

Preface

This is the latest in a series of monographs which propose a framework for the explanation of complex human behavior such as purchase and consumption. This interdisciplinary task is primarily an exercise in theoretical economic psychology and, as such, it draws also upon aspects of behavioral economics, philosophy and biology that are relevant to the quest for a more unified theory of consumer choice. In *Context and Cognition: Interpreting Complex Behavior* (Foxall, 2004), I derived a system of explanation founded upon a critique of both behavioral and intentional psychologies. The argument led to the conclusion that a strictly behaviorist, descriptive or extensional behavioral science, while essential to the prediction and possibly the control of choice, was inadequate to the job of explaining such aspects of behavior as its continuity and its experience at the personal level. Intentional terms, referring to desires and beliefs, must be incorporated within a behavioral science that could achieve these requirements of theory. Two levels of the necessary contextual – intentional theory were put forward: *intentional behaviorism,* in which the basic requirements of a theory of complex behavior are proposed in the absence of ontological conjectures with respect to cognitive mechanisms; and *super-personal cognitive psychology,* in which an attempt is made to specify the functions of a cognitive system that would be consistent with observed patterns of behavior and the evolutionarily-consistent neuroscience that underlies them.

Understanding Consumer Choice (Foxall, 2005) took this development further by applying it to patterns of purchase and consumption uncovered by the empirical research program, consumer behavior analysis (described more fully by Foxall, Oliveira-Castro, James and Schrezenmaier, 2007). The aim was to show how the kinds of contextual – intentional psychology proposed elucidate consumer choice in affluent, marketing-oriented economies and to demonstrate the relevance of the more abstract theoretical developments made in *Context and Cognition* to the more concrete world of everyday consumer decision making. (Most of the papers reporting empirical work in the behavioral economics of consumer choice have been gathered into a companion volume: Foxall, Oliveira-Castro, James and Schrezenmaier, 2007).

The present volume, *Explaining Consumer Choice*, takes this progression further by examining in greater depth the philosophical assumptions that underlay the theories of contextual – intentional influence on consumer choice proposed in the earlier books. Although some familiarity with those works may be useful, *Explaining Consumer Choice* is intended to stand alone for those who encounter the subject for the first time at this level. It introduces new perspective to the quest for an understanding of consumer choice: the various schools of behavioral economics that have provided explanations of consumer behavior, especially in its extreme forms like compulsion and addiction. The import of matching analysis for consumer research lies in its demonstration of the tendency of humans to choose smaller but soon rewards (SSRs) over larger but later rewards (LLRs), to maximize current options but not to optimize overall returns as rational choice theory predicts. This process, known as melioration (Herrnstein, 1997), contains an inbuilt drive toward addiction, and its treatment by the three intellectual giants of behavioral economics – Herrnstein, Rachlin (2000a) and Ainslie (2001) – throws light not only on the components of a theory of such extreme consumer choice but of the everyday choices inherent in the selection and consumption of products and brands. I identify the systems of explanation advanced by these authors with extensional behavioral science, intentional behaviorism, and super-personal cognitive psychology respectively, and argue that a comprehensive account of consumer choice must incorporate all three.

The focus of the book is the theoretical and empirical researches that make up the consumer behavior analysis program. This has two aspects: the assessment of the theoretical adequacy of the framework that has guided much of the program, the Behavioral Perspective Model (BPM), and the explanation of the results which our applied research has revealed. These operations call upon a wider disciplinary base than has hitherto been the case: in addition to the economic psychology that underlays the entire research process, it has become natural to extend the task of explanation into cognate areas of biology and philosophy. In addition, the work of behavioral economists such as Herrnstein, Rachlin, and Ainslie has become more central. First, it helps clarify the more philosophical departures which the process of social scientific explanation necessitates; these in turn elucidate the nature of the behavioral economic theories these authors have proposed. Second, it brings the inescapably abstract nature of the philosophical discussions down to the level of real consumer behavior. The main spheres of consumer choice on to which these theoretical deliberations are brought to bear are, nevertheless, the empirical findings of the consumer behavior analysis program.

An increasingly important issue for this research program is the demonstration that the proposed models and the explanations they propose as essential to the explanation of consumer choice are consistent with considerations that arise from evolutionary reasoning. The fundamental biologically-based implications of an explanation of complex human behavior which arise at the neurophysiological level must be consonant with natural selection (Dennett, 1969); in addition, patterns of human behavior must be shown to be consonant with the selection of responses according to their environmental consequences (van Parijs, 1981); these analyses suffice for what I have called intentional behaviorism. But the higher levels of theory demand other strands of explanatory content that draw more deeply upon biological and anthropological considerations. It is necessary to demonstrate, for instance, the links between the systems that reward and punish behavior and the neurophysiological mechanisms and processes that are correlated with them; and it is also important to ensure that the behaviors which one is seeking to explain by reference to biological and cultural means are themselves consistent with evolutionary considerations. Especially in a system of explanation in which the ascription of intentional terms is so central is it incumbent upon one to seek these links.

Gordon Foxall
Penarth
25 December 2006

Acknowledgments

I am grateful to members of the CBAR Group for their discussion of these ideas over several years, notably to those to whom the volume is dedicated, who must feel they have lived with this book longer than I have! I am grateful to all of these for reading part or all of earlier drafts as well as Michael Kirton and Tony Ellson.

Vicky James and Jorge Oliveira-Castro devised the revised summation of the Behavioral Perspective Model shown in Figure 1.1. Figure 2.1 is reproduced with gratitude from http://www.training.seer.cancer. gov; funded by the U.S. National Cancer Institute's Surveillance, Epidemiology and End Results (SEER) Program, via contract number N01-CN-67006, with Emory University, Atlanta SEER Cancer Registry, Atlanta, Georgia, U.S.A. Permission to reproduce Figures 9.1, 9.2 and 9.3 was kindly given by Dr. George Ainslie. Figure 9.4 is reproduced by kind permission of Dr. Paul Kenyon, School of Psychology, Plymouth University. Figure 9.5 is reproduced from Phillips, H., Just can't get enough, *New Scientist*, 26 August 2006, p. 33.

I have reproduced some material from my papers, "Explaining consumer choice: Coming to Terms with Intentionality", and "Intentional behaviorism", for which I thank the publishers of *Behavioural Processes* and *Behavior and Philosophy* respectively.

Part I
Foundations

1
Consumer Behavior Analysis

Now, when we attempt to describe and to understand developments of this kind in a general way, we are, of course, obliged to appeal to the existing forms of speech which do not take them into account and which must be distorted, misused, beaten into new patterns in order to fit unforeseen situations (*without a constant misuse of language there can not be any discovery, any progress*). (Feyerabend, 1975, p. 27, emphasis added.)

Academic marketing takes much for granted, largely because it is not a discipline in its own right, but an application area that relies on the perspectives, theories, methodologies, and techniques provided by disciplines such as economics and psychology. At a theoretical level, it generally incorporates rather than creates. As a result, it frequently makes philosophical and methodological assumptions that stem directly from the deliberations of other scientists pursuing other ends. Whatever discipline forms the predominant underlying intellectual basis of marketing science at the moment – it was once economics, has been and continues to be economic psychology, but sociology and anthropology have had their days too – tends to provide a philosophical and theoretical foundation of a sort, ad hoc and temporary but sufficient unto the day. There may not be an easy alternative to this, given the nature of marketing inquiry, but it raises certain difficulties of explanation. For the methodological imperatives imported into marketing are, inevitably, not constructs that are in some way absolutely characteristic of the discipline involved but only those that are currently acceptable to the exponents of that discipline or a subdisciplinary section of it. Disciplines and their imperatives change; in the social sciences, methodologies are coeval. Feyerabend's dictum to the effect that "without a constant misuse of language there can not be any discovery, any progress" is a subtle reminder of the ambiguities involved in social and behavioral research. It is a warning, perhaps, but certainly it is an invitation.

While the deliberate misuse of language is inimical to scientific inquiry, the active consideration of alternative modes of expression, metaphor and nuance, even a conscious seeking for ambiguity in the terminology one uses, can all be critical to the quest for explanation. And all of these are likely to increase through the multidisciplinary attempt to understand and explain marketing phenomena; especially, perhaps, by the competition of *intra*disciplinary methodologies. Because the understanding of consumer behavior is fundamental to that of marketing itself, because the theory of the marketing firm cannot be pursued in the absence of a preexisting theory of consumer choice, the series of monographs, of which this is the latest, has concentrated particularly upon the philosophy and methodology of *consumer behavior analysis* as the basis for a comprehensive marketing theory. The intense excitement generated by this intellectual journey stems directly from this juxtaposing of alternative explanations. Consumer research presents an enthralling opportunity to pursue this kind of inquiry because the predominant means of explanation, cognitive psychology, albeit the leading paradigm within psychology itself, is not the only psychological perspective that illumines marketing behavior. However cognitive and behaviorist paradigms, for instance, may separately enhance our understanding of consumer choice, their interaction may do more as they force us to consider alternative hypotheses, means of testing them, methods of data collection and analysis, and a range rather than a monolith of theoretical viewpoints entering into their explanation. For science sometimes progresses not by a clash of competing theories in which one eventually wins out by achieving a consensus within the intellectual community, but by the acceptance of a superordinate framework of conceptualization and analysis into which hitherto conflicting explanations can be harmoniously accommodated. Each may retain its unique perspective while finding a place in a broader matrix where its conflict with other approaches is minimized while the overall enterprise enhances the growth of knowledge. I should like to propose such a framework for the role of behavioral science in the explanation of consumer choice in natural settings. It is that broader theoretical matrix that is the focus of this volume.

In pursuing these themes, we are taking some terms and constructs that can be very precisely defined in the context of the laboratory and using them to interpret everyday life. Moreover, the very interdisciplinarity of our work, while it is a constant source of inspiration and encouragement, calls for a framework of interpretation as a central means of analysis. You do not have to be a firm believer in the indeterminacy of translation to work out that this sometimes means construing those terms and constructs somewhat less precisely than would the experimental scientist. Nor is it always possible to use words in a multidisciplinary context with the exactness they command in their originating field of study. The results we get are the fruits by which we judge the constructs, necessarily tailored to the sphere of reality with which we dealing, by which we generate them. Feyerabend's point is a good one: perhaps progress lies this way.

In answer to the question what is an explanation? I offer no more than a broad response. In Boden's (1972, p. 32) words, "At this point, it is convenient to regard an 'explanation' as any answer to a why question that is accepted by the questioner as making the event in question somehow more intelligible. A 'scientific explanation' may be defined as an explanation that is justified by reference to publicly observable facts, and which is rationally linked to other, similar explanations in a reasonably systematic manner." In seeking a scientific explanation, I am not trying to provide criteria that might establish by verification or falsification whether a particular hypothesis or proposition should be accepted or rejected. Rather, I understand the actual behavior of scientists to be that of classifying evidence as supporting or not supporting a hypothesis or proposition. There is no question of ultimately rejecting a hypothesis, as long as it is devised within the usual canon of scientific practice and derived from a generally accepted theoretical framework of conceptualization and analysis, any more than there is of enthroning such a hypothesis on the basis of its empirical correspondence as a truth of science. What is not supported today may be established tomorrow as new evidence is adduced or may suggest new lines of inquiry that would otherwise be overlooked. Our aim is not to say what causes what in any final, deterministic sense, let alone how; it is to identify what legitimates the use in science of a particular kind of explanatory language. Hence, Chapters 2–6 seek a "framework of exposition," a way of talking about the explanation of consumer choice rather than a definitive theory thereof.

The aim, therefore, is not to propose a single theory or philosophy that does all the work of explanation but to point to some of the considerations that must be taken into account in the formulation and testing of such theories and philosophies. The original aim of the research program remains, with the result that the following pages are addressed to behavior analysts as well as economic psychologists and marketing scientists. If the book sometimes seems to be addressing the concerns of one of these groups to the exclusion of the others, that is a necessary consequence of inter-disciplinary work. But it brings a great bonus, for it is only by understanding the intellectual concerns of other groups with a claim on our subject matter that we learn fully the nature and implications of our own.

Consumer behavior analysis

Consumer behavior analysis is concerned with the extent to which a radical behaviorist account of consumer behavior is feasible and useful, and the epistemological status of such a model of choice (Foxall, 1994b). The associated research program has involved the generation of a philosophy of behavior analysis in consumer behavior, a model of consumer behavior, a means of interpreting complex consumer choices, and an empirical agenda that has resulted in a body of know-ledge about consumer behavior that is novel. *Understanding Consumer Choice* (Foxall, 2005) presented a summary of that empirical work and of recent theoretical and philosophical developments. The present book takes the theoretical and philosophical implications of the empir-ical results further by considering the ways in which they might be interpreted beyond the confines of a strictly radical behaviorist approach but still within the framework of a contextual psychology.

Consumer behavior analysis draws upon behavioral psychology and behavioral economics to further understanding of the nature of con-sumer choice in the context of the contemporary marketing-oriented economy (Foxall, 2002a). It originated as an attempt to demarcate the limits of radical behaviorism as a means of explaining consumer behavior and contributing to marketing theory. As a result, although it majored in the feasible contribution of this school of psychology to consumer and marketing research, it was never confined to it. The purpose of the research program was to determine at what point, if any, the simple models of behavior with which the adherents of radical behaviorism were content would break down as explanations of consumer choice and require augmentation by other schools of inquiry.

The resulting research program initially took the form of a critique of the conventional wisdom by which consumer behavior was explained in the context of marketing study, indicating for instance how notions of attitudinal – behavioral consistency, generally and somewhat uncritically accepted within that realm, might be subjected to critical examination and supplemented or replaced by alternative explanations (Foxall, 1983). This process was subsequently extended to areas of research such as consumer innovativeness (Foxall, 1987), and the program entered a fruitful phase with the development of the Behavioral Perspective Model (BPM) of consumer choice (Foxall, 1990/2004) which permitted the behavioral interpretation of purchase and consumption, saving and domestic financial management, innovative consumer choice, "green" consumer behavior, and of marketing management (Foxall, 1994a, b, 1995, 1996, 1998). This model also led to the first empirical research in consumer behavior analysis, a continuing project which is concerned with the prediction of consumers' verbal behavior with respect to their emotional reactions to environments of purchase and consumption (Foxall, 1995, 1997a, 1999; Foxall and Greenley, 1998, 1999, 2000; Foxall and Yani-de-Soriano, 2005; Soriano and Foxall, 2001, 2002; Yani-de-Soriano and Foxall, 2006). Further empirical work has been concerned with the extent to which the methodology of behavioral economics can be employed to elucidate patterns of consumer choice (Foxall and James, 2001, 2003; Foxall and Schrezenmaier, 2003; Foxall, Oliveira-Castro and Schrezenmaier, 2004; Oliveira-Castro, Foxall and Schrezenmaier, 2004, 2005, 2006). It has also proved possible to extend the interpretation of consumer behavior through the employment of the model (Foxall, James, Oliveira-Castro and Chang, 2006), and to develop the theoretical and philosophical bases of the research program. It is with these developments that this book is principally concerned.

Without any attempt at theorization beyond that of establishing empirical generalizations, we can say that most consumers of a product category are multi-brand purchasers, penetration levels for brands within a product category are remarkably similar, differences in market share account for the commercial differences among such brands, and so on. These are results that have been established by Ehrenberg (e.g., 1972/1988) and his colleagues for numerous consumer goods markets in several countries, over decades. Subsequent work within the consumer behavior analysis framework has shown measures of brand performance to be predictable and stable with respect to environmental stimuli. With the basic theoretical goal of identifying the stimulus conditions that enable the prediction of behavior, our research shows that: consumer brand choice is described by the matching law; consumers tend to face downward sloping demand curves, and show maximization in their brand choices; consumers who purchase a specific combination of utilitarian (functional) and informational (symbolic) rewards differ from purchasers of other combinations in terms of the elasticity of demand shown by their purchases; consumer behavior varies with the scope of the current behavior setting; relatively open settings (those in which several behavioral choices are available to the consumer) evoke longer time periods and more money spent in the setting, and stronger verbal reports of dominance than closed settings (where typically only one behavior is available; consumers' attitudes and behavior are highly inconsistent in the absence of situational correspondence in the measurement of these variables.

These analyses enable us to predict consumer behavior and identify the factors that control it. But is there anything more to be said about how we are to *explain* the findings? Is there a level of theory that would take us beyond the identification of controlling stimulus conditions? These are questions that behaviorists have heard many times, and I agree that identifying the environmental determinants of behavior is *an* explanation thereof, one that fits the requirements of Machian positivism and that is therefore generally sufficient for the goals of behavior analysis – prediction and control.

The behavioral perspective model

In line with the stated goal of consumer behavior analysis of testing radical behaviorism to destruction as a means of explaining consumer behavior, early empirical work has been conducted within the framework of this extensional behavioral science. The variables employed in empirical studies derive from a general model of consumer behavior designed to capture the essential components of the three-term contingency of radical behaviorism as it applies to economic behavior: the Behavioral Perspective Model (BPM) which is summarized in Figure 1.1.

The BPM relates patterns of consumer choice to their differing environmental consequences. Detailed accounts of the derivation and application of the model are available (Foxall, 1990, 1992a, 1992b, 1992c, 1993a). The following is, therefore, only a summary. There are three kinds of effective consequence of consumer behavior. Utilitarian reinforcement derives from the satisfaction produced by buying, owning, and consuming economic goods. Informational reinforcement is provided by feedback on the consumer's performance, especially the social status produced by conspicuous consumption. Aversive conse-

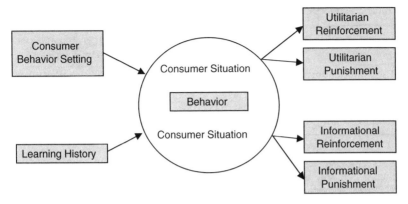

Figure 1.1 Summative Behavioral Perspective Model

quences are the costs of consuming: relinquishing money, waiting in line, forgoing alternative products, etc.

The antecedent events that set the scene for consumer behavior form the behavior setting. This consists of all the physical, social, and temporal elements that signal the likely consequences of behaving in a particular way. Behavior settings facilitate or inhibit consumer movement and choice and form a continuum from the most open (where consumers are positively reinforced, free to choose their behavior) to the most closed (where agencies other than the consumer largely determine the pattern of pre-purchase, purchase and consumption behaviors). The consumer is represented in two ways: their learning history is the cumulative effect of rewarding and punishing outcomes of past behavior; it represents the personal factors influencing consumer choice and primes the consumer's approach/avoidance responses; and state variables, moods, ability to pay, deprivation, influence momentary purchase and consumption, etc.

Four broad classes of consumer behavior can be inferred from the pattern of high/low utilitarian and informational reinforcement that maintains them (Table 1.1). *Maintenance* consists of activities necessary for the consumer's physical survival and welfare (e.g. food) and the fulfillment of the minimal obligations entailed in membership of a social system (e.g. paying taxes). *Accumulation* includes the consumer behaviors involved in certain kinds of saving, collecting, and installment buying. *Hedonism* includes such activities as the consumption of popular entertainment. Finally, *Accomplishment* is consumer behavior reflecting social and economic achievement: acquisition and conspicuous

Table 1.1   Operant Classes of Consumer Behavior

	High utilitarian reinforcement	*Low utilitarian reinforcement*
High informational reinforcement	ACCOMPLISHMENT	ACCUMULATION
Low informational reinforcement	HEDONISM	MAINTENANCE

consumption of status goods, displaying products and services that signal personal attainment. Both types of reinforcer figure in the maintenance of each of the four classes, though to differing extents.

Adding in the scope of the current behavior setting, leads to the eight-fold way depicted in Table 1.2 which shows the variety of contingency categories that exclusively constitute a functional analysis of consumer behavior. This theoretical development has inspired not only the empirical research described briefly below but a means of interpreting familiar aspects of consumer behavior such as saving and purchasing, the adoption and diffusion of innovations, and "green" consumption.

Brand and product choices

Comparatively few consumers seem amenable to the recommendations of marketing textbooks. While many of these tomes exhort managers

Table 1.2   The BPM Contingency Matrix (CC = contingency category)

	BEHAVIOR SETTING SCOPE		
	Closed ⬅——————➤ *Open*		
ACCOMPLISHMENT	Fulfillment	*CC2*	Status consumption	*CC1*
HEDONISM	Inescapable entertainment	*CC4*	Popular entertainment	*CC3*
ACCUMULATION	Token-based consumption	*CC6*	Saving and collecting	*CC5*
MAINTENANCE	Mandatory consumption	*CC8*	Routine purchasing	*CC7*

to ensure the loyalty of their customers and assume that buyers tend to explore the entire array of brands on the market, the consumers themselves staunchly practice multi-brand purchasing within a small repertoire of available brands. This repertoire or "consideration set" is composed of tried and tested brands which the consumer knows well through purchase and consumption, a mere subset of the full range of brands within the product category. Each brand of course attracts its quota of "sole purchasers," those who are totally loyal to it, but the majority of consumers select seemingly randomly within their consideration set, sampling several competing versions of the product in the course of a succession of shopping trips.

A customer who purchases a new brand within an established product category is likely to be already a substantial user of the product, someone who is well-versed in the requirements consumers have and the capacity of existing brands to fulfill them. At best, the new brand consumer initially *tries* the new version. If the brand meets the expectations of the consumer, that is, if it performs at least as well as other members of the product category, it might be included in her repertoire, something that guarantees nothing other than that it is likely to be chosen again at some future time. Most new consumer goods fail at this point, but some go on to be repeat-purchased sufficiently often that they meet their revenue and profit targets and are retained within the firm's portfolio as well as enough consumers' repertoires.

Although work in this tradition has described patterns of consumer choice, it has not, except in a few cases, been concerned to establish the determinants of the observed patterns in terms of price and non-price marketing mix variables. True, some of the research has documented the effects of price promotions on brand purchases, but there has been little systematic analysis of the effects of small differences in price on routine weekly or monthly brand selections. Nor has there been any discussion in this literature of the goals of consumers, their tendencies to maximize or satisfice, for instance, or the underlying motives that propel consumer decision-making. Equally importantly, the analysis of aggregate patterns of consumer choice has rested on certain assumptions which, while plausible, have not been supported by systematic empirical evidence. It has been presumed, quite reasonably but without other than face validity, that brands within a product category are functional substitutes for one another. Developments in behavioral psychology and experimental economics have provided the means to overcome these difficulties.

The experimental analysis of behavior has demonstrated that choice and consumption in the confined context of the operant chamber adhere to the laws of neoclassical microeconomics (Kagel, 1988; Kagel et al., 1995). Moreover, the extension of behavioral economic methods to the more complex situations of human consumption through applied behavior analyses of more open settings – such as token economies, therapeutic communities, environmental conservation programs, and the purchasing of familiar consumer products in simulated shopping malls – has indicated the robustness of this methodology as a general approach to economic analysis. The recent findings that, even in the relatively open settings of the modern marketing-oriented supermarket, consumer choice also conforms to the patterns established by behavior analysis and behavioral economics has revealed the possibilities of consumer behavior analysis as a means of both extending operant psychology into new areas of human endeavor and enriching that analysis through the absorption of results that are neither apparent nor predictable from prior work in behavioral economics be it with humans or non-humans.

Patterns of demand

Traditional behavior analysis has employed the idea of a schedule of reinforcement as a principal component of the contingencies that control behavior. In interpreting the realms of human behavior that lie beyond the laboratory, however, it is often impossible to assign schedules of reinforcement with any hope of precision. It may be that much of the complex human behavior that is the subject of such interpretation cannot be understood in these terms. A more appropriate means of categorizing the environmental contingencies that impinge on and shape complex choice is called for. Recent theoretical work in this domain has proposed that the contingencies in terms of which complex choice is to be understood have two sources: the functional or technical reinforcement that is common to both human and non-human animal behavior (that which is "contingency-shaped" in the words of Skinner's pioneering article) plus the symbolic depiction of reinforcement that provides performance feedback (that which is verbal, indeed "rule-governed" in Skinner's terms). We have styled these *utilitarian* and *symbolic* reinforcements, respectively.

Instead of the notion of schedule of reinforcement as embodying the relevant contingencies, it is vital to the intelligible interpretation of complex human behavior to move to the idea of the *pattern of reinforcement* as embodied in the combination of utilitarian and symbolic reinforcements that correlates with a persistent sequence of behavior. The pattern of reinforcement has proved especially useful in elucidating the behavior of consumers whose purchases have been reinforced by various combinations of utilitarian and symbolic reinforcement: for example, each group of such consumers in our sample showed behavior that was marked by a distinct elasticity of demand (Foxall et al., 2004; Oliveira-Castro, Foxall and Schrezenmaier, 2005, 2006; Oliveira-Castro, Ferreira, Foxall and Schrezenmaier, 2005).

An extensional behavioral science such as radical behaviorism is sufficient to account for the incidence of these behaviors, to predict them and perhaps control them (or at least to identify the factors that control them). All of the behaviors listed in the first two columns of Figure 9.2 can be described sufficiently by radical behaviorism, behavioral economics, the BPM. If we are content to call a statement of how behaviors are related to their environmental correlates an explanation, then clearly a radical behaviorist account can explain to the extent that it permits the prediction and control of such behaviors in similar environments. However, if we wish to explain these behaviors further, if we seek answers to "why" questions that allow us to understand how the personal level is necessary to account for behavioral continuity and change, why behavior persists or is modified as environmental contingencies alter, and how sure we can be that our broader interpretations are consonant with an operant methodology, we require intentional behaviorism and cognitive psychology, particularly as exemplified in teleological behaviorism and picoeconomics.

Before proceeding to those explanations, however, two additional strands of research which also figure in the consumer behavior analysis research program and have produced results that are important to the overall pattern of findings and their explanation in terms of these three theoretical stances need to be briefly noted. These strands are, first, consumers verbal and affective responses to consumer situations and, second, the quest for attitudinal – behavioral consistency in consumer choice. Both of these were considered at length in *Understanding Consumer Choice* (Foxall, 2005).

Consumers' verbal and affective responses

Another way in which complex consumer behavior can be better interpreted by the idea of the pattern of reinforcement than in terms of schedule effects is apparent from work on the verbal and emotional responses to consumer situations. In this research, consumers evinced a unique pattern of affective responses in terms of pleasure, arousal and dominance for each of the eight possible "contingency categories" composed of varying levels of utilitarian and symbolic reinforcement, and the relative openness or closedness of the consumer behavior setting (Foxall, 1995, 1997; Foxall and Greenley, 1998, 1999, 2000; Foxall and Yani-de-Soriano, 2005; Yani-de-Soriano and Foxall, 2001, 2002, 2006). The results were discussed at some length in *Understanding Consumer Choice* (Foxall, 2005) but can be briefly summarized here. It was hypothesized that each of the basic emotional responses to environments posited by Mehrabian and Russell (1974) would be uniquely associated with a particular structural element of the consumer situation: pleasure with utilitarian reinforcement; arousal with informational reinforcement, and dominance with the openness of the consumer behavior setting. The findings corroborate this: verbal responses that refer to the experience of pleasure are significantly related to situations defined in terms of utilitarian reinforcement; verbal responses that refer to the experience of arousal are significantly related to situations defined in terms of informational reinforcement; and verbal responses that refer to the experience of dominance are significantly related to situations defined in terms of openness. Moreover, approach behavior increases with higher levels of utilitarian reinforcement and informational reinforcement and is highest where high levels of both are combined (Accomplishment) and lowest for combinations of low levels of both (Maintenance). The cross-cultural validity of these results – projects were executed in England and Venezuela, the latter in Spanish – suggest a robust methodology. Table 1.3 summarizes the expected and actual results. Where an emotional response is in upper case it is relatively higher than when it is in lower case.

Attitudinal–behavioral consistency

When psychologists measure "attitudes," they are actually measuring behavior, generally verbal behavior, and using it to predict other, generally non-attitudinal, behavior. Despite the success of attitude psychology over the last two or three decades, its findings substantiate a behavioral rather than a cognitive model of human action. Recent research on attitude-behavior relationships supports this in two ways. First, attitude research has sought to make measures of attitude, intention and behavior far more situation-specific than has traditionally been the case. As a result of the emphasis on such tight situational correspondence among the measures it employs, attitude research has

Table 1.3 Results of the PAD Research

| | BEHAVIOR SETTING SCOPE | |
	Closed ◄————————► Open	
	CC2	CC1
ACCOMPLISHMENT	PLEASURE AROUSAL dominance	PLEASURE AROUSAL DOMINANCE
	CC4	CC3
HEDONISM	PLEASURE arousal dominance	PLEASURE arousal DOMINANCE
	CC6	CC5
ACCUMULATION	pleasure AROUSAL dominance	pleasure AROUSAL DOMINANCE
	CC8	CC7
MAINTENANCE	pleasure arousal dominance	pleasure arousal DOMINANCE

actually pointed up the situational or contextual determinants of behavior rather than having shown that behavior is caused (or is most accurately predicted) by cognitive precursors. Second, attitude researchers increasingly measure respondents' behavioral histories in order to predict their behavior. The variable most predictive of current and future behavior is past behavior in similar contexts. However, because of the fixed adherence of the investigators to the social cognitive metatheory, the findings are cast in the language of information processing. The challenge for attitude researchers is to appreciate the environmental influences responsible for both the verbal and nonverbal responses and for any continuity between them. The need is not for a paradigm shift, of the kind documented by Kuhn, so much as an "active interplay of competing theories" as advocated by Feyerabend.

Behavior analysts have surmised that behavior is rule-governed only on its initial emission; thereafter, it comes under contingency control. The analysis undertaken in this paper suggests a more elongated process. At first the consumer has no specific learning history with respect to the consumption behavior in question. Perhaps presented with a new brand in a new product class, there is no accumulated experience or knowledge of buying and using the item and the consequences of doing so.

However, in proportion to the consumer's having a learning history for rule-following, other-rules may be sought out for guidance and action. These might take the form of the advertising claims which first created awareness of the innovation; alternatively, they might come significantly from others, acquaintances and opinion leaders. Whatever their source, these rules are not passively accepted by the consumer but used as the basis of a sequence of deliberation and evaluation, first of the claims themselves, and their comparison with similar claims for other products and brands, then of accumulated consumption experience. The consumer's actions involved in the trial and repeat purchase/consumption of the product develops a learning history. Moreover, reasoning with respect to personal experience of the item, and the evaluation of this experience, will lead to the formation of self-rules which henceforth guide action without constant deliberation. The consumer has moved from the central route to the peripheral, from deliberation to spontaneity, from systematic reasoning to the application of heuristics. The initial lack of a relevant learning history prompted a search for other-rules; the acquisition of such a history means that self-rules can be extracted from experience. Only the acquisition of such an extensive history can transform the behavior finally from rule-governed to contingency-shaped and even then the distinction between self-rule governance and contingency shaping is not empirically available. The import of this analysis lies not in its reiterating the sequence of consumer decision-making found in cognitive models of initial and subsequent information processing but in its capacity to account for these phenomena without extensive reliance on theoretical entities posited at a metabehavioral level.

Interpreting consumer behavior

Broad patterns of consumer behavior are amenable to interpretation in terms of the BPM, as witness the following accounts of consumers' saving and wealth management, adoption of innovations, and environmental conservation attest.

Saving and wealth management

In everyday consumer behavior conflict arises principally between purchasing and saving, something that needs to be phrased carefully. Rather than speaking of immediate or delayed gratification, we must think in terms of immediate or delayed spending, imminent or delayed consumption. "Imminent" permits not only immediate consumption (e.g., of a restaurant meal) and consumption that is slightly delayed to fit into the consumer's usual consumption pattern: buying this breakfast cereal now for consumption in the course of the next seven days. Even this represents a kind of saving insofar as consumption is planned and set out over a period of time. Storing goods for a world catastrophe (as some stocked food for the "Y2K" disaster of fond memory, or as people stock up with basic commodities against a rainy day) involves an extended timeline during which consumption is put off. Saving by definition requires delayed consumption in some form or other which can be classified in terms of how the accumulated funds or wealth are eventually disposed of. Several authors have identified categories of saving behavior and shown their significance in consumer psychology (Wärneryd, 1989a). Katona (1975), for instance, defines several kinds of saving: *contractual* (e.g. regular payments of life insurance premiums), *discretionary* (e.g. saving for a planned vacation), and *residual* (e.g. holding money in a current account against irregular expenditures). Lindqvist (1981) goes further by proposing a hierarchy based on four sequential motives for saving: *cash management*, the most frequent motive, arising from the need to synchronize unpredictable payments and cash availability, *buffer saving*, a reserve of funds to meet unforeseen emergencies and their financial consequences, *goal-directed saving* – for a better car or home, etc., and *wealth management*, the creation and deployment of wealth in order to achieve more with the assets at one's disposal.

A BPM analysis of saving at the extensional level avoids motives and goals as explanatory constructs and seeks to relate observed patterns of savings behavior to the contingencies likely to maintain them. (For more detailed consideration, see Foxall, 1994). At early stages of the consumer life cycle, saving is related to Maintenance. In open settings, such cash management consists of residual saving, cash held in current accounts for the purpose of harmonizing receipts and expenditures, saving by default. In closed settings, it takes the form of contractual saving, payments made for credit, insurance, pensions schemes, and so on. In both cases, it is likely to be predominantly contingency-shaped rather than rule-governed. The consumer comes directly into contact with the environmental factors that maintain these behaviors and, although some rules may affect specific choices (e.g., regulating the payment of premiums in contractual saving), the behavior is, for the most part, determined by its direct effects.

Additional income is likely to be saved for purposes of Accumulation, i.e. with a view to gaining consumer durables, a better home, and so on. In open settings, it takes the form of a basic kind of discretionary saving, saving as a buffer against future misfortune (Katona, 1975; Lindqvist, 1981; Wärneryd, 1989a). This implies formal saving, the regular putting aside of funds into an account which attracts interest. In closed settings, the saving is of a token-economy kind. It consists of accumulating tokens (perhaps though the purchase of products which confer bonuses in the form of additional products – as in frequent customer programs that confer additional air tickets or free gifts – or by a commitment to saving regularly which, when adhered to, provides a higher rate of interest) which give access to other products or prizes which provide mainly utilitarian reinforcement. In both open and closed settings, initially at least, other-rules of a specific nature are likely to influence consumer behavior; such rules specify, for instance, the rate of interest, the number of times a saving act needs to be repeated in order to earn benefits. Tracking is the consumer's likely verbal behavior as he or she follows instructions to: 'Do this and that will follow'; to initiate and sustain early saving, however, some plying and augmentals may be necessary. The actual contingencies are likely to assume an important effect as regular saving is maintained by the addition of interest or other benefits.

Further gains in income and/or wealth are likely to lead to saving which will eventually facilitate higher levels of discretionary spending, perhaps on more luxurious items. In open settings, this could mean saving related to pleasure and fun: saving for vacations, luxuries, entertainment equipment such a video recorders, camcorders, and the like. In closed settings, it would refer to dutiful saving, as for school fees for one's children, for instance. The benefits of such saving are long deferred and rules are necessary to instigate and sustain this behavior; the contingencies are likely to assume greater control as saving plans mature, enabling spending, which motivates further long-term saving. Both of these are discretionary saving in Katona's terms, though of a more affluent nature than that which was described as Accumulative saving. This is what Lindqvist (1981) refers to as goal-oriented saving (see Wahlund and Wärneryd, 1987). The final stage is Accomplishment, which manifests in personal asset management, the use of wealth to create more wealth (Lindqvist, 1981; Wärneryd, 1989b). In open settings, this wealth management takes the form of speculation for gain and in closed setting as the management of investments. Rules play an important part in both cases: self-rules in speculative investment, and advice from others, such as brokers, in the context of investment management. Tracks and augmentals are likely to be particularly important.

The BPM approach does not simply redescribe the categories developed in other systems but relates patterns of consumer behavior with respect to saving and asset management to the changing patterns of contingencies likely to be operative at different stages in the consumer life cycle. However, it might be objected that, while the interpretation appears plausible, and at least indicates that a behavior analytical account of some specialized aspects of consumer behavior is feasible, it proceeds largely in terms of two components of the model. These are the scope of the behavior setting defined primarily in terms of the nature of the physical and social surroundings in which purchase and consumption occur, and the nature of the pattern of reinforcement apparently maintaining the chosen exemplar behaviors. An interpretative account of a broader sequence of consumer behavior is needed, if we are to adjudge the usefulness of the remaining variables in the model, particularly the role of consumers' verbal behavior. An appropriate sequence is that provided by the adoption and diffusion of innovations. Consideration of the sequence of consumer behaviors that occur over the product-market life cycle permits the extension of the applicability of the model in two ways. First, it allows assessment of the explanatory status of the setting and consequential variables that have not yet been covered, namely effects of consumers' verbal behavior on their non-verbal responses, and the distinction between utilitarian and informational reinforcement. Secondly, it demonstrates the capacity of the model to account not simply for a sequence of consumer behavior within the context of an individual's economic experience but for an entire sequences of consumption responses involving diverse consumer groups and occurring within a broad social and economic context.

The adoption and diffusion of new products

In place of the usual depiction of consumer decision-making for new products, brands, ideas and practices in terms of a sequence of cognitive effects (Rogers, 2003), the operant classes of consumer behavior defined in terms of the BPM have been used to suggest a process of adoption based on the changing patterns of reinforcement made available in the course of the product life cycle by the marketing and socioeconomic environment. Since this interpretation is described in Chapter 11, further discussion is deferred until that point.

Environmental conservation

The spoliation of the physical environment is the result of consumer behaviors that are influenced by their consequences, in fact, the pattern of reinforcement that defines the behavior in question as accomplishment, hedonism, accumulation, or maintenance (Table 1.4). Each of the major areas of behavior analytical research in this field – the pollution and depletion of fossil fuels caused by private transportation, the similar depletion and pollution caused by domestic energy consumption, the wanton disposal of the products of consumption leading to landfill problems, and the usage of a scarce naturally occurring resource, water – corresponds to one of these classes of operant consumer behavior. The problem of private transportation is one of accumulation: the behavior is maintained by high levels of both utilitarian reinforcement (such as the fun of driving, comfort, flexibility, and the control of one's journey) and informational reinforcement (speed, low and flexible journey times) and can, therefore, be categorized as accomplishment. A successful demarketing strategy would need to replace this pattern of consequences with one equally motivat-

Table 1.4 Types of Environmental Spoliation Defined by Pattern of Reinforcement

	Utilitarian	*Informational*	*Aversive*
Private transportation	Control, Privacy, quiet, speed, fun, safety, protection	Travel time reduction, cargo capacity, predictability, status	Traffic congestion, stress, costs of purchase, maintenance
Bus-riding/Public transport	Social contact, healthiness, reading opportunity	Cost savings, fitness, pro-social	Slowness, fares, exposure, crowds inflexibility, lack of control
Domestic energy use	Comfort, convenience	Status, level of warmth	Charges
Waste Disposal	Ease of disposal	Conspicuous consumption, prestige, social status approval	Social disapproval, loss of aesthetic benefits
Domestic Water use	Satisfaction, ease, cleanliness, hygiene	Status, prevention of Disease, social approval	Taxes, charges, rationing, pricing, metering

ing (e.g., in the provision of public transportation). Domestic energy usage is based on consequences which include convenience and comfort, and so are generally maintained by high levels of utilitarian reinforcement. Its over-consumption is thus a problem of hedonism. While informational reinforcement (or feedback) is less obvious, it may be important in social situations where visitors are also affected by usage. In recent research, both incentives and feedback have been used alone and in combination to reduce domestic energy consumption with an indication that incentives have the largest effect (cf. Hayes and Cone, 1977; Foxall, Oliveira-Castro, James, Yani-de-Soriano and Sigurdsson, 2006). Waste disposal is classed as accumulation but the problem is actually manifested in the opposite of accumulation: disposal. Indiscriminate waste disposal has relatively few utilitarian reinforcers other than convenience, but its informational outcomes are extensive if subtle. It confers status through the assumption that someone else will clear up, and it may also imply conspicuous consumption. Intervention may take the form of increasing informational reinforcement by linking the individual's attempts at recycling or saving resources and feeding this information back to them. In the case of domestic water consumption (classed as maintenance) both utilitarian and informational reinforcers are low, compared to the other class of consumer behavior but are not absent. They are related to the consumer's state of deprivation, as domestic water consumption allows us to drink, clean and wash which are basic human needs. Due to the low levels of both reinforcers it may be the case that the most successful intervention strategy might be punishment. The utilitarian and informational positive consequences are not strongly motivational, and the price elasticity of demand for the commodity is high, so an increase in price would be particularly effective.

Some early observations on explanation

Some obvious questions that arise from the findings of consumer behavior analysis are: how and what do consumers maximize, i.e., how do they make decisions? Given that consumers tend to maximize, what is the role of melioration (implied by their matching) in their decision processes? How do emotional responses contribute to the explanation of consumer choice? There are two kinds of question here in each case: the ontological and the methodological. The first concerns what is actually going on (in terms of private events or mental processing) when consumers carry out these functions; the second is bound up with the explanatory components required by a theory of consumer choice. They are obviously linked at one level but not entirely; it may be necessary to include some aspects of processing, some intentional terminology, in a theory of consumer behavior regardless of what is known about the calculating or decision-making of consumers. A more complete account of consumer choice requires that we address both types of question. I have argued that the first kind of question, the ontological, can be answered largely by the extensional sciences of neurology and behavior, but that the second requires, in addition to knowledge of these levels of analysis, the use of intentional terminology.

Even in order to make the sense we have of our data, we have had to modify the basic contingency that radical behaviorism takes as its conceptual paradigm. Although the model has successfully embraced a radical behaviorist interpretation of the results, has its adoption required subtle theoretical amendments to the basic Skinnerian scheme? We have had, for instance, to make a bifurcation of reinforcement (which stems from the nature of human economic behavior itself as something that is both instrumental and social. While utilitarian reinforcement is contingency-based reinforcement, informational reinforcement depends upon verbal behavior. Further, in order to explain differences in consumers' verbal and non-verbal buying and consumption behaviors, we have had to introduce the idea of the scope of consumer behavior settings, treating them as relatively open (those in which a variety of behaviors is available) and relatively closed (in which a single behavior is induced) in order to make consumers' responses intelligible even in radical behaviorist terms. The resulting Behavioral Perspective Model (BPM) has been used in a variety of studies of consumer behavior including brand and product choice, and consumers' verbal and non-verbal responses to retail and consumption environments. The BPM, as we have used it in this chapter, remains nevertheless an elaboration of the three-term contingency, and its use *need* not depart from the scientific canons enjoined by radical behaviorism. Like radical behaviorism itself, it is, as it stands, an extensional model of behavior, denying explanatory reference to intentional terminology such as likes and dislikes, attitudes and intentions. But, can its application to the explanation of consumer behavior, while remaining contextual in its comprehension of the causation of behavior, be extended by theoretical considerations and taken for granted elsewhere in the social and behavioral sciences? The question can be answered only by enquiring further of the epistemological status of radical behaviorism itself.

Questions have arisen from the empirical findings that require a deeper level of explanation than that provided by the kind of descriptive behavioral science that radical behaviorism prides itself on being. In a consumer science based on a philosophy of psychology, behaviorism, that is satisfied that a behavior has been explained when the environmental contingencies that control the rate of its emission have been identified, how are we to account for behavior at the personal level, whether this be understood subjectively or objectively? How are we to account for the continuity of behavior over time and circumstances when this cannot be achieved solely in terms of the continuity of environmental stimuli, verbal behavior such as rules of conduct, or physiological changes within the individual? And, given that much of our account of the complex behavior involved in purchase and consumption must involve an element of interpretation rather than experimental analysis, how can we properly delimit the range of behavioral consequences that should be taken into account in those interpretations?

Finally, the question arises how the explanation of the relatively routine consumer behavior that we have studied, everyday consumer choices, is related to the kinds of explanation that have recently been forthcoming among behavioral scientists of those more extreme consumer behaviors that are best described as impulsive or compulsive, those involved in addictions to alcohol and other drugs, gambling and compulsive purchasing. The pioneering work of behavioral economists such as Rachlin (e.g., 2000a) and Ainslie (e.g., 2001) has yet to be incorporated fully within consumer research but it provides keys to explanation that are highly germane to the understanding of more mundane consumer choices.

However, the contribution of the behavioral sciences inaugurated by these authors to the understanding of consumer choice in general can be fully realized only if the nature of their explanations is more completely spelt out than is currently the case. The earlier chapters, which may appear on the surface to have little to do with consumer choice but which are essential to understanding and explaining it, develop an approach to behavior as influenced by both environmental contingencies and neurophysiology. In later chapters, this is applied to the explanation of both "extreme" and "routine" consumer choice.

2
What is Intentionality?

At the very least behaviorists should consider the problem of intentionality to be a most interesting case of verbal behavior, not to be dismissed but to be explored and understood. The standard behavioristic line that the mental is the fictional is just not good enough. (Schnaitter, 1999, p. 239)

Scientific explanation is verbal behavior. Any attempt to comprehend behaviorism as a philosophy of psychology requires an appreciation of how its practitioners use language. It also requires some familiarity with the ways in which competing systems of explanation use language. For this reason alone, we cannot avoid intentionality. Some behaviorist rebuttals of intentional explanation do not even mention that it inheres above all in a particular form of linguistic usage, even before any ontological questions have been settled. Dennett, for example, is repeatedly cited by behaviorists, though sometimes without understanding of what he said and how it has changed over the decades. It seems essential, therefore, to understand the nature of intentionality and to contrast it with the extensional explanation towards which behaviorism has traditionally striven. *For, whatever our aims, if we use intentional language, we are using intentional explanation.* Intentional explanation is both in widespread use among behaviorists, and in any cases necessary to a behavioral science approach. Better, therefore, to identify where it is used, perhaps where it needs to be used, than to simply deny it. In particular, I want to address the question: To what extent does intentionality, as well as behaviorism, elucidate the findings of consumer behavior analysis?

Social cognitive psychology accounts for choice by arguing that the consumer buys this or that brand because she *prefers* it, *likes* it, *wants* it or *needs* it, *has a positive attitude* toward it, or *intends* to purchase it, and despite the increased complexity of social cognitive psychology in recent decades, this level of understanding suffices for much semi-popular marketing writing and as the foundation of more serious research. Indeed, the ubiquity of mentalistic terminology and explanation in consumer research is evidenced by both standard textbook treatments and the research reported in leading journals. Consumer behavior is ascribed generally to mental processing and its outcomes in the form of brand beliefs, brand attitudes and brand-related purchase and discontinuance intentions. *But what justifies this cognitive stance?* Although there is no shortage of discussion of the most appropriate methods by which this assumption can be demonstrated, it is seldom questioned that the cognition–behavior approach is a legitimate source of explanation, and rare among consumer researchers to go beyond the formalism of social cognitive psychology in order to examine the philosophical basis of the explanation that is being offered. Usually in empirical work it is sufficient that coefficients reach a conventional level of significance for hypotheses to be accepted, for knowledge of the phenomena under investigation to be assumed. And critical theoretical work is rare enough to constitute no threat to the prevailing order.

The italicized words in the opening sentence are all intentionalistic terms: as such, they represent not just an alternative way of expressing what we mean when we describe someone's behavior but a radically different kind of explanation of that behavior. The reason for giving a special designation to words of the kind italicized is that they are all *about* something other than themselves. (For exposition, see, inter alia, Anscombe, 1957; Chisholm, 1957; Dennett, 1969; Searle, 1983). Most terms that we think of as mentalistic are intentional in referring to or representing something outside themselves: it is impossible just to *know*: we know that something; or just to *believe*: we believe that this or that is the case; or just to *desire*: again we desire some thing or other. These words are therefore different from many others that do no have mentalistic import: we do not walk *that*, or push *that*, or sit *that* in the sense that these verbs imply something other than themselves in an aboutness sort of way. The precise meaning of these "attitudes" as they are known to philosophers is denoted by the proposition that follows them. We might say, for instance, "Steve knows that the person who heads the Roman Catholic Church is the Pope." Yet we it might not be true to say "Steve knows that the person who heads the Roman Catholic Church is Benedict XVI," since he might not know that Benedict XVI is (as I write) the Pope. "The Pope" and "Benedict XVI" are different *intensions* or *meanings* that we may wish to delineate when expressing the content of Steve's knowing. But it is not possible to substitute one for the other; and the reason for this has to do with what we can assume, and therefore write, about what Steve "knows." This is a different way of using language from the way scientists usually do: their *extensional* use of language where we can substitute codesignative terms and retain the truth value of the sentence (Quine, 1960). We can say, for instance, "That planet is the fourth from the sun," and we can quite truthfully substitute "Mars" for "fourth from the sun." The reason that this is important is that the intentional has – at least since Brentano (1874) – been proposed as the defining characteristic of the mental. It is, as a result, precisely what behavioristic theories have sought to avoid since they eschew mentalistic explanations of behavior. Acquaintance with the writings of Skinner, for instance, since his inaugural definition of radical behaviorism in his paper of 1945 to his primer in basic behaviorism (1974), demonstrates his constant striving to maintain the extensionality of the language in which his explanations are couched. This is of the utmost significance to the establishment of behaviorism as an extensional behavioral science because intentional sentences are not reducible to extensional sentences, e.g., through paraphrase. No extensional account can thus substitute for or take the place of the intentional. Dennett also argues that behaviorism has failed, though it is not immediately obvious on what grounds he claims this. It appears superficially that he is claiming that behaviorism has failed on its own terms to produce an experimental science that permits the prediction and control of behavior. It is difficult to countenance this in view of the success of behaviorism on this level. Dennett also appears to be criticizing behaviorism here on the basis of its lack of an adequate explanatory basis for its observations: the experimenter can predict learning but cannot specify what is learned or how it influences subsequent behavior.

Brentano emphasized intentionality as "the mark of the mental," i.e., as a means of making an ontological distinction. Chisholm (1957) makes a crucial advance in rendering Brentano's thesis as a linguistic phenomenon; hence, "We may now re-express Brentano's thesis – or a thesis resembling that of Brentano – by reference to intentional sentences. Let us say (1) that we do no need to use intentional sentences when we describe nonpsychological phenomena; we can express all of our beliefs about what is merely 'physical' in sentences which are not intentional. But (2) when we wish to describe perceiving, assuming, believing, knowing, wanting, hoping, and other such attitudes, then either (a) we must use sentences which are intentional or (b) we must use terms we do not need to use when we describe nonpsychological phenomena." (Chisholm, 1957, pp. 172–3)

Most important from our point of view is Chisholm's re-expression of Brentano's irreducibility thesis, the argument that it is impossible to recapture the meaning of an intentional sentence in an extensional sentence, that the exact translation of one to the other is not feasible. We might easily stretch linguistic usage by inventing "a psychological terminology enabling us to describe perceiving, taking, and assuming in sentences which are not intentional (emphasis added)." (Chisholm, 1957, p. 173) "Instead of saying, for example, that a man *takes* something to be a deer, we could say 'His perceptual environment is deer-inclusive'. But in so doing, we are using technical terms – 'perceptual environment' and 'deer-inclusive' – which, presumably, are not needed for the description of nonpsychological phenomena. And, unless we can re-express the deer-sentence once again, this time as a nonintentional sentence containing no such technical terms, what we say about the man and the deer will conform to our present version of Brentano's thesis." (p. 173) Chisholm objects that the translation requires the invention of non-intentional psychological terms like "perceptual environment" and "deer-inclusive" are not otherwise used for the purpose of characterizing non-psychological phenomena. It would be necessary to recast the sentence about man and deer in non-intentional terms that did not include these technical neologisms before we had satisfied Brentano's thesis to the effect that our sentence was non-intentional. What Chisholm is getting at is that these invented technical terms are psychological, even if they are non-intentional, that they have no place in the usual range of physical explanations, and therefore the translation does not fully render the sentence in purely physical terms. Until this is done, we are still in the realm of Brentano's intentionalism.

Quine (1960, p. 220) confirms this by pointing out that it is impossible to translate this intentional sentence such as "He said that it was raining" into an extensional sentence without adding meaning. "He said, 'It is raining,'" adds meaning. It is an alternative to "He said, 'You bet!'" or "He said, 'Il pleut.'" While the intentional sentence is true, the extensional statements could behavior false. As Dennett, from whom this example is derived, comments: "If so overt an act as saying that something is the case is not subject to behavioural, extensional paraphrase, what hope is there for such hidden, private phenomena as believing and imagining?" (Dennett, 1969, p. 31). Nor is the problem overcome by Schnaitter's (1999) suggestion that we parse the sentence functionally. A structural parsing would be: He (pronoun); said (verb); that it was raining (noun clause object). A functional parsing of the clause would be: that (autoclitic); it was raining (tact). But this does not alter the meaning of the sentence. If we "parse" the sentence according to its construction in terms of propositional attitudes, it exhibits the phenomenon of referential opacity whether we construe it structurally or functionally.

Quine (1960, p. 219) also shows the relevance of the foregoing to our attempt to understand human choice behavior when he states that Brentano's divisions between intentional idioms and "normally tractable ones" "divides referential from non-referential occurrences of terms. Moreover [he continues], it is intimately related to the division between behaviorism and mentalism, between efficient and final cause, and between literary theory and dramatic portrayal." Indeed, he finds Chisholm's work relevant to his doubts re "the propositional attitudes and other intentional locutions." (p. 220). He summarizes Chisholm's linguistic rendering of Brentano's thesis as "roughly that there is no breaking out of the intentional vocabulary by explaining its members in other terms. Our present reflections are favorable to this thesis.... Brentano's thesis of the irreducibility of intentional idioms is of a piece with the thesis of indeterminacy of translation" (Quine, 1960, pp. 220–1)

Speaking as a behaviorist, Quine concludes from this is that Brentano, Chisholm, and the other intentionalists are mistaken in permitting an intentional mode of explanation to coexist with or even replace an extensional: "One may accept the Brentano thesis either as showing the indispensability of intentional idioms and the importance of an autonomous science of intention, or as showing the baselessness of intentional idioms and the emptiness of a science of intention. My attitude, unlike Brentano's, is the second." (Quine, 1960, p. 221) But my point is a third one: If we persist in using intentional idioms, if they appear essential to the exposition of our science, we are whether we like it or not employing not only intentional locutions but intentional explanation. We ought to be at the very least extremely careful about this if we wish to derive from our behaviorist philosophy of psychology an extensional behavioral science. Or, if we are not careful in that sense, it is because we are acknowledging that we have embraced intentional explanation.

The inevitability of intentionality

The question whether intentional explanation is necessary in the behavioral sciences can be answered by examining the nature of an extensional behavioral science in relation to its capacity to fulfill three theoretical requirements: that it deal with the personal level of analysis, that it account for the continuity of behavior across situations, and that its interpretations of the complex realities of human behavior that is not directly amenable to an experimental analysis can be effectively delimited to the reinforcing stimuli that can be reasonably held to influence them. In this section, I argue that radical behaviorism, for all the prowess of behavior analysis in the prediction and control of behavior especially in experimental and quasi-experimental settings, cannot of itself accomplish these imperatives of behavioral theory.

Radical behaviorism

Radical behaviorism as a philosophy of psychology is strictly extensional: it strives to account for its subject matter, behavior, in sentences that are referentially transparent, in which codesignatives are substitutable because they have the same extension (Skinner, 1938, 1945, 1974). It is thus distinguished from cognitivism by its rigorous avoidance of intentional language, and from both cognitivism and other neo-behaviorisms by its inclusion of thinking and feeling ("private events") as phenomena that require explanation on the same terms as public responding. Its focus is the prediction and control of behavior by reference to its environmental consequences and the antecedent stimuli that set the scene for reinforcement or punishment; in its adherence to Machian positivism, it holds that when the environmental stimuli that control behavior have been identified the behavior has been explained. The truth criterion it applies to this endeavor is pragmatism rather than realism (Foxall, 2004).

The scientific arm of this philosophy, behavior analysis, seeks the prediction and control of behavior in the environmental–behavioral contingencies which in the familiar "three-term contingency" (Exhibit 2.1). Behavior analysis seeks to proceed extensionally, i.e., in verbal behavior that avoids propositional content, describing its observation in language that is referentially transparent. It has two components or modes: the experimental analysis of behavior which is a laboratory-based investigation, and radical behaviorist interpretation which uses the principles of behavior gained in that analysis to provide an account in operant–contingency terms of the complex behaviors that are not amenable to direct experimental examination. Radical behaviorist interpretation frequently involves the use of mediating events, something ostensibly ruled out by Skinner's avoidance of "theoretical terms" but which appears necessary at this level of explanation. However, these mediating events are not intentionalistic: they remain part of an extensional account whose explanatory terms are extrapolated from the experimental to the non-experimental sphere.

Exhibit 2.1 The Three-Term Contingency

The "three-term contingency" is a theoretical construal which proposes that $S^D : R \rightarrow S^R$ where S^D is a cue or *discriminative stimulus*, R is a response, and S^R is a reward or *reinforcing stimulus*. The discriminative stimulus (S^D) sets the occasion (:) for, but does not elicit (as does the unconditioned stimulus of classical conditioning) a response (R) which produces ($\rightarrow$) a reinforcing consequence (S^R), i.e., on which makes the future enactment of this or a similar response in similar circumstances more probable (Moore, 1999). The behavior in question is *operant* behavior, that which by operating on the environment generates the consequences that control its future rate of emission. It is said to have been explained when the environmental variables of which it is a function (S^R and by implication S^D) have been identified.

Each element of the three- or n-term contingency is described in extensional language: its operation is not dependent upon wants or beliefs, desires or intentions (Smith, 1994). Radical behaviorism describes both contingency-shaped and rule-governed behaviors in terms of "a system of functional relationships between the organism and the environment" (Smith, 1994, pp. 127–8). Hence, an *operant response* "is not simply a response that the organism thinks will have a certain effect, it does have that effect". Further, a *reinforcer* "is not simply a stimulus that the organism desires to occur. It is a stimulus that will alter the rate of behavior upon which its occurrence is contingent". And a *discriminative stimulus* "is not simply a stimulus that has been correlated with a certain contingency in the organism's experience. It is one that successfully alters the organism's operant behavior with respect to that contingency". Descriptions of contingent behavior do not take propositions as their object; rather their object is relationships between an organism's behavior, its environmental consequences, and the

Exhibit 2.1 – *continued*

elements that set the occasion for those contingent consequences. So behavior analysis does not attribute propositional content to any of the elements of the three-term contingency. "Instead of accepting a proposition as its object, the concept of reinforcement accepts an event or a state of affairs – such as access to pellets – as its object" (Smith, 1994, p. 128). Mentalistic description: "The animal desires that a pellet should become available". The behavior analytic description is not "The animal's lever presses are reinforced that a pellet becomes available". It is: "The animal's lever presses are reinforced by access to pellets". A discriminative stimulus would not be described as a signal *that* something will happen but simply that a contingency exists. "It attributes an effect to the stimulus, but not a content". Whereas the substitutability of identicals fails in mentalistic statements (such statements are said to be logically opaque), behavioral categories are logically transparent, suggesting that "behavioral categories are not a subspecies of mentalistic categories" (Smith, 1994, p. 129).

Neither is the proposition that "reinforcer" merely denotes "desire" feasible: desires are not equivalent to reinforcers, nor reinforcers to desires. Common-sense notions imply that if a stimulus is (positively) reinforcing it is desired, and if it is desired it is because it is a (positive) reinforcer but in fact neither holds. Objects of desire may not be attainable (the fountain of youth, perpetual motion) and so cannot be (linked to) reinforcers. Nor are reinforcers necessarily desired: on FI schedules, electric shock maintains responding for monkeys, pigeons, and rats. The shocks are easily avoidable, but are not avoided. They cannot be "desired," yet they reinforce behavior. Nor do functional units of the speaker's verbal behavior such as mands and tacts (Skinner, 1957) have propositional content. They are simply statements of contingencies that account for an individual's behavior in the absence of his or her direct exposure to those contingencies. A mand is "a verbal response that specifies its reinforcer" (Catania, 1992, p. 382): for example, "Give me a drink" plus the unspoken, "You owe me a favor" or "Else I shall ignore your requests in future". Even if this is expressed as "I desire that you give me a drink...", it is actually no more than a description of contingencies. A tact is "a verbal discriminative response... in the presence

Exhibit 2.1 – *continued*

of or shortly after a stimulus" (Catania, 1992, p. 399): "Here is the bank". Even if this were expressed as, "I want you to see the bank", its function would be confined to establishing the stimulus control of the word "bank", as when the listener replies, "Oh, yes, the bank." More technically, the *mand* denotes the consequences contingent upon following the instructions of the speaker or of imitating his or her example. Much advertising consists of mands – "Buy three and get one free!" "Don't forget the fruit gums, mum" – which indicate contingencies that are under the control of the speaker. *Tacts* present a con*tact* with part of the environment and, depending on learning history, a potential for behavior on the part of the recipient. A trade mark or logo may be followed by making a purchase or entering a store. The definitive source is Skinner's *Verbal Behavior* (1957).

The functional units of the listener's verbal behavior, as proposed by Zettle and Hayes (1982) similarly describe contingencies rather than express propositional content. Pliance, for instance, is the behavior of the listener who complies with a verbal request or instruction: hence, "Pliance is rule-governed behavior under the control of apparent socially mediated consequences for a correspondence between the rule and relevant behavior" (Hayes, Zettle and Rosenfarb, 1989, p. 201). Pliance is thus simply the behavior involved in responding positively to a mand. Tracking is "rule-governed behavior under the control of the apparent correspondence between the rule and the way the world is arranged" (Hayes et al., 1989, p. 206). It involves tracking the physical environment as when following instructions how to get to the supermarket. Once again, its form – for example, "Turn left at the traffic light" plus the unspoken "And you'll get to Sainsbury's" – is a basic description of contingencies rather than an expression of propositional attitudes. Precisely as Smith has concluded with respect to contingency-shaped behavior, we may conclude with respect to rule-governance: "Beliefs and desires have propositional content. … Designations of discriminative stimuli and reinforcing stimuli, by contrast, do not accept *that*-clauses." (Smith, 1994, p. 128) A third functional unit of listener behavior has no corresponding unit for the speaker: the *augmental* (Zettle and Hayes, 1982) is a highly motivating rule that states emphatically how a particular

Exhibit 2.1 – *continued*

behavior will be reinforced or avoid punishment. "Just one more packet top and I can claim my free watch!"

The private events which distinguish radical behaviorism are not "cognitive" or "mental" rather than material or physical. They are essentially private, collateral responses under the influence of the same environmental stimuli that control overt – or, better, public – responding. As such their ontological status is fixed by their place in the three-term contingency: they are responses in need of operant explanation by means of an account that causally links them with antecedent and reinforcing stimuli occurring in the extra-personal environment, rather than discriminative or reinforcing stimuli which are capable of determining the frequency of a response. They are dependent variables. Radical behaviorism explains verbal behavior in similar terms to non-verbal: that of the speaker as a series of functionally defined speech (and quasi-speech) units – tacts, mands, autoclitics, echoics, intraverbals; that of the listener as a series of functionally defined verbal units that prescribe the consequences of rule-following – tracks, plys, and augmentals.

Sidman (1994) proposes that *n*-term contingencies can be invoked to explain increasingly complex behavior. In the 4-term contingency, for instance, the presence of an initial stimulus controls the subsequent $S^D \rightarrow R \rightarrow S^R$ relationship. Michael (1982, 1993) has drawn attention to the possibility that motivating stimuli can fill the role of this initial stimulus, making the reinforcer that completes the sequence more desirable. A social rule such as ply or, more probably, an augmental might enhance the reinforcing capacity of the S^R or even transform a neutral consequence into a reinforcer or punisher. For an examination of the use of this fourth element in the behavioral contingency, see Fagerstrøm, Foxall and Arntzen, 2006. For recent application of this theoretical construct, see Tapper, 2005.

Radical behaviorist explanation thus proceeds on the basis of the *contextual stance* (Foxall, 1999) which states that behavior is predictable in so far as it is assumed to be environmentally determined; specifically, in so far as it is under the control of a learning history that represents the reinforcing and punishing consequences of similar behavior previously enacted in settings similar to that currently encountered. The contextual stance thus portrays behavior as taking place at the temporal and spatial intersection defined by learning history and behavior setting. It is this intersection that defines the situation (precisely as it is defined in the BPM).

While there is no doubting the capacity of behavior analysis within the framework of radical behaviorism to predict and control behavior, at least in the relatively closed setting of the operant laboratory, there is a need for further conceptualization if we wish to account further for certain aspects of that behavior. Explanation of this kind is optional for behavior analysts, who may wish to remain within the philosophy of science set by Machian positivism, as did Skinner. (Smith, 1986; Mach, 1893/1974, 1896/1959, 1905/1976) But there is no compelling reason to confine inquiry to this extensional level of analysis. In seeking to extend the conceptual framework here, I am concerned with methodology, with instances in which it is impossible to proceed with inquiry in the absence of intentional language, rather than with ontological questions. I should like to pursue three areas in which I believe explanation that goes beyond the n-term contingency can yield answers to questions that would be asked as a matter of course in most scientific endeavors but which have not usually found a place within radical behaviorism. These concern the treatment of the personal level of analysis, accounting for the continuity of behavior, and delimiting behavioral interpretations of behavior by delineating the scope of behavioral consequences that can be called upon to provide a causal explanation thereof.

The personal level

The personal level of explanation is that of "people and their sensations and activities" rather than that of "brains and events in the nervous system" (Dennett, 1969, p. 93). The latter belong to the sub-personal level, that at which an extensional science such as physiology (neuroscience) operates, its mechanistic explanations inappropriate to the explanation of so-called mental entities such as pain which can be understood only at the personal level. The personal level is that at which the organism as a whole can be said to act. As Ryle (1949) and Wittgenstein (1953) have pointed out it is a stage of explanation that is quickly exhausted because so little can be said at this level. Of his pain, the bearer can say little more than that it hurts, for instance. In Dennett's system, as we shall see, it is the level at which beliefs, desires and other intentional idioms are ascribed, but for now we are concerned only with the personal level as an analytical tool in extensional behavioral science and its implications for the explanation of behavior.

The personal level has two aspects, a first-personal perspective (that from which I actually feel my pain as an inner-body experience) and a third-personal viewpoint (that in which I attribute pain to another person who is sobbing and holding her head as well as using the word "migraine" a lot.) The acceptance of these "subjective" and "objective" understandings of the personal level does not divide cleanly along behaviorist/non-behaviorist lines. Skinner's analysis of private events can be read as embracing both at one time or another. Dennett's cognitive approach concentrates on the objective, third-personal level which he associates unremittingly with a scientific standpoint, while Schnaitter's (1999) behaviorist view is ready to endorse the first-personal level. Others, such as Searle, fully accept the necessity of speaking in terms of both the first- and the third-personal levels, and that is the approach taken here.

The difficulty for radical – or any other brand of extensional–behaviorism is that it deals inadequately with neither aspect of the personal level, largely because it confuses them. First note that in the case of the first personal or subjective level of personhood, radical behaviorism simply has no means of accounting for some behaviors without resorting to intentional language. This stems from the irreducibility of intentional language to extensional and is illustrated by the following examples of people acting contrary to their desires, beliefs and expectations in ways that cannot be entirely captured in a purely extensional description. Take, for instance, the couple who found themselves married because they went through the motions of a Jewish wedding ceremony, they with all the other participants thinking that they were engaged in an elaborate joke, only to discover that they were in fact married. No-one intended this outcome; one member of the couple fully intended to marry someone else. Another example concerns the Muslim acting with his real life wife in a television production who, having followed the script to the letter, found himself divorced from both his screen wife and his actual spouse, unable to live with her on pain of being found guilty of adultery. This, again, was contrary to the expectations the entire cast and production team held about the situation. (Both examples are taken from Juarrero, 1999). The point is not that a radical behaviorist interpretation of these behaviors is impossible, or even whether they are actual or anecdotal, but that it can never capture the entire behavior in question without resorting to intentional idioms, i.e., without deviating from its commitment to extensional behavioral science.

So how does it cope? Skinner's approach to interpretation is to seek the explanation of an individual's current behavior in his or her history of reinforcement and punishment, i.e., *learning history*. Despite the way in which the three-term contingency is usually symbolized as showing the factors that cause a response as the consequences that necessarily follow it, Skinner does not try to explain behavior by reference to future events. He avoids teleology by explaining current behavior in terms of the consequences that have followed similar responding in the past. Hence, when we see someone rummaging about among the objects on her desk, we infer that she is looking for her glasses. But the information available to us to make sense of her behavior is identical to the information she has to do the same. All she can say in explanation is that she has found her glasses in the past when she has engaged in behavior of this kind. The behaviorist strategy of "discovering" a learning history in order to interpret complex behavior evidently accords with the philosophy of behaviorist explanation. (Baum and Heath, 1992) Although it eschews the mentalistic fictions Skinner so strongly repudiated, it nevertheless extends the analysis of human behavior beyond the confines of a scientific enquiry (Foxall, 2004).

But the clincher comes from Skinner's statement that a man who is looking intently at his desk, moving papers to look underneath them, knows that he is "looking for his glasses" only because the last time he behaved in this way he came across them. His knowledge of what he is doing is gained from the same source as our knowledge of what he is doing: the observations of an external witness:

> When we see a man moving about in a room opening drawers, looking under magazines, and so on, we may describe his behavior in fully objective terms: "Now he is in a certain part of the room; he has grasped a book between the thumb and forefinger of his right hand; he is lifting the book and bending his head so that any object under the book can be seen." We may "interpret" his behavior or "read a meaning into it" by saying that "he is looking for something," or, more specifically, that "he is looking for his glasses." What we have added is not a further description of his behavior but an inference about some of the variables responsible for it. There is no *current* goal, incentive, purpose or meaning to be taken into account. This is so even if we ask him what he is doing and he says, "I am looking for my glasses." This is not a further description of his behavior but of the variables of which his behavior is a function; it is equivalent to "I have lost my glasses," "I shall stop what I am doing when I find my glasses," or "When I have done this in the past, I have found my glasses." These translations may seem unnecessarily

roundabout, but only because expressions involving goals and purposes are abbreviations. (Skinner, 1953, pp. 89–90).

But, in everyday life, it is only very rarely that we base our statements about our emotions, say, on self-observation. A person does not come to understand that he is nervous because he sees his hands shaking and hears his voice quavering. He does not come to *conclude* that he is nervous on the basis of evidence of this kind any more than his saying he has a headache depends on his prior observation of his flushed features, his holding his temples, and his having taken aspirin. As Malcolm (1977) says, "If someone were to say, *on that basis*, that he has a headache, either he would be joking or else he would not understand how the words are used." He argues further that behaviorists have erred by assuming that a psychological sentence expressed in first-personal terms is identical in content and method of verification to the corresponding third-personal sentence. We verify that another person is angry by the way the veins stand out on his neck, by the redness of his face and by her shouting. But we do not verify our own anger in this way. As Malcolm points out, we do not as a rule attempt to verify it at all. Verification is simply not a concept or operation that applies to many first-person psychological reports, those which are not founded on observation. An individual's statement of purpose or intention belongs in a different class from one made by someone else on the basis of observing that individual. If we see someone turning out his pockets and recall that on previous occasions he has done this before producing his car keys from one of them we can reasonably conclude that he is looking for this car keys this time too. But it would be odd indeed if he himself were to work out what he was doing by observing that he was emptying his pockets as he had done in the past when looking for his car keys. If he announced that he must be looking for his car keys at present because he was doing what he had done in the past when finding them had eventuated, we should think him most odd, crazy, to be treated in future with circumspection. The avoidance of such convoluted locutions, which seem to fulfill no function other than to avoid the intentionality of "looking for," "knowing that," and "remembering" involves not only a different kind of verbal description but a different form of explanation.

The continuity of behavior

The plausibility of an extensional radical behaviorist interpretation depends vitally upon its capacity to account for the continuity of behavior. Why should behavior that has been followed by a particular ("reinforcing") stimulus in the presence of a setting stimulus be re-enacted when a similar setting is encountered? Why should a rule that describes certain physical or social contingencies be followed at some future date when those contingencies are encountered? Why can I tell you now what I ate for lunch yesterday? The whole explanatory significance of learning history is concerned with the continuity of behavior between settings and this implies some change in the organism, some means of recording the experience of previous behavior in such a way that it will be available next time similar settings are encountered. There is no other way in which the individual can recognize the potential offered by the current behavior setting in terms of the reinforcement and punishment signaled by the discriminative stimuli that compose it.

The radical behaviorist account of behavioral continuity requires that a common stimulus or some component thereof is present on each occasion that a response is emitted. The stimulus must be either a learned discriminative stimulus and/or a reinforcer. The difficulty with this is that it is not always possible to detect each element of the three-term contingency when behavior is learned or performed. The tendency is, then, to suppose that something occurs within the individual, presumably at a physiological level, that will one day be identified as sufficient to account for the continuity of behavior. But the problem is less one of ontology than of methodology, of the theoretical imperatives involved in explaining the continuity of behavior and therefore the language employed to account for it.

The issue revolves around what is learned. Whether one assumes that learning takes place as a result of initial exposure to a reinforcing stimulus and that behavioral control us transferred contingently to a paired setting stimulus that acquires discriminatory significance – the standard radical behaviorism view – or that learning usually occurs as a result of observing a conspecific's behavior and its consequences, the only way in which such learning can be described requires the use of intentional idioms. A purely descriptive account can, where this is possible, relate responses to the stimuli with which they correlate, and by which they are therefore predictable and open to influence. This is the essential program of an extensional behavioral science, and I do not wish in any way to argue that it be other than enthusiastically executed. Indeed, it is important to my research program that it is. However, it is not always feasible to make the required connections between environment and behavior, and that this acts as a stimulus to the discovery of an explanation rather than a mere description of behavior and its contextual determinants. The quest for explanation will always be there, should behaviorists choose to adopt it, but the failure of the extensional approach is a catalyst to its implementation. The behaviorist account is both incomplete (Foxall, 2004) and fails to come to terms with what is learned in the process of learning (Exhibit 2.2).

Exhibit 2.2   What is Learned?

"The difficulty the behaviorist has encountered is basically this: while it is clear that an experimenter can predict rate of learning, for example, from the initial conditions of his mazes and experience history of his animals, how does he specify just *what* is learned? ... What [the animal in the maze] learns, of course, is *where the food is*, but how is this to be characterized non-Intentionally? There is no room for 'know' or 'believe' or 'hunt for' in the officially circumscribed language of behaviorism; so the behaviorist cannot say that the rat knows or believes that his food is at x, or that the rat is hunting for a route to x." (Dennett, 1969, pp. 33–4)

It is considerations such as these that have led behavioral scientists to theorize about the nature of learning. Mediational theories such as those of Hull and Tolman have given way to the explicit use of intentionality to explain behavior: not on the basis of positing intervening variables but as an inevitable linguistic turn (Foxall, 2004). Berridge (2000) makes the progression from mediationism to intentionalism clear in his description of the history of behavioral psychology. Bolles's (1972) account of behavior in terms of the expectation of utilitarian consequences of Bolles follows the S–S theory of Tolman rather than the S–R theory of Hull but suggests that what is learned are S–S associations of a particular kind and function: an association is leaned between a conditioned stimulus (CS) and a subsequent utilitarian stimulus (S*) that elicits pleasure. The first S does not elicit a response but an expectation of the second S (S*). Bolles (1972) developed a "psychological syllogism" in which, as Dickinson (1997, p. 346) puts it, "Exposure to stimulus–outcome (S–S*) and response–outcome (R–S*) contingencies leads to the acquisition of S–S* and R–S* expectancies, respectively, that represent these relations. The two expectancies are 'synthesized' or combined in a 'psychological

Exhibit 2.2 – *continued*

syllogism' so that in the presence of the cue, S, the animal is likely to perform response R." The response becomes more probable as the strengths of the expectancies increases and as the value of S*, which is influenced by the animal's motivational state, increases. Bolles employs this theory to explain why animals sometimes act as though they have received a reward when they have not: e.g., the raccoon that washes a coin as though it were food, "misbehavior," or autoshaping, or schedule-induced polydipsia, all empirical instances that research in the 1960s had shown to be contraindicative of the reinforcement model.

Berridge (2000) argues that useful as this is it fails to explain why the animal still approaches the reinforcer (say food) rather than waiting for it to appear and enjoying the S* in the interim. He discusses the approach of Bindra (1978) who proposes the utilitarian transfer of incentive properties to the CS. Bindra accepts the S–S* theory but argues that the S does not simply cause the animal to expect the S*: it also elicits a central motivational state that causes the animal to perceive the S as an S*. The S assumes the motivational properties that normally belong to the S*. These motivational properties are incentive properties which attract the animal and elicit goal-directed behavior and possibly consumption. Through association with the S*, the S acquires the same functions as the S*. An animal approaches the CS for a reward, finds the signal (S) attractive; if the CS is food, the animal wants to eat it. If it is an S for a tasty food S*, the animal may take pleasure in its attempt to eat the CS (Berridge, 2000, p. 236; see also Bouton and Franselow, 1997). But if CSs were incentives one would always respond to them whether or not one were hungry. The question is to explain how CSs interact with drive states. Toates (1986), therefore, builds on the Bolles–Bindra theory by positing that both cognitive expectancy and more basic reward processes might occur simultaneously in the individual. All of these theories are necessarily intentionalistic since they deal in expectancies.

Delimiting behavioral interpretation

The ubiquity of apparent three-term contingencies as we survey life beyond the lab raises difficulties for an interpretative account which is meant to be more than 'plausible'. As radical behaviorism stands, its program of interpretative research based adjudged solely on the criterion of plausibility, there is no way of successfully delimiting the scope of its interpretations so that they meet the standards of validity and reliability that are decisive in qualitative as well as quantitative research.

This problem is inherent in Rachlin's (1994) interpretation of observed behavior, *teleological behaviorism*, as long as it is understood as an extensional behavioral science. (I shall, in a later chapter, propose that it belongs properly within the category I shall define as "intentional behaviorism," and that this overcomes the difficulty I am going now to outline. However, that does not invalidate the following argument, and provides an opportunity to introduce at this relatively early stage one of the most important theoretical stances in behavior analysis and behavioral economics.) Teleological behaviorism proposes an interpretation of complex behavior based on final causes, i.e. the consequences of behavior. Final causes extend serially outwards from the individual who behaves, each fitting or nesting into the pattern the next. Hence, "eating an appetizer fits into eating a meal, which fits into a good diet, which fits into a healthy life, which in turn fits into a generally good life. The wider the category, the more embracing, the 'more final' the cause." (Rachlin, 1994, p. 21). The process of finding the causes of behavior is one of fitting the behavior into an ever-increasing molar pattern of response and consequences. Rachlin's system has no time for private events or intrapersonal phenomena; yet, unlike both radical and methodological behaviorism it freely employs mentalistic terminology. Rachlin asserts that mind is behavior, sequences or patterns of behavior rather than single acts. This molar view means that mental phenomena such as attitudes, intentions and even pain are all defined by extended patterns of behavior. We know that our friend is in pain because of the behaviors he emits: grimacing, groaning, holding his arm, and so on. But this is not the central concern of this account. That lies in the fact that interpretations based on this system are unbounded and require an intentionalistic overlay of interpretation in order to be useful.

A whole series of final causes may each be nested within one another, diffused over time, the whole sequence being necessary to a full explanation of the behavior that produced them. But, since the events that explain a behavior are temporally extended, the compilation of its explanation may require the elapse of a significant period before the full complexity of the behavior's consequences can be noted and understood (Rachlin, 1994, pp. 31–2; see also Rachlin, 2000b). The search for final causes as ultimate explanations may, nevertheless, be convoluted and unscientific in the sense that the propositions employed in explication of a behavior may never be brought into contact with the empirical events that could substantiate them or lead to their refutation. Rachlin's search for plausible extensions fails because the extension identified is untestable (at least during the period of the interpretation). To say that a or the (final) cause of the physics research undertaken by Rutherford and his colleagues that included the splitting of the atom was the death of millions of Japanese civilians is a travesty. The two events are undoubtedly linked but the invocation of a causal relationship between them is hardly adequate to account for either. But even if we try to confine the range of consequences, as Rachlin surely intends, to those that can be said to enter into an individual's utility function (Rachlin, 1989, 1994), we still face the difficulty of determining exactly what these might be. Do the procedures involved in my preparing a meal with the foodstuffs I purchased this morning enter into that function equally with the feelings of nausea I experienced after eating it? Are both to be assigned equal significance as causes of my behavior? More satisfying explanations, certainly more complete explanations, must be sought at the intensional level.

The responsible ascription of intentionality

Since we cannot avoid intentionality (unless we stick rigidly to the prediction and control aims of radical behaviorism), how are we to ascribe intentional terms responsibly? Dennett (1969) proposes that we can do so on the basis of the evolutionary consistency of the afferent–efferent linkages identified in (extensional) neuroscience. The result is an a-ontological basis for intentional explanation as an additional interpretation of physiological mechanisms, a "heuristic overlay" of intentional interpretation placed upon neuroscience but not part of its extensional program. However, Dennett's scheme does not take behavior sufficiently into consideration, at least not in a systematic manner, and we require an extensional *behavioral* science to balance the extensional neuroscience on which it depends. Moreover, by the time Dennett had – in the late 70s – begun to apply the intentional stance – the view that it is legitimate to ascribe intentionality to any system if we can thereby predict its behavior – to non-human and especially non-living entities such as computers, he had committed the *mereological fallacy*, the application to the parts of a system of attributes that properly belong only to the system as a whole. We should then be able to ascribe intentionality responsibly on the basis of evolutionarily consistent patterns of contingency-controlled behavior (as well as contemporaneously following Dennett's physiology-based method where this is feasible). This position might be called *intentional behaviorism.*

If intentional ascription is necessary, how can it be accomplished responsibly? Dennett (1969) argues, in language reminiscent of behaviorists' criticisms of the proliferation of mental "explanations," that a purely intentionalistic psychology is impossible because its explicative terms are tautologically derived from its observations of that behavior. A more appropriate basis for psychology would be to add a layer of intentionalistic interpretation to the theories and findings of physiology. Those theories cannot of themselves account for the personal level of analysis, that of "people and their sensations and activities" rather than that of "brains and events in the nervous system" (Dennett, 1969, p. 93). It is the level at which the person knows what it is to feel pain but cannot express this in a way that is further analyzable. It is at this level that the abstractions of intentional analysis (beliefs, desires, and so on) are attributed. The resulting heuristic overlay adds nothing to the neurophysiological account but provides a means of prediction. The sub-personal level provides mechanistic explanations but these are not appropriate to the explanation of the so-called mental entities such as pain. While there is a good understanding of the neurological basis of pain, Dennett raises the question whether the presumed evolutionarily-appropriate afferent-efferent networks underlying this understanding are sufficient (they are certainly necessary) to account for the "phenomena of pain". This resolves itself into the question whether pain is an entity that exists in addition to the physical questions that constitute this network (Dennett, 1969, p. 91).

There are no events or processes in the brain that "exhibit the characteristics of the putative 'mental phenomena' of pain" that are apparent when we speak in everyday terms about pain or pains. Such verbalizations are non-mechanical, while brain events and processes are mechanical. It is unclear for instance how an individual distinguishes a sensation of pain from a non-painful sensation. The only distinguishing feature of pain sensations is "painfulness" which is an unanalyzable quality that allows of only circular definition. But people can do this and the personal level is the level at which pains are discriminated, not the sub-personal. Neurons and brains have no sensation of pains and do not discriminate them. Pains, like other mental phenomena, do not refer: our speaking of them does not pick out *any thing*; pain is simply a personal-level phenomenon that has, nevertheless, some corresponding states, events or processes at the sub-personal, physiological level. This is not an identity theory: Dennett does not identify the experience of pain with some physical happening; he maintains two separate levels of explanation: one in which the experience of pain, while felt, does not refer, and one in which the descriptions of neural occurrences refer to actual neural structures, events and states in which the extensionally-characterized science deals.

The task now becomes that of ascribing content to the internal states and events. The first stage is straightforward: since intentional theory assumes that the structures and events they seek to explain are appropriate to their purpose, an important link in this ascription is provided by hypotheses drawn from the natural selection not only of species but, as we have seen, of brains and the nervous system. A system which through evolution has the capacity to produce appropriate efferent responses to the afferent stimulation it encounters, it clearly has the ability to discriminate among the repertoire of efferent responses it might conceivably make. Its ability so to discriminate and respond to the stimulus characteristics of its complex environment means that it must be "capable of interpreting its peripheral stimulation", to engender inner states or events that co-occur with the phenomena that arise in its perceptual field. In order for us to be justified in calling the process intelligent, something must be added to this afferent analysis: the capacity to associate the outcomes of the afferent analysis with structures on the efferent portion of the brain.

What is Dennett referring to when he speaks of "afferent-efferent linkages"? Afferent refers to moving or carrying inward or toward a central part and may refer to vessels, nerves, etc. So blood vessels carrying blood toward the heart, or nerves conducting signals to the brain would be referred to as *afferent*. Blood vessels or nerves carrying blood or signals away from the hear or brain are, by contrast, known as *efferent*. Closer to the present context, the terms denote functions of neurons which are cells in the nervous system that transmit impulses to other neurons. Figure 2.1 shows the structure of a typical neuron. The important components from the point of view of the current discussion are the cell body itself which is broadly similar to other types of cell, containing for instance a nucleus (though differing in other respects that do not concern us here), and the fibers that project from it, dendrites and axons. Dendrites, of which there are a number to each cell, receive signals from other neurons and are accordingly known as

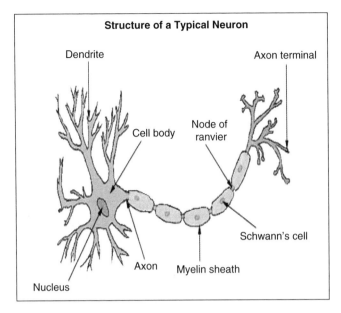

Figure 2.1   The Structure of a Typical Neuron

afferent. Axons, of which each cell has only one, transmit signals to other neurons and are, therefore, known as *efferent.*

Closer still is the sense in which these terms are used to denote the functions of neurons by reference to the direction in which they transmit impulses: *towards* the central nervous system (CNS) in the case of afferent or sensory neurons, *away from* the CNS in the case of efferent or motor neurons. (Connecting the two types of neuron, within the CNS, is a third kind of nerve cell known as interneurons). Although both afferent and efferent neurons are found primarily in the peripheral nervous system (PNS), they are defined functionally and in relation to the CNS. The import of Dennett's argument is that the linkages between afferent and efferent neurons evolved in the course of natural selection (as it were) to solve the problem of how the organism "knows" the appropriate response to produce in the face of a particular stimulus. If sensory neurons signal the availability of food to a hungry animal, for instance, it produces the appropriate response of approaching the stimulus and devouring it. Dennett argues that in this instance, we are justified in saying that the animal *desires* the food and *believes* that acting in this manner will procure it. The purpose of his inquiry is to determine how intentional terms, inescapable because of their general usage and carrying important implications for explanation in view of the meanings assumed by sentences that carry them, can be legitimately employed in psychology.

For instance, in order to detect the presence of a substance *as food*, an organism must have the capacity not only to detect the substance but thereafter to stop seeking and start eating; without this capacity to associate afferent stimulation and efferent response, the organism could not be said to have detected the presence of the substance *as* that of food. Dennett uses this point to criticize behaviorists for having no answer to the question how the organism selects the appropriate response. There is a need to invest the animal which has discriminated a stimulus with the capacity to "know" what its appropriate response should be. (In fact, behaviorists have ducked this problem by designating it a part of the physiologist's assignment and drawing the conclusion that the behavioral scientists need be concerned with it no longer. The conventional behaviorist wisdom over the kind of cognitive ascription to which Dennett refers is that it amounts to no more than "premature physiology".)

The content of a neural state, event or structure relies on its stimulation *and* the appropriate efferent effects to which it give rise, and in order to delineate these it is necessary to transcend the extensional description of stimulus and response. It is necessary to relate the content to the environmental conditions as perceived by the organism's sense organs in order that it can be given reference to the real-world phenomena that produced the stimulation. And it is equally important to specify what the organism "does with" the event or state so produced in order to determine what that event or state "means to" the organism. An aversive stimulus has not only to be identified along with the neural changes it engenders to signify that it means danger to the animal; in addition, the animal has to respond appropriately to the stimulus, for example, by moving away. Failure on its part to do so would mean that we were not justified in ascribing such content to the physiological processes occurring as a result of the stimulation. If we are to designate the animal's activities as "intelligent decision making" then this behavioral link must be apparent. Only events in the brain that appear appropriately linked in this way can be ascribed content, described in intentional idioms.

How are the intentional ascription and the extensional descriptions provided by neuroscience related then? The ascribed content is not an additional characteristic of the event, state, or structure to which it is allocated, some intrinsic part of it discovered within it, as its extensionally-characterized features are discovered by the physiologist. They are a matter of *additional interpretation*. The features of neural systems, extensionally-characterized in terms of physiology or physics, are describable and predictable in those terms without intentional ascription which makes reference to meaning or content. Such a scientific story, consisting in an account of behavior confined to talk of the structure and functions of neural cells and so on, is entirely extensional in character. But such an extensional story could not, according to Dennett, provide us with an understanding of *what the organism is doing*. Only an intentional account can accomplish this, "but it is not a story about features of the world *in addition to* features of the extensional story; it just describes what happens in a different way". Such an extensional theory would be confined to the description/explanation of the *motions* of the organism rather than of its *actions*.

The legitimate ascription of content relies emphatically upon the clear understanding of the nature of the personal level of analysis, a matter on which Dennett has proved extraordinarily flexible over the years. Later chapters examine the changes in his thought and argues for the preservation of this level in order to make clear that the ascription of content cannot take place at any other. The logic of intentional ascription derives from the evolutionary imperative that a creature must in order to survive and reproduce generate environmentally appropriate behavior – its responses must be suitable to the stimuli that impinge upon it. Only an intelligent creature can produce the right behavior in the circumstances it faces, i.e., a creature whose nervous system can generate the efferent behavior that matches the afferent stimulus in order to increase its biological fitness. There is a need to invest the animal which has discriminated a stimulus with the capacity to "know" what its appropriate response should be, and such an intelligent capacity can be specified only in intentional terms. We have not identified some additional characteristic of the physiology of the creature by ascribing content to it in order to account for the intelligence it exhibits: we have simply provided *additional interpretation*. Such ascription is unnecessary to the research program of the physiologist who characterizes the features of neural systems via extensional physics or biology, and who for the purposes of neuroscience has no need of intentional ascriptions that refer to meaning or content. But Dennett argues that the extensional account provided by the physiologist cannot provide us with an understanding of *what the organism is doing*. Only an intentional account can accomplish this, "but it is not a story about features of the world *in addition to* features of the extensional story; it just describes what happens in a different way". A simple example of the kind of afferent–efferent linkage Dennett is talking about is: sight of a particular foodstuff (afferent sensory input) leading to approach behavior mediated by motor neuron activity in requisite muscles: the intentional inference is that the organism *wants, needs, has a positive attitude toward, intends to get* the food. But the ascription of wanting, intending, and so on, is not part of the physiology: it is not part of extensional neuroscience which deals with the sub-personal level: it belongs only at the level of the person since only a whole organism can be said to do these things.

3
Intentionality and Mind

> Private events are observable, even if only by an audience of one. They are just as real as public events... Mental (fictional) events, in contrast, are unobservable because they are non-physical. (Baum and Heath, 1992, p. 1313)

Although the view of intentionality being taken here would be agreed by many philosophers of mind, elaborate and remold it how they might, it requires to be stated explicitly and its implications understood. Searle (2004, p. 28) writes that "'Intentionality' is a technical term used by philosophers to refer to that capacity of the mind by which mental states refer to, or are about, or are of objects and states of affairs in the world other than themselves." However one defines "mind," this captures the essence of aboutness and mentality that we have espoused so far. It is true to Brentano in being capable of embracing intensional inexistence and the opacity of intentionalistic expressions. Now, save to emphasize that intentionality is a verbal phenomenon (following Chisholm, 1957; Dennett, 1969), one that concerns sentences and types of explanation rather than something that refers ontologically to mental and physical realities, the view taken here does not depart from this understanding. This view is neither Dennettian nor Searlean in its entirety, however, something which requires further elaboration.

Intrinsic and derived intentionality

Searle distinguishes the original or intrinsic intentionality just described from the "derived intentionality" possessed by say a shopping list. Whereas a shopping list displays intrinsic intentionality when it exists in my mind, as soon as I commit it to paper the marks on the paper derive their intentionality, their aboutness, from the original intentionality of my mental list. This seems to abstract unnecessarily from the idea of intrinsic intentionality by (i) removing the mental level: the intentional is no longer the "mark of the mental" (or, better, the mark of a particular kind of explanation), but anything created by a mind capable of original intentionality. Moreover, the concept of intentionality is in this way stripped of any peculiar analytic value since everything in the world it appears has intentionality: a bookcase is about books, a stone is about breaking windows, a hosepipe is about botanical longevity, and so on, and so on. The precise intentionality of any of these things is of course interestingly contingent on the original intentionality of its user or creator: a bookcase could be about storing my butterfly collection, a stone about writing the ten commandments, a hosepipe about goading my horse. But unraveling any or all of these connections hardly requires the concept of intentionality: there are other concepts (such as motivation) that do as well without blunting the precision of the notion of intentionality that uniquely picks out the nature of sentences and explanations. And there are stances such as the physical and design that cope better with these phenomena.

Dennett (1995, pp. 50–5) goes further than Searle by claiming that *all* intentionality is derived intentionality, that even a mental shopping list is secondarily intentional. In one respect this need not detain us since we have already agreed upon the lack of usefulness or even plausibility of derived intentionality. But Dennett's reasoning is nonetheless instructive. He argues that a "representational artifact" such as a written shopping list possesses derived intentionality by virtue of the role it plays in the activities of its creator. It is intentional solely because of the intentionality of the agent that made it; and, by extension, a mental shopping list has derived intentionality for exactly the same reason. "It is internal, not external, but it is still an artifact created by your brain and means what it does because of its particular position in the ongoing economy of your brain's internal activities and their role in governing your body's complex activities in the real, surrounding world." (p. 52) The brain can obtain such states only by deriving them from "the ongoing economy of the larger system of which it is a part – or, in other words from the intentions of its creator." (p. 53).

Several objections may be offered to this. First, what is the origin of these broader intentions? To enter this avenue of reasoning is to become involved in an infinite regress. Second, to ascribe intentional states to brains is to commit the mereological fallacy (Bennett and Hacker, 2003), the ascription to parts of a system of characteristics that can be attributed only to the system in its entirety. Third, the "creator" is established here as an entity other than the brain which smacks of dualism. Fourth, the notion of intentionality has lost the key incisive role of which Dennett (1969) makes so much, its role as a divider of one kind of sentence (and therefore explanation) from another.

The main reason for steering clear of derived intentionality is that it blunts the precision instrument that Dennett (1969) has been at pains to set up to provide an incisive means of delineating the mental and its role in behavioral explanation. Tenaciously accepting intrinsic intentionality as an a-ontological construct (albeit parting company with Searle) that is primarily a means of distinguishing sentences, means to retain the advantages of a method of analysis that reveals intentional inexistence and the opaqueness of intentional sentences as opposed to the transparency of extensional sentences. The central analytical competence that inheres in distinguishing these two kinds of sentence, hence two types of scientific explanation, is lost if all intentionality is reduced to the derived. Dennett's embracing derived intentionality complicates at the very least the simple plan he put forth in *Content and Consciousness* (1969), and perhaps departs from it entirely.

Dennett's assuming this position fits with his broader philosophy in two ways. First, it is convenient to employ the notion of derived intentionality exclusively since this legitimates and naturalizes the idea that *things* are properly designated intentional systems, that the intentional stance can be applied at the sub-personal level. Second, since Dennett insists on a third-person account of intentionality, it is useful to emphasize that intentionality is always ascribed no matter at what level. The upshot is that by taking a quasi-instrumental approach here, Dennett can argue that even the intrinsic intentionality of the mind (not brain) is ascribed by a third party.

It follows that if intentionality is to be understood as a property of sentences rather than the mark of an ontologically distinct mental realm, then such "intrinsic" intentionality involves not only aboutness but some or all of the linguistic logic of intentionality, i.e., referential opacity and intentional inexistence. Intentionality that is a property of things (a bookcase is about books) is derived and has only the vague quality of aboutness. (Although such derived intentionality does not feature in the present discussion, it will assume interest in the context of rules, which are about something other than themselves but which are not necessarily expressed in opaque sentences.)

Moreover, in order to distinguish intrinsic from derived intentionality, it is necessary to talk about the mental in some sense because referential opacity depends on what the individual knows (first-person) or can be said to know (third-person). What, then is "knowing"? It might be construed as a behavior (Skinner, 1974), a position that avoids an ontological commitment to mentalism. Alternatively, some kind of ontological reality might be accorded a first-personal level of experience through which believing, knowing, desiring, and so on are experienced by the individual. This experience would then be the basis by which the individual can define such terms, albeit through social interaction with a verbal community (Skinner, 1945, 1957). Although I have argued that it is desirable to avoid undue mentalism in defining intentionality, to confine the phenomenon to sentences, this personal level of experience through which the *contents* of intentionality are initially and fundamentally experienced and defined, through which the way to use intentional sentences is initially learned, cannot be escaped. This is not to make the intrinsic/derived distinction in another way. We are still speaking of the meaning of sentences and how such meanings are learned and conveyed; we are invoking a subjective level of experience as the method by which such learning initially takes place.

Mind and consciousness

Hence, the originating source of third-personal intentionality, that which is ascribed in the process of heterophenomenology (Dennett, 1991b), is the first-personal (subjective) experience of intentionality that each person has as he or she thinks and feels, for him- or herself, privately. The term "mind" denote this subjective experience of the world, unique to the individual, that includes having beliefs and desires. We only know such things (can be said to) exist because subjectively we believe and desire (or have experience of believing and desiring, or come to learn through contact with a verbal community that the experience we know inwardly is called believing and desiring). This emphatically non-Wittgensteinian position proposes that we can attribute these acts to others – in order to understand, explain or predict their behavior – only because we "have had them ourselves." Dennett's (1991b) heterophenomenological procedure would be otherwise impossible. A conclusion is that it is feasible to speak of mind in first-personal or third-personal terms.

Searle (2004) argues for the first personal (experiential, subjective) level by noting that all conscious phenomena have three properties.

The first is qualitativeness: "...every conscious state has a qualitative feel to it" (Searle, 2004, p. 134). This is what is referred to by the term *qualia*, though in opposition to some philosophers of mind, Searle includes both cognitive and affective consciousness in this term. (Searle's objection to the term *qualia*, on the grounds that it suggests that "some conscious states are not qualitative," exemplifies well what I have elsewhere called "the manner of philosophers" (Foxall, 2004). His objection arises apparently because some authors use "qualia" to refer only to emotional feels whereas Searle (quite rightly) wants to include thinking/conscious cognition. It might have been more straightforward simply to make this point rather than to "object" to the term itself. He goes on to make the perfectly acceptable point that having defined qualia in this broader way, he can equate consciousness with qualia.) In fact, we only know that there are such states because we experience them in this subjective way. Our only suspicion that others might have them too arises in this way. There would be no third-person analysis of intentionality or cognition or consciousness if there were not a preexisting first-person experience thereof. Heterophenomenology is only possible because there is already "homophenomenology" (or, of course, just phenomenology).

The second is subjectivity. The qualitative character of consciousness means that "conscious states exist only when they are experienced by a human or animal subject" (pp. 134–5). This is their *ontological subjectivity* or *first person ontology*. It exists only from a first-person point of view and to know ones own consciousness is to have a kind of knowledge that is different from knowing (about) some else's. (Scholars as disparate as Malcolm (1977) and Skinner (1945, 1974) seem to agree on this; an interesting question is where Dennett fits. He makes strong claims to be objectively third-personal even in *Content and Consciousness* (1969) and at best has a dismissive attitude to what most people would regard as first-personal experience. Yet his discussion of the personal level of analysis (1969, pp. 90–6) seems to rely on a subjective experience of pain, for instance.

There can, Searle points out, nevertheless, be a scientific, objective or third-person study of consciousness. In an *epistemic* sense, there are statements whose truth value can be determined independently of the feelings and attitudes of speaker or listener. "Tom weights 200 pounds" is one such epistemically objective sentence. However. "Tom is more fun to be with than Alice" is epistemically subjective: it has truth value only in the context of a particular individual's evaluations. It is also possible to make a distinction based on mode of existence. Conscious states have a subjective mode of existence in that they exist only when experienced by human or animal; they differ in this from pretty well anything else that exists. Searle (2004, pp. 135–6). So the fact that conscious states are ontologically subjective does not preclude an objective study of them: "*ontological subjectivity of the subject matter does not preclude an epistemically objective science of that very subject matter.*" Neurologists try to establish objectively the causes of subjectively experienced pain. This has to tie in with the personal level/sub-personal level distinction.

Searle does not, moreover, mention explicitly that we can only embark on a third-person objective scientific study of consciousness – insofar as this applies to other people – if we assume that other people have minds and consciousness like our own. This is a plausible working assumption but we can make it only by considering the behavior and speech acts of others, i.e., by providing an answer to the perennial question of the ontological and methodological availability of other minds. In other words, our objective study is not independent of our making this assumption; rather the making of the assumption is itself a part of the objective study of consciousness which it supposed to legitimate. (This problem does not arise if, as in the case of Dennett, minds are ascriptions made for the sole purpose of predicting behavior). Now, having said this about the existence of a first-personal mind, there is no need to propose that first person subjectivism is the determinative factor in behavior or that its workings can be fully known through introspection (Ross, Spurrett and Vuchinich, 2005, pp. 17–19.)

The third is unity, by which he means that the various modalities of consciousness work together to produce an overall experience of what is going on. Hence, argues that qualitativeness, subjectivity and unity are a single whole, something that jars with Dennett's (1991b) repudiation of the notion that there is a "Cartesian theatre where it [consciousness] all comes together." Nevertheless, our conscious experience suggests on a common-sense level that there is such an arena (and, as has frequently been pointed out, it is this experience that Dennett fails to explain.) We can explore this more thoroughly in terms of what Strawson (1994) refers to as *agnostic materialism.*

Strawson is a thoroughgoing materialist, basing this stance on physicalism (the belief that there is a physical world, which is "much as it is ordinarily supposed to be,") and monism (the view that the universe comprises only on kind of stuff which constitutes everything.) Mental events, whatever they may be, are subject to these assumptions: they are realized entirely by the physical and, since evolution provides an authentic account of human origins, the nature of mind must be approached naturalistically. But he is an "agnostic materialist." Since Strawson believes that materialism must be accepted "on faith" (at least the faith justified by this reasoning), whence his agnosticism? The first stage in answering this question is Strawson's understanding of the nature of experience. He uses this term much as other philosophers use conscious/consciousness: hence, all experience is conscious experience. But this experience has no neurological substrate. Hence, there is an incompatibility between the physical and the mental: "...when we consider the brain as current physics and neurophysiology presents it to us, we are obliged to admit that we do not know how experience – experiential what-it's-like-ness – is or even could be realized in the brain... [I]t just leaves out the phenomenal or experiential character of my experience." (pp. 81–2). The result is that "Our existing notions of the physical and the mental or experiential cannot possibly be reconciled or theoretically integrated as they stand." (p. 104)

This position may become clearer by comparison with that of a philosopher such as Dennett whose view is that while individuals may seem to have subjective experiences of the kind Strawson takes for granted, these apparent phenomena are actually illusory. Hence, Strawson, in line with his common-sense view of experience, takes issue with "Philosophers [who] may conceivably propose a radically new theory of what pain really is, and say that relative to this theory, our experience of pain can correctly be characterized as illusion or mere seeming. The reply is immediate, however: *whatever* the proposal, the seeming is itself and ineliminably a real thing, and whatever the nature of the universe, it is what we denote when we use the word 'pain'." "For this seeming is already experience." (p. 51) With Dennett in mind he goes on:

> It has been suggested that experience might not really be a matter of qualitative character or phenomenology at all, that it might somehow be wholly the product of some cognitive faculty, the "judgment module" or "semantic intent module," and that we might to that extent be entirely deluded about its nature. Thinking along such lines, Dennett has suggested that "there is no such thing [as] ... phenomenology." "*There seems to be phenomenology,*" he concludes, "but it does not follow from this undeniable, universally attested fact that *there really is* phenomenology" (Dennett, 1991b, 365–6; compare Rey, 1993).

What Dennett argues in those pages is that just as the characters in a novel have no independent life of their own, though they can be investigated by literary critics taking the third-personal viewpoint of science, so the life of the mind that seems so real to the individual thinker has no real existence, but is amenable to heterophenomenological procedures. (See Dennett, 1991b, pp. 365–6). Dennett is rejecting the view that consciousness is a "plenum", a whole that brings together into one entity the various strands of awareness provided ultimately via the separate sense modalities. It may *seem* as if there is a "Cartesian theatre" in which this occurs but the lack of any central processing sector of the brain rules this out, brands it as no more than illusion. (See also Dennett, 1991b, pp. 406–11). Here, in words that support the attribution "behaviorist" made by some philosophers of Dennett, he describes first his experiencing a beautiful external scene of sunlight and trees on a spring day, synchronized in some way with the Vivaldi to which he was listening. He marvels how "my conscious thinking, and especially the enjoyment I felt in the combination of sunny light, sunny Vivaldi violins, rippling branches – plus the pleasure I took in just thinking about it all – how call *all that* be just something physical happening in my brain? How could any combination of electrochemical happenings in my brain somehow add up to the delightful way those hundreds of twigs genuflected in time with the music? How could some information-processing event in my brain be the delicate warmth of the sunlight I felt falling on me? ... It does not seem possible." (p. 407). Yet, in applying his heterophenomenological methodology, he arrives at the answer to the question, *But what about the actual phenomenology?* – "There is no such thing." (p. 365) Commenting on the text created by his description of his sitting in his rocker on the spring day described above, he says "...we should not suppose that when he looked out the window, he 'took it all in' in one wonderful mental gulp – even though this is what his text portrays. It seemed to him, according to the text, as if his mind – his visual field – were filled with intricate details of gold-brown buds and wiggling branches, but although this is how it seemed, this was an illusion. No such 'plenum' ever came into his mind; the plenum remained out in the world where it didn't have to be represented, but could just be." (pp. 407–8; see also pp. 408–11).

It becomes necessary to ask again what has happened to the personal level of analysis, so central to Dennett's reasoning in *Content and Consciousness*. (It is interesting that Dennett's comment about the plenum being out there in the world but not part of his experience (in

Strawson's term) is reminiscent of Skinner's statement that it was Pavlov who associated the metronome and the meat powder (US and CS), not the dog, and that this association was a physical one taking place in the external environment. Similarly behavioristic; similarly doctrinaire in its ontology.)

There, (see especially pp. 90–6), Dennett seems to be arguing that the personal experience of, say, pain, is a necessary assumption for the third-personal ascription of pain. Strawson argues, as I have done above, that whatever *seems* like personal conscious experience – e.g., that resulting from listening to music – *is* the conscious experience that philosophers ought (a) to recognize actually exits and (b) try to explain. The view of the philosophers who deny this "seems to be one of the most amazing manifestations of human irrationality on record" (p. 53.) While Dennett is saying, in effect, "There is no neurophysiological evidence for the kind of experience of which Strawson speaks: therefore it does not exist," Strawson is saying, in effect, "It does exist: therefore the neurophysiological evidence does not or has not been discovered yet. Hence my agnostic materialism."

Strawson speaks, moreover, of the "inescapability of metaphysics" (pp. 78–9): "... one cannot get out of metaphysics. As soon as one admits that something exists – and one must do that – one has to admit that it has some nature or other. And as soon as one admits that it has some nature or other, either one has to hold that one knows what its nature is – in which case one endorses a particular metaphysical claim about the nature of reality – or one has to admit that one might be wrong about its nature, at least in the sense that one might have an *incomplete* picture of its nature – in which case one admits that there are various metaphysical possibilities, even if one can never know for sure which one is correct." (p. 78)

The conscious experience of mental behavior has neural and behavioral correlates but neither of these is mind itself. This is very close to what Skinner calls private or covert behavior, the realm of the private events of thinking and feeling. I would add: (1) that the processes I am talking about could be unconscious as well as conscious, (2) while they may be determined by external contingencies as Skinner proposes, they may be modified to some degree by the individual's own creative interpretations (Horne and Lowe, 1993a, b, c); this is the basis of cognitive activity, (3) they may function as what Skinner (1988a, b, c) calls non-initiating causes insofar as they embody rules that influence covert and overt behaviors, (4) though they may be creatively modified by the individual to whom they belong, and may be insensitive to changing contingencies in the short term, they will ultimately be brought into conformity with the contingencies that prevail (Catania, Matthews and Shimoff, 1982), (5) contra Skinner, when one speaks of the mental as coterminous with the covert or private, this does not imply that the mental is composed of non-material stuff; it is reasonable to accept that the world will doubtless be found to be composed only of matter, even though it is not necessarily possible to find the neural substrates of personal experience at present (Strawson, 1994) or ever (McGinn, 1989b, 1991). To the extent that the mental consists in behaviors, it is material because behavior is material. What I conclude is that covert behaviors, because they consist in intentional behaviors such as believing and desiring, knowing and deciding (Skinner, 1974), must be spoken of in a different kind of language from that which is appropriate for extensional behavioral science – the language of intentionality. This modifies our explanation (as I have argued earlier). Mind has both neural and behavioral substrates but is not reducible to either, though each is essential to it and it arises from their interaction (Greenfield, 2001).

Third-personal ascription of intentionality

The question arises what entities can be treated – when we come to apply a third-personal, scientific approach – as minds or as having minds? In other words, to what entities can heterophenomenology be sensibly applied? The criteria are the order of intentionality that can be ascribed to them, and the possibility of more appropriately applying a stance other then the intentional to them.

The criterion is the concern of theory of mind. An entity is said to have theory of mind (ToM) if at least second-order intentionality can be ascribed to it. (Note that no ontological assumption is needed here with respect to what is actually going on within this entity, its mental or other components and their functioning. This is a linguistic and methodological ascription. It operates at the level of IST abstracta.) Intentional behaviorism requires the ascription of just first-order intentionality: he believes that p, or desires p, etc. Super-personal cognitive psychology, however, requires higher-orders of intentionality to be ascribed to the entities it attempts to predict and explain. It is uncertain that any non-human animal or thing displays second-order intentionality. This must, however, remain an empirical question: the behaviors of apes, but not monkeys or dolphins, appear to verge on second-order intentionality (Dunbar, 2004).

Another consideration here is that no non-human animal has been shown to display stimulus equivalence. If, as I have argued (Foxall, 2004), this phenomenon can be accounted for only by the attribution of intentionality, this follows naturally enough from what I have just said about theory of mind. Even if one takes a firmly radical behaviorist line with respect to stimulus equivalence, however, there is an enigma here. It is also interesting that the age at which children acquire the verbal skills necessary to devise their own rules about the nature of the concurrent schedules operating in matching experiments (Horne and Lowe, 1993) is that at which ToM emerges.

The second criterion revolves about the need to invoke the intentional stance at all. For physical entities the physical and design stances suffice; for animals, the contextual stance; only for humans the intentional stance and even then only for the whole person. *Mind* is a theoretical entity that may be seen either as a device that "saves the theory" or as an integral element in the theory insofar as it seeks to explain and act as a stimulus to further research and thought rather than simply to predict. There is an ontological argument for using the concept of mind in our theories as well as a linguistic case for talking about minds. The underlying reason for positing mind and its contents is that we cannot reduce experience to physics (Strawson, 1994; cf. McGinn, 1989a).

This is not to deny the materiality of experience and consciousness; nor to deny that experience has a physiological substrate which is modified by further experience. But this amounts to no more than an "agnostic materialism" since we do not know the mechanisms involved in getting from experience to neurology. The neurology may at times be the only evidence of the existence of mind – e.g., when we are asleep or otherwise unconscious. But its dependence on conscious experience (fetal pain issue) mean that when we are "awake," our minds are more than our brains. This is the ontological argument for speaking in terms of minds and for conceptualizing them as requiring the interaction of neurophysiological development and conscious experience. The linguistic case we have already encountered: it is the phenomenon of intentional vs extensional language. For we tend to understand the content of our own subjective experience in terms of beliefs, desires and other intentions, and we can reconstruct the conscious experience of others, whether to predict them or explain them, only in these terms. Dennett's three kinds of intentional psychology are three levels on which such heterophenomenology may be undertaken. And, in speaking of beliefs and desires, we are engaging in a form of expression that is importantly different from those of the neu-roscientific and behavioral sciences, the sciences of extensionality, in which we ordinarily conduct our research. The four kinds of contextual psychology and the integrated cognitive-behavioral model portray the means by which behavioral experience may enter into the definition of mind.

We cannot avoid intentional idioms when we seek to explain behav-ior beyond identifying the environmental influences with which it covaries. It is necessary, as we have seen, in order to account for the personal level of explanation, account for behavioral continuity, and delimit our interpretations of complex behavior. Moreover, when behavioral scientists employ intentionalistic language they are present-ing a different kind of explanation from the extensional approach which Skinner/radical behaviorism strives to maintain. This is because, as I have pointed out, intentional sentences are not translatable into extensional sentences without adding either information or mentalistic neologisms. But it is not a matter of either/or. We need both. Hence when Baum and Heath (1992, p. 1316) argue that

> When the history is unavailable, the behaviorist speculates in the light of what is already known, exactly as in other sciences... In the absence of information, one guesses at the appropriate history... The great advantage of speculating about history, in contrast to fictional present causes, is that it holds out the possibility of replac-ing guesswork with observation

they are entirely correct – as far as an extensional account is con-cerned. But an explanatory account that seeks to show why things are this way, a necessarily intentional account, is required also. They are not competing accounts: they are seeking to fulfill different functions.

Mind includes that subjectively available consciousness in which we are aware of acting cognitively or affectively. It has both neurophysio-logical and behavioral correlates, perhaps "causes." Although it is sub-jectively experienced and apparent, it is the basis, when attributed to others, of a universal means of understanding, predicting and reacting to the behavior of others. This experience (or verbal reports of it if we wish to be fastidious) correlate with both physical events in the brain and external conditions that are contingent upon behavior, but they are a separate entity from either of these. Just as material as the neu-ronal substrates and environmental superstrates with which they corre-late, they are private and subjective, not amenable as the correlates are to examination by extensional neuroscience or extensional behavioral science but existing and reportable only in the first person. This is the only way in which a person can know his or her own mental events such as pain, depression, or anxiety. That others are having similar experiences is inferable from physiological measures, from their verbal and non-verbal reports of what is going on, and from the third-personal analysis of their life conditions. But the mentality in which they experience these events (as well as joys and affections) are not the same as any of these. The heterophenomenological reconstruction of these events is a third-personal activity that is indispensable to their being fully understood. Hitherto, many scientists have concentrated on one cause of these mental events (almost) to the exclusion of the other. Kagan (2006, pp. 54–5) comments, "Scientists are now demonstrating what they had believed but had been unable to prove: namely, that a psychological symptom, such as depression or a panic attack, requires both a genetic vulnerability and a set of life conditions. Either one alone is insufficient to produce the disabling state. For example, intense feelings of depression occur in children when early parental abuse, lack of social support, and a genetic vulnerability that affects the amount of seratonin in the brain are combined. In this and other examples there is no single cause. A coherence of several factors is necessary to produce a particular phenomenon."

I want however to contrast these subjective feelings with the cognitive processes that inhere in the generation of sentences expressing beliefs and desires, the sentences containing propositional content that behave differently from extensional sentences. By the time our desires and beliefs reach the stage of being expressed in such fully formed sentences they are already the outcome of a process of ascription to them of intentionality based on the kind of deductive reasoning that has led to their formation in the first place. They differ therefore from the direct raw feels or qualia that are our affective reactions such as pains. They are something over whose formulation we have some control as a result of the grammatical and syntactic operations we impose on sentence formation, structuring, and utterance.

I want also to distinguish these intentions (expressible in intentional sentences) from the dispositions of which Ryle has made us aware. To speak of a person having "strength of character" because of he manner in which her behavior perseveres toward a goal in the face of constant obstructions is to attribute to her a disposition that is not separate from the behavior itself. It is another way of conceptualizing or organizing the behavior from that of seeing each act as a separate event. It is a relational category in that it links separate acts together into a pattern. Desires and beliefs (and other intentions) are dispositional too, but they have the special property that they can be expressed in the kinds of sentence that has been explored. It is principally with these intentions that I am concerned. They are not the whole of mind or mentality but they are an element of it that must be taken firmly into consideration in the explanation of choice.

Part II
Kinds of Contextual Psychology

4
Intentional Psychologies

> The recently arrived Martian does not take his umbrella when
> it is cloudy because he has never learned to connect the pres-
> ence of clouds with the possibility of rain. The behaviorist asks
> us to believe, however, that nothing has changed inside of us
> who have made that link. (Juarrero, 1999, p. 51).

Juarrero is not entirely fair to behaviorists, whose aim was only ever to
predict and control behavior rather than to explain it any further; nor
has the behaviorist denied that internal change at the physiological
level accompanies our learning. But the explanation of such behavior
requires, as we have seen, some inference or other about intentionality.
Dennett (1969) proposed a plausible scheme for the scientifically-
compatible ascription of the necessary content but the clearcut distinction on which that early work was based has become clouded in his
later writings. Indeed, having drawn the personal/sub-personal division
so vividly and usefully in *Content and Consciousness*, Dennett subsequently loosened the argument that content was ascribable only at the
personal level of non-mechanical explanation, and proposed that
mechanistic sub-personal systems may be treated as intentional
systems in their own right via the ascription of content that permits
their prediction. Dennett's introduction of the idea of sub-personal
cognitive psychology is a particular source of confusion of his original
personal/sub-personal dichotomy. The next chapter attempts to lay an
unambiguous basis for behavioral psychology in which the level of
analysis at which content ascription may properly be made is established as the personal level, and the range of non-personal levels of
analysis which provide the basis for such attribution is extended from
the sub-personal to the super-personal in order that behavior may be

systematically incorporated in the scheme of explanation to which Dennett has given rise. It argues, moreover, that only at the personal level is it possible to ascribe intentionality in order to explain behavior; of particular importance in the present context, it is the only level at which cognition and consciousness can be ascribed. The development in Dennett's thought with respect to the personal–sub-personal distinction is specifically addressed, and the confusion in philosophical psychology that has arisen from the proliferation of levels of explanation is examined. It is argued that the personal level, which is at least severely de-emphasized in Dennett's continuing work, is of central importance to the philosophical basis of cognitive psychology since it is the sole level at which cognition can be said to occur.

The personal level of explanation is, moreover, vital to both intentional and behavioral psychologies: to the first because it is at this level alone that intentional content can be legitimately ascribed, to the second because of the necessity of making sense of private events and their status in a causal theory. Perhaps no-one has argued more convincingly for the theoretical necessity of this level of analysis, nor has anyone sought to undermine its theoretical value, more so than Daniel Dennett. For, the grounds provided by Dennett for the legitimate ascription of content have with time become vaguer insofar as they have become explicitly detached from the logic of evolutionarily-consistent reasoning that originally underpinned the distinction. Admittedly, the rules for ascribing beliefs and desires to a rational system in order to predict it (i.e., the execution of the intentional stance or as Dennett refers to it *the intentional strategy*) include consideration of what beliefs and desires it "ought" to have given its position and circumstances, and this is bound to include considerations that stem from its phylogenetic history as well as its current setting. But this is a less detailed and less logically constructed version of the procedure for allocation content than that given in *Content and Consciousness* (Dennett, 1969). This procedure involves the ascription of content to the theories and findings of the extensional sciences that proceed at the sub-personal level, but it leaves them intact in the process. It is an additional level of interpretation; it does not take place in the terms of the extensional science on which it is built and is thus not a contribution to neuroscience; rather, it comprises a heuristic device that is composed of intentional idioms, which do not belong in an extensional science. It exists on a level other than the sub-personal which characterizes neuroscience: the personal level, the only level at which it is legitimate to ascribe content, according to the early

Dennett. This is the process in which the ascription of intentional idioms takes place and the process produces the personal level by prescribing in a way that is highly circumscribed by the logic of evolution by natural selection the content that an evolved entity "ought" to have by virtue of its phylogeny.

But there is more to the prediction and explanation of the organism's behavior than the ascription of content according to the principles of evolutionarily-consistent reasoning. The intentional strategy (Dennett, 1987) assumes that the behavior of an organism can be predicted only by the ascription of content relating not only to its evolution but also to its current position, those of its circumstances which signal the rewards and punishments of following a particular course of action *primed by* the organism's learning history gained in similar circumstances. It requires in other words the ascription of content (again to arrive at the personal level) on the basis of the theories and findings of extensional science that deals with the effects of social and physical context on the ontogenetic development of the organism, including its acquisition of a behavioral repertoire. I submit that this science is behavior analysis in which the fundamental unit of analysis is the environment–behavior contingency (Lee, 1988). Content may be legitimately attributed to the findings of this science on the basis of the principle of "selection by consequences" (Skinner, 1981) which includes not only natural selection but the process in which a behavioral repertoire is acquired in the course of operant conditioning. Behavior analysis thus provides an extensional basis for a super-personal level of analysis. How would the process of ascription be determined in this case?

While there is a good understanding of the neurological basis of pain, Dennett raises the question whether the presumed evolutionarily-appropriate afferent-efferent networks underlying this understanding are sufficient (they are certainly necessary) to account for the "phenomena of pain." Commentators on *Content and Consciousness* seem often to overlook the ambitious nature of Dennett's project: the resolution of the claims of extensional science with the inevitability of intentional explanation of behavior. This is to be achieved not by the super-conceptual integration of the two systems of explanation, which retain their individual claims to uniqueness as explicators of one or other facet of natural phenomena, but to ground the intentional in a basis of materialism that rescues it from apparently unlimited phenomenological speculation.

Dennett notes the unfeasibility of S-R theorists' – under which term he seem to subsume advocates of both respondent and operant behaviorisms – showing how a novel stimulus can arrive at or select the appropriate response. He points out, for instance, that an animal might detect a stimulus but not "know" what the appropriate response is (the stimulus in question could as well be discriminative stimulus as unconditioned or conditioned.) No afferent can be taken by the brain to have significance unless it is recognized by the efferent side of the brain as having it, i.e., until the brain has produced the appropriate response. The content of a neural event or state depends not only upon its "normal state of stimulation" but also whatever additional efferent effects it produces. The determination of these factors necessarily takes us beyond the extensional description of stimuli and responses. Indeed, the lack of an account of behavior at the personal level imposes a severe restriction on radical behaviorist explanation (Foxall, 2004).

The categorical distinction

Content can accordingly be ascribed to a neural event when it is a link in an *appropriate chain* between afferent and efferent which has been selected in the course of the phylogeny of the organism in question. The content is not something to be discovered *within* this neural event but is an extra interpretation, the rationale of which is not to understand better the operation of the subsystem *per se* but to provide a local justification for the ascription of appropriate content at the personal level. The ultimate justification for such ascription is provided by evolutionary thinking – the intelligent brain must be able to select the appropriate response to a specific stimulus. Why should this be less the case for the link between extensional operant analysis and the personal level of analysis than for that between physiology and that level? A totally biological theory of behavior would still not be able, Dennett claims, to account for *what the person is doing*. Intentional ascription simply describes what a purely extensional theory would describe, nothing more, but in a different way. This different way may be useful to the physiologist, however. Neuroscience that does not view neural events as signals, reports, or messages can scarcely function at all. No purely biological logic can tell us why the rat knows which way to go for his food. Nor can any purely contextualistic logic reveal this in the absence of some sort of "Dennettian overlay." In neither case does the proposed intentional ascription detract from the extensional version of events but adds an interpretation that provides greater intuitive understanding of the system.

Hence, the sub-personal level is coterminous with that of an extensional science such as physiology, which is mechanistic in the explanations it provides. Intentional explanation simply *does not belong at this level* and we cannot add content to this level without violating its integrity as a conventionally scientific (i.e. extensional) approach to theory. But we can use it as the basis of appropriate content ascription (i.e. the attribution of intentional idioms that make certain behaviors of the organism intelligible – pain, for instance, or other emotional activity – but in so adding content, we arrive at the personal level of explanation. This is the sole level at which pain, etc. can be comprehended. There is a sharp epistemological dichotomy here between the personal and sub-personal levels of explanation: at one of which it is appropriate to include intentional explanations, the other serving as a basis for legitimately doing so but remaining intact as an extensional level of understanding. The guiding principle by which content is added is evolutionary logic: the process of natural selection that produced the findings identified at the level of physiology (or other sub-personal science) must provide the logic by which activities that are proposed in order to explain or predict the behavior of the whole organism.

The intentional stance

By the time of Dennett's (1981) distinction among three *kinds* of intentional psychology, however, his thinking demonstrates some subtle changes in the use of the terms personal and sub-personal levels and their relationships with psychology. He argues that folk psychology (the first kind of intentional psychology) provides a source of the other two: "intentional systems theory" and "sub-personal cognitive psychology." Folk psychology provides a non-specific and unhelpful causal theory of behavior: a more systematic and useful predictive tool requires refinement. The distinction between logical constructs or *abstracta* and causally interacting *illata* provides a key. While the beliefs and desires of abstract and instrumental folk psychology are abstracta, the interactive theoretical constructs of sub-personal cognitive psychology are illata.

Each of the two additional intentional psychologies Dennett proposes rests integrally on one or other. *Intentional systems theory* (the second kind of intentional psychology) draws upon the notions of belief and desire but provides them with a more technical meaning than they receive in folk psychology. It is a whole-person psychology, dealing with "...the prediction and explanation from belief–desire profiles of the actions of whole systems... The *subject* of all the intentional attributions is the whole system (the person, the animal, or even the corporation or nation [see Dennett, 1976] rather than any of its parts..." (Dennett, 1987, p. 58). Intentional systems theory is a competence theory in that it specifies the functional requirements of the system without going on to speculate as to what form they might take. The necessity of this general level theory is that of providing an account of intelligence, meaning, reference, or representation. Intentional systems theory is blind to the internal structure of the system.

A person who has only been a passenger in a motor car might pursue such an approach to a theory how the engine works by conjecturing that it must have a means of generating motive power or, even, that it must be capable of transforming linear movement into rotary. "Motive power" and "transformation" are, at this stage, no more than highly abstract notions that point to the more specific parts out of which the engine and other apparatus within the car must be constituted, abstracta. This theory, highly abstract as it is, could still lead to predictions such as that a car without such means of power and transformation would not move.

The capacity of abstracta to interrelate, predict, and partly explain behavior itself suggests some underlying mechanism to which intentional systems theory does not on principle address itself. Any intentional system of interest would surely have a complex internal structure and chances are this will be found to resemble closely the instrumental intentional interpretation. The third kind of intentional psychology, "*sub-personal cognitive psychology*," is tasked with explaining the brain as a syntactic engine (as opposed to the task of intentional systems theory which is to explain it as a semantic engine).

This terminology and leap in analysis are in themselves misleading and confusing. The level of illata is simply that of cognitive psychology: there is no need to designate it further *sub-personal*. This immediately suggests a source of confusion with the sub-personal level of analysis, especially as it has been defined in terms of the extensional rather than the intentional. It appears, moreover, that Dennett is thinking of cognitive psychology as requiring no other qualification than sub-personal: he is not contrasting this with super-personal cognitive psychology, for instance, something which does not enter into his thinking at all. The distinction he is making is that between the personal level, at which abstracta operate, and that of another level at which illata do. For him, this is the sub-personal. But, as I aim to show in this paper, cognitive psychology may require sub-personal *and/or* super-personal qualification depending upon which source of justification for the ascription of cognitive variables at the personal level of analysis is being alluded to. In the case of sub-personal cognitive psychology this remains the naturally selected afferent–efferent linkages embedded in neurology; in the case of super-personal cognitive psychology it is environment–behavior linkages. I shall argue, further, that both abstracta and illata are phenomena of the personal level. The analysis appropriate to what is internal to the organism is neuroscience; intentionalistic psychological theories must perforce deal at the personal level.

The underlying mechanism to which even abstracta appeal in their capacity to explain and which (sub-personal) cognitive psychology attempts to uncover and explicate must surely be physiological in nature and requires an extensional neuroscience to reveal it. Cognitive psychology remains as theoretical an enterprise as intentional systems theory: its focus is the explanation of the brain as syntactical through its identification of the cognitive variables that may be legitimately ascribed at the personal level. In doing this it draws upon both its sub-personal and super-personal inputs, neurology and behavior, both of which are approached through an extensional science. But itself, cognitive psychology, remains an intentional science. To deviate from this "pure" dichotomy of the personal and sub-personal/super-personal is to invite the mereological fallacy. (For an alternative view of Dennettian philosophy of psychology and mereology, and its application to economic theory, see Ross, 2005).

The subtle difference that accompanies Dennett's later usages inheres in his (1978, p. 154) argument that the behavior of the person as a whole is the outcome of the interactive behavior of its various subsystems (Hornsby, 2000, pp. 16–17). This is a departure from his earlier insistence that to move to the sub-personal level, i.e., to the operation of the central and peripheral nervous systems, is to leave behind the personal level of explanation of sensations, intentionality, and behavior. Hornsby argues that this is inconsistent with the proscription on using sub-personal level findings to understand the personal level. Why-questions about the behavior of an actor in an environment can be answered only at the personal level. It is Dennett's later claim that the program of sub-personal cognitive psychology is to show how the physicalist findings of sub-personal extensional science can be used to interpret a fully-realized intentional system operating at the personal level that is the problem.

Hornsby (2000, pp. 20–1) seeks to maintain the distinction between personal and sub-personal levels of explanation by arguing that intentional phenomena are real at the levels of persons but merely as-if constructions at the sub-personal level. The attraction of this is that it maintains the independence of the personal level as a basis of explanation but permits the intentional stance to be operated at the sub-personal level for purposes of predicting the behavior of subsystems. Her somewhat arbitrary assertion however makes a ontological distinction between persons and non-persons (animals, subsystems, machines) that Dennett has sidestepped by adopting an instrumental approach to the ascription of intentionality (ascription is justified if it facilitates prediction, to have a mind or its constituent beliefs, desires, etc. is simply to have behavior that is predictable on the assumption that one has a mind, beliefs, desires, and so on.) Dennett seems to have dealt with her position already (Dennett, 1978, pp. 272–3). Again, it is the distinction between Dennett's earlier and later positions on instrumentalism versus realism that seems to be at the heart of the misunderstanding.

This problem clearly rests on the more limited project in *Content and Consciousness*, which focused on the materialistic delineation of the intentional by reference to a genuinely sub-personal level of neuroscience, and Dennett's later enterprise focusing on the development of sub-personal cognitive psychology as the basis of a philosophy of cognitivism. In *Content and Consciousness*, Dennett was concerned primarily with establishing how the findings of an extensional neuroscience could be brought into a single framework of analysis along with the conclusions of a mental science which recognized, albeit critically, the reality of intentional phenomena. The overall framework was to be consistent with materialism and thus to eschew an easy metaphysical reconciliation. The aim was to devise an a-ontological basis for the systematic ascription of content to the findings of physiology (a science of the sub-personal), the purpose of which was not enhance or contribute to neuroscience per se but to justify the intentional ascriptions that could be legitimately made to the whole person. What could an individual with this physiology, produced in the process of natural selection in order to generate appropriate afferent–efferent connections that enhanced the fitness of the individual, the propagation of the selfish genes for which it acted as a replication machine, be said to have by way of beliefs and desires? The ascriptions are not part of physiology but an additional interpretation that makes possible analysis at the personal level, that prevents the unwarranted ascription of intentional content simply to explain behavior on mentalistic, uncritical folk-psychological grounds. They are, moreover, the ascriptions that account for personal level experience, such as that of pain, which cannot *by their nature* be accounted for in terms of neuroscience, the unanalyzable nature of felt pain, of which the individual experiencing it can say no more than "It hurts", thereby bringing analysis to a quick end.

The implications for cognitive psychology which are drawn in a rudimentary way in *Content and Consciousness* are that it is an activity of the personal level that inextricably involves intentional phenomena but that it has been reconciled with extensional science through the agency of natural selection. It is when Dennett (1978) seeks to clarify the nature of intentional psychology by introducing a distinction between intentional systems theory and sub-personal cognitive psychology that potential confusion arises. The difficulty revolves around the status of sub-personal cognitive psychology.

In seeking to resolve it, it is important to appreciate that the sub-personal level of explanation that Dennett (1969) describes differs from the sub-personal cognitive psychology he introduced later (Dennett, 1981), and how. While the sub-personal level consists in extensional science, sub-personal cognitive psychology, being derived from folk psychology, adds to this the heuristic overlay of ascribed intentional content that properly belongs at the personal level. However many levels of explanation emerge from Dennett's scheme, the most prevalent current cognitive psychology, *social cognition*, is founded upon another: the super-personal level, an extensional psychology founded upon the "contextual stance," that relates behavior to the environmental contingencies that shape and maintain it (Foxall, 1999), and which is linked to the personal level of explanation by means of the ascription to the theories and findings of that extensional science of intentional content (Foxall, 2004). The three stances, pre-empirical methodological prescriptions for the prediction and partial explanation of systems, that Dennett proposes provide a key to the number of levels of explanation at which psychology may operate and clarify some of their interrelationships. In particular, the design stance, which Elton (2003) shows to be bifurcated in Dennett's writings, is highly relevant to the distinction between the sub-personal level of explanation and sub-personal cognitive psychology.

Sub-personal cognitive psychology

Perhaps the distinction between competence and performance cannot always be made with finality in connection with actual theories of behavior; more likely is it that many theories have elements of compe-tence-specification and performance-specification and heat there is often a to-ing and fro-ing between these levels among scientists in the way they use theories. (Certainly, as Dennett notes, the same terms appear in both, treated variously as abstracta and illata. This fact implies, however, a degree of commonality in the concepts the terms describe that would be overlooked by preserving too strict a dichotomy between them.) Nevertheless, the distinction provides an exploitable analytic model of how theories are built and how they interrelate. As ever with such schemes, the evaluation of the distinction depends on its capacity to elucidate the research process, and I think it presents us with a valuable function in the case of Dennett's kinds of intentional psychology and the kinds of contextual psychology which proposed in the next chapter.

Useful as a competence theory is, moreover, there has to be some underlying internal structure that accounts for the capacity of the various abstracta that are the components of intentional systems theory to predict systemic behavior at the personal level so well. Discovering this structure and its workings is the task of the third kind of intentional psychology: sub-personal cognitive psychology, the task of which consists in "[d]iscovering the constraints on design and implementation variation, and demonstrating how particular species and individuals in fact succeed in realizing intentional systems" (Dennett, 1987, p. 60).

The task of the brain, according to intentional systems theory and evolutionary biology is *semantic*: it must decipher what its stimulus inputs mean and then respond with appropriate behavior. But in fact to the physiologist the brain is no more than a *syntactic* engine: it "dis-criminate[s] its inputs by their structural, temporal, and physical fea-tures and let[s] its entirely mechanical activities be governed by these 'syntactic' features of its inputs" (Dennett, 1987, p. 61). Hence "it is the task of sub-personal cognitive psychology to propose and test models ... of pattern recognition or stimulus generalization, concept learning, expectation, learning, goal-directed behavior, problem-solving – that not only produce a simulacrum of genuine content-sensitivity, but that do this in ways demonstrably like the way people's brains do it, exhibiting the same powers and the same vulnerabilities to deception, overload and confusion. It is here that we will find our good theoretical entities, our useful *illata*, and while some of them may well resemble the familiar entities of folk psychology – beliefs, desires, judgments, decisions – many will certainly not... The only similarity we can be sure of discovering in the *illata* of sub-personal cognitive psychology is the intentionality of their labels (see *Brainstorms* [Dennett, 1978], pp. 23–38). They will be characterized as events with content, bearing information, signaling this and ordering that" (Dennett, 1978, p. 63).

"In order to give the *illata* these labels, in order to maintain any intentional interpretation of their operation at all, the theorist must always keep glancing outside the system, to see what normally produces the configuration he is describing, what effects the system's responses normally have on the environment, and what benefit normally accrues to the whole system from this activity... The alternative of ignoring the external world and its relations to the internal machinery... is not really psychology at all, but just at best abstract neurophysiology – pure internal syntax with no hope of a semantic interpretation. Psychology 'reduced' to neurophysiology in this fashion would not be psychology, for it would not be able to provide an explanation of the regularities it is psychology's particular job to explain: the reliability with which 'intelligent' organisms can cope with their environments and thus prolong their lives. Psychology can, and should, work toward an account of the physiological foundations of psychological processes, not by eliminating psychological or intentional characterizations of those processes, but by exhibiting how the brain implements the intentionally characterized performance specifications of sub-personal theories" (Dennett, 1978, p. 64).

Preserving the personal

We should now take stock of Dennett's altering conception and attribution of importance to the distinction of personal and sub-personal levels of explanation. Four distinct phases are apparent in his thought. The first is the so-called "categorical" distinction (held in varying forms by Davidson, 1980; Davies, 2000; Elton, 2000; Gardner, 2000; Hornsby, 2000) which maintains the analytical difference between these levels of explanation that Dennett set out in 1969. Dennett here holds to a strict personal/ sub-personal distinction, using the latter to ascribe intentionality at the personal level. He also maintains a strict difference between extensional and intentional sciences, claiming that both are necessary. The role of behavior appears important here because it is to its explanation that the ascription of intentionality is ostensibly directed. But it receives no explicit definition or analysis: it is taken as a given, albeit an important one.

In the 1970s, and certainly by 1980, Dennett's criterion for the ascription of content changed from one that was explicitly justifiable on biological grounds to that of the predictability of behavior. This progression, by means of the introduction of the intentional stance, marks the abandonment of the personal level as a seriously entertained analytic category. The distinction between personal and sub-personal, crucial to the originally argued basis for the legitimate ascription of content, is lost as the intentional stance comes to be applied to sub-personal units in order to predict them (see also Hornsby). We have seen that the mereological fallacy, inherent in Dennett's reasoning, rules out such a move, despite the stand on realism that Dennett takes. Behavior is still important because its predictability is a criterion of the legitimate ascription of the mental. But it still receives no additional analysis nor yet definition.

The third phase comes with Dennett's attempt to include cognitive functioning at the sub-personal level: the so-called "sub-personal cognitive psychology" that he has made the center of his philosophy of psychology. The sub-personal that is now the focus of attention is that of an intentional level of analysis that spans the divide between neurology and the personal. The categorical distinction is being further eroded. Behavior now is more sidelined than before. But is the notion of sub-personal cognition sustainable? Or does cognition belong at the personal level?

The final phase (so far) is Dennett's explanation of consciousness. By now any suggestion that the personal is important appears to have been lost – though Elton disagrees – as the quest is for the heterophenomenological interpretation of behavior at the third-personal level. But Elton claims that consciousness can only be entertained at the personal level. Behavior … is presumably important again because it is the basis of heterophenomenological attribution of the content of consciousness. But what are the rules for legitimately ascribing content now? It seems that Dennett has lapsed into the very loose mode of intentional attribution that *Content and Consciousness* was to guard against!

Some sources of confusion

The definition of the sub-personal level as being a target for intentional ascription (i.e., the view that the intentional stance can be used at any level of analysis at which it permits prediction superior to that provided by other stances), something which jars with Dennett's views in

Content and Consciousness though not with his later opinion, reflects the fact that Dennett uses the term sub-personal in two ways (Elton, 2000). In the first, the sub-personal level is devoid of ascribed intentionality in its own right – in *Content and Consciousness*, he speaks of neuroscience in this capacity; the intentionality is something additional to the extensional science and bringing them together results in the personal level analysis by making legitimate in terms of evolutionary reasoning the ascription of appropriate content at that level. The extensional science is coterminous with the sub-personal level of analysis. In the second usage, the sub-personal level *incorporates* intentionality per se: this is the sub-personal cognitive psychology he speaks of in "Three Kinds of Intentional Psychology" (Dennett, 1981). There is no contradiction here since the sub-personal level he defines in *Content and Consciousness* and the sub-personal cognitive psychology he speaks of later are different levels of explanation, each of which draws upon the design stance in its own way (Elton, 2003, 38–41). The first is the "causal blueprint perspective" in which the design of a system is closely related to its causal structure: whether the system is performing as designed can be ascertained by comparing its functioning with the blueprint of its causal structure. How well a chess computer for instance is operating can be judged by comparing its operation with that specified by the program that regulates it. This design gives no indication of what the system is for: even a non-chess playing person could make a judgment of the efficacy of its operations in this manner. The design purpose of the machine does not attract consideration. The "teleological interpretation" of the design stance is, however, vitally concerned with the purpose of the system. The purpose that the system was designed to fulfill can be specified and its progress towards fulfilling that purpose monitored without reference to the causal blueprint of the system. We may know what a spark plug is designed to do and determine its success without knowing how it does it at the level of its sub-operations. We can nevertheless make predictions about the behavior of the spark plug and assess its efficacy in reaching its goal. In the case of the teleological perspective we are concerned with what the system as a whole is designed to do; with the causal blueprint perspective we are concerned with what the subsystems are designed to accomplish and with their interactions.

The result of acknowledging the two kinds of sub-personal analysis results, however, in the proliferation of levels of analysis and raises the question of where any particular psychological theory fits among them. This is particularly clear in the case of social cognitive psychology which is revealed to have connections with both the personal level and sub-personal cognitive psychology but to derive its distinctive purview of human behavior predominantly from yet another level of analysis, the super-personal level of explanation. The sub-personal level that Dennett identified in *Content and Consciousness* is guided in practice by that design stance that Elton understands in terms of the causal blueprint perspective in which physiology attempts by reverse engineering to establish how the organism's subsystems have been designed in the process of evolution by natural selection; the physical stance is also apparent here. By contrast, sub-personal cognitive psychology involves the teleological perspective of the design stance in which intentionality is invoked and ascribed in the attempt to reverse engineer the system as a psychological entity in order to permit the prediction of the system as a whole.

Now Dennett claims that sub-personal systems can be treated as intentional systems, i.e., the intentional stance can be adopted towards them. Elton (2000, p. 4) notes that contrary to Dennett's initial clear distinction between the personal and sub-personal levels, he later, notably in *Consciousness Explained* (Dennett, 1991b), spoke as though the autonomy of the personal level were in doubt and as though an analysis in personal terms could be given of the sub-personal. He notes McDowell's (1994) claims that instead of maintaining the distinction between on the one hand (i) the relationship between a person and her environment, and on the other (ii) the relationship between different components of a person, Dennett conflates them. Hence, Dennett's claim that consciousness inheres in a person's capacity to access the content carried by a subsystem mixes stories that must by their nature be kept separate. According to Elton, however, Dennett does indeed want to pursue the idea of sub-personal processing as a prelude to his conclusions about consciousness, and the problem is that of reconciling this with the force of Dennett's original distinction between the personal and sub-personal. He claims that this is possible if pursued with understanding of how Dennett conceptualizes the ascription of content to systems and their component parts. Dennett has never denied that subsystems can be content-bearing but he has not provided much clue to how such ascription is to take place. Elton suggests that the procedure is as follows. Intentional states (attitudes towards contents) can be attributed, Dennett says, to intentional systems which include people, frogs, chess machines, and robots. They can (Elton says of Dennett) also include *parts* of such systems which can be seen as constituting smaller systems in themselves. On the assumption that the system under investigation has some goals (e.g., to survive, to win, to avoid injuring humans) and some "rational" means to achieve them (e.g. perceptual apparatus, powers of action), *"one then ascribes a whole network of intentional states (both cognitive and motivational) that best make sense of the system's behavior."* (Elton, 2000, p. 6) The constraint on this ascription process is knowledge of what intentional states the system "ought" to have, given its circumstances, and what, in view of the imperfections of the system; it is likely to have in actuality. This is the adoption of the intentional stance.

Elton (2000) proposes, as a means of comprehending so wide a range of systems and of remaining true to Dennett, that a content bearing state be understood liberally as "no more than a state that is semantically evaluable and behavior guiding... what the state represents may or may not be the case and the behavior of the system will, in appropriate circumstances, be suitably affected by the presence of the state. Thermostats represent the temperature of the room – but of course a thermostat may do so incorrectly if place it in a draught – and this representation affects what they do, e.g. switch the boiler on or off." (Elton, 2000, p. 6). So general a view of content requires that different kinds of content must be distinguished. Elton distinguishes content ascribed to a dog from that (less structured content) ascribed to a frog or (less structured still) that ascribed to a chess machine. While "The content ascribed to persons has a structure such that it can figure in chains of reasoning, in expressions of justification and explanation, and so forth, the content ascribed to less cognitively sophisticated systems does not have a structure that is amenable to such uses. It does not, because there is no behavior that such systems can engage in that could count as, say, deliberative reasoning, justifying, or explaining. And ascription of content, in the view in question, cannot be divorced from the cognitive capacities of the system in question." (Elton, 2000, pp. 7–8).

Elton states also that to adopt the intentional stance is to use "an autonomous level of explanation of the activity of that system" (Elton, 2000, p. 8) The behavior of the person (say) whose behavior is predicted by the intentional stance is not being explained in terms of the component parts of that person qua intentional system whether this is treated as an intentional system in itself or otherwise. Confusion arises because on the one hand, in the earlier Dennett, intentional ascription is something that can be justified only in terms of appropriate afferent–efferent linkages, while on the other, the later Dennett argues that intentional idioms, consonant with a broader understanding of the system's evolution and its present position, can be ascribed as long as they enable the system to be predicted. Although there may be an argument that any system that is so evolved and so placed that it can be predicted must have evolved the apt afferent–efferent linkages, this is too easy a way of overcoming the fact that we are presented in the earlier and later Dennett with essentially alternative devices for legitimately ascribing intentionality.

The complication that arises from this analytical uncertainty might be overcome in two ways: first, by accepting that Dennett is speaking of sub-personal cognitive psychology when he says subsystems can be treated as intentional systems, or, second, by arguing that any system can be addressed with any of the stances he proposes and can, therefore, be studied as either a personal level system or a sub-personal system. However, the conclusion is that whatever the merits of adding content *at* the sub-personal level, this action removes the justification in evolutionary terms of adding content to extensional science in order to arrive at what may be legitimately explained in intentional terms at the personal level. It opens the way for the identification of neurological activities as behavioral substrates, a rather different emphasis.

5
Contextual Psychology (1): Intentional Behaviorism

> Whether or not Skinner can be said to have discovered a different type of conditioning, he is certainly responsible for formulating the conception of "operant conditioning" and analysing it. In my estimation this is the sum total of Skinner's contribution to psychology... Of course, both he and his followers have a grossly inflated view of the importance of this discovery. (Dilman, 1988, p. 8).

Although Dennett refers often to behavior as that which is to be explained, he does not incorporate an extensional behavioral science into his scheme of explanation to counterbalance the extensional neurology on which he (at least originally) relies. Yet behavior is the criterion of the intentional and needs to be systematically related to its causal environment in order that it may play its vital role in the framework of analysis proposed here. Nor does the intentional strategy provide other than outline information on the attributions that are to be made in order to predict an intentional system. To say that these attributions consist in the beliefs and desires it "ought" to have is of itself little more than an abstract formula. Yet, the heterophenomenological device that Dennett (1982, 1991b) proposes invites a careful scrutiny of the system's prior behavior, applying the intentional stance to people's verbal behavior, treating it as a text to be interpreted in terms of their beliefs and desires. Much as one examines the text of a character in a novel in terms of what he or she says, what they do and what others say of them, plus background information about the author and his or her other writings, so one can produce an inter-subjective account of the text provided by another person. The heterophenomenology of the person consists in an account of "*what it is like to be* that subject – in the subject's own terms, given the best interpretation we can muster" (Dennett, 1991b, p. 98). The resulting account is, like a scientific hypothesis, subject to testing in the face of the evidence, hence corrigible.

Now this is only a highly generalized method of interpretation. It does not amount to a systematic means of incorporating behavior and its determinants into the framework. In order to accomplish that we shall need a more complete understanding of the requirements for a behavioral science, with its attendant means of interpretation, and its role in a comprehensive framework for psychological research that incorporates both the intentional and the behavioral. For now, however, we face the immediate problem of determining what the link between behavior and ascribed intentionality might be in a more specific context. So how might we proceed?

In establishing his appeal to neurology as criterion for the ascription of intentionality at the personal level, Dennett acknowledges what we might call the intentionalist fallacy: a science of pure intentionality fails because it rests on a circular logic in which the source of explanation is inferred from the behavior it is used to interpret.

But the brilliance of Dennett's approach as a means of circumscribing the intentionalist fallacy may hide a major flaw in it: it is still too vague a means of ascribing intentionality than is desirable. Does an animal's reaching out towards food as a result of the appropriate afferent–efferent linkages having been operationalized legitimize the interpretation that the animal *wants* the food, or *likes* it, or *prefers* it, or what? On its own the observation that the afferent–efferent links in question are evolutionarily consistent does not make one of these attributions more probable than another. Some other criterion is required and I suggest that what Dennett's scheme lacks is an extensional behavioral science which plays the same role as extensional neuroscience in permitting the rational attribution of content and which in fact balances the contribution of the physiological basis of content ascription that Dennett proposes. The neuroscience required by Dennett's approach is sub-personal in character, linking external environmental with behavioral responses via processes within the individual organism. The extensional behavioral science I am proposing would be super-personal in character and would link external environmental stimuli and behavioral responses by reference to operant conditioning. Dennett points out that the method of content ascription he advocates is not perfect but sufficiently accurate to make broad behavioral predictions. The inclusion of a systematic account of the causation of behavior will not make the system perfect either but may increase both its predictive accuracy and the validity of the intentional attributions to which it leads. The additional accuracy with respect to the latter must depend above all on the inclusion of verbal behavior into our scheme. We are in the realm of interpretation here as well as that of science but that does not mean that we are unable to draw general conclusions with respect to the meaning of observed behavior which can lead to the inclusion of scientific insights that help us be more specific about the causation of the behavior in question both in terms of the stimuli that immediately shape it and the theoretical terms that may be legitimately invoked to account for its continuity, the intentional content that completes the explanatory picture. I have argued at length that radical behaviorism provides an extensional behavioral science *par excellence* (see Foxall, 2004, 2005).

Contextual psychologies

It is possible now to derive some new theoretical frameworks for the explanation of consumer choice. They derive in part from Dennett's kinds of intentional explanation that stem from folk psychology. His view of folk psychology it will be remembered was that of a somewhat unsophisticated everyday attempt to make sense of and predict the behavior of ourselves and others by the attribution. Let us call this Folk Psychology 1 (or FP1) because I want in a moment to introduce a competing notion of folk psychology. Dennett's intentional systems theory (IST) consists of a formalization of folk psychology in which refined definitions of contentful terms such as attitude and intention serve to predict the behavior of an intentional system. The intentional stance is thus applied at the level of the system in order to predict it, and there is thus a degree of instrumentalism in the definition, ascription, and employment of intentional terms. The concepts of IST are "abstracta," logical constructs that can be related to one another in a formal system but which lack the precision of the illata that comprise scientific theories. IST is, furthermore, a "competence theory," one that shows what mechanisms would be required to account for behavior but which does not delve into the nature and operations of those mechanisms. These functions belong to what Dennett styles sub-personal cognitive psychology, in which cognition is justified on the basis of neurophysiological links which proceed in terms of the more specific illata that lead to empirically testable theories and interpretations. Sub-personal cognitive psychology represents the sophisticated application of the intentional stance at the level of the sub-personal, notably that of neurophysiology. Sub-personal units are treated as predictable from the attribution to them of contentful terms. Employing as its constructs the illata that Dennett defines as the specific and refined variables that can enter into scientific theories, sub-personal cognitive psychology is a performance theory, one which explores the structure and functioning of the cognitive mechanisms that account for behavior.

Unlike folk psychology, IST and sub-personal cognitive psychology rest upon the use of the intentional stance by which not only entire systems but their parts can be predicted and partially explained by the ascription of the intentional terms that make these tasks easier. In the theoretical structures that I wish to propose for the analysis of consumer choice, which might be terms "kinds of contextual psychology," I shall, contra Dennett, maintain a clear distinction between the personal and other levels of analysis, in line with what has been said about the mereological fallacy. Moreover, although Dennett seems by the time of his introduction of "three kinds of intentional psychology," to de-emphasize the personal level and, particularly, the categorical principle that content be ascribed only at that level, it seems that the principle he announced in 1969 to the effect that the ascription of content (at the personal level) be consistent with the evolution by natural selection of afferent–efferent linkages (at the sub-personal level of neurophysiology) must nevertheless underlie both IST and sub-personal cognitive psychology. It remains central to the three kinds of contextual psychology I now describe.

The first is Folk Psychology 2 (FP2), the unsophisticated everyday attempt to make sense of and predict the behavior of ourselves and others by the attribution of rewards and punishments. A considerable amount of daily prediction and understanding of our own behavior and that of others rests on the calculation of what we or they are likely to receive as a consequence of acting in a particular way in specific environments. These predictions and explanations reflect what has happened to ourselves and other in these circumstances at earlier times. They thus represent a fundamental application of the contextual stance at the mundane level. In other words, this is a strand of folk psychology in which casual definitions of the rewards of behavior and experience are used to predict a contextual system.

Intentional behaviorism, the second kind of contextual psychology is the formalization of this common usage. The result of its application is also however to explain the behavior of the system by attributing to it the intentionality that would be legitimate based on observed molar environment–behavior relationships. Intentional behaviorism can be used to explain operant behavior in experimental settings but is especially useful in arenas where behavior can only be interpreted (i.e., not directly subjected to an experimental analysis). The interpretation of such complex behavior must be undertaken according to strict guidelines that permit the reliable identification of antecedent and consequential stimuli as well as genuine operant responses. (Foxall, 2004). The application of the contextual stance will automatically operate in a way that is consistent with the principle of selection by consequences (Skinner, 1981) and thus parallel the evolutionarily-consistent relationships inherent in Dennett's thinking on IST and sub-personal cognitive psychology. Operant conditioning the appropriate evolutionary analogy for this level of theory because there is no attempt to derive intentional ascription form other than environmental–behavioral linkages; the evolutionary analogy actually makes operant behaviorism the appropriate extensional behavioral science here for the very reason that it operates in a manner analogous to natural selection. Competence theory: says what would be necessary in order for the environment–behavior theory to hold, but only in terms of theoretical entities that "save the theory". These are not scientific terms; they explain, but no causal significance is accorded them.

Finally, the third kind of contextual psychology, super-personal cognitive psychology, represents the refinement of the intentional terms employed in intentional behaviorism so that they can enter into scientific theories that employ the contextual stance. This is a performance theory, but the questions remain (a) of the ontological status of the entities proposed; and (b) of their causal significance. There is no need to accord them either table-and-chair reality (though they may be real in Dennett's sense that parallelograms of forces are "real," i.e., that physical theory must treat them as so in order to predict and explain physical phenomena), or causal efficacy unless this is derived from molar patterns of environment-behavior relationships in which the contingencies can be shown to control behavior. There is limited acceptance that humans can be creative in formulating personal or self-rules, but there is (can be) no evidence that these procedures are not environmentally determined through environmental–behavioral conditioning. I suggest that the link with evolution comes in this case through evolutionary psychology. The reason is that we are now seeking cognitive ascriptions that can be justified directly in terms of evolutionary processes; evolutionary psychology, which is concerned with the development of cognitive structures that were appropriate

Table 5.1   Kinds of Intentional and Contextual Psychology

Folk psychology	*Intentional (FP1)*	*Behavioral (FP2)*
Competence theory	*Intentional systems theory*	*Intentional behaviorism*
Performance theory	*Sub-personal cognitive psychology*	*Super-personal cognitive psychology*

during the Pleistocene period and which are an amalgam of biological and mental/behavioral selection.

Although the kinds of contextual psychology I have outlined here do not exactly parallel the intentional psychologies proposed by Dennett, they are arranged as alternative hierarchies in Table 5.1. Each has its origins in a version of folk psychology, and goes on to explore the possibility of constructing from this first a competence theory of behavior and then a performance theory. Theory-building need not end here, however. Having specified these levels of theoretical understanding, it becomes possible to propose an integrated cognitive-behavioral psychology which brings together the various strands of reasoning that have justified the preceding levels of theoretical analysis. It ascribes intentional and cognitive terms principally on the basis of molar environmental–behavioral relationships as in intentional behaviorism and super-personal cognitive psychology but seeks to relate the behaviors it studies also to neurophysiological and processes that evolved in the course of natural selection and which are necessary to the performance of those behaviors. Only if these various circles can be squared can we speak legitimately in terms of cognitive processes explaining behavior.

Some comparisons may clarify the arrangement of theories that is proposed. Compared with intentional systems theory, in first introduces a behavioral criterion for the ascription of intentional content that parallel's Dennett's (1969) approach by invoking an extensional (this time, behavioral) science as the basis for such attributions. The ascription of content takes place at the personal level but this time – in consonance with what I have called the categorical distinction – on the basis of super-personal extensional science. By contrast with IST, therefore, it does not commit the mereological fallacy (IST makes intentional systems of subsystems which is inimical to the arguments made in Chapter 3). There is no objection in intentional behaviorism to the use of extensional neuroscience in the way that Dennett (1969) proposes, to augment or corroborate the environment–behavior patterns criterion. In fact, an intentional behaviorist analysis would be completed by the identification of the means to establish the consistency of the behavioral pattern with evolutionarily consistent afferent–efferent linkages, and an account derived from evolutionary reasoning of he emergence and maintenance of the environment–behavior pattern.

Whereas intentional behaviorism is a competence theory that ascribes intentional content, super-personal cognitive psychology is a performance theory that seeks to establish the cognitive operations that would be consistent with the behavior sequences on which such ascription is founded. While in intentional behaviorism the goal of ascription is to account for gaps in an extensional behavior theory, the goal of super-personal cognitive psychology is to propose the information processing mechanisms that would accompany those behavior patterns. This does not of itself imply that the cognitive operations in question are causative of the behavior; it merely asserts that in order to establish the continuity of those patterns, to account for activity at the personal level (even in terms of the private events of Skinner's bareboned account, i.e., thinking and feeling), and to delimit behavioral interpretations, it is necessary to consider concomitant information processing operations. The principal criterion for the ascription of this cognitive apparatus and functioning remains the patterns of molar behavior that can be shown to be contingency-based or rule-governed. However, it becomes increasingly necessary, at what is still a highly theoretical level of analysis, to establish (1) the neurological basis of the ascribed cognition – and this may be accomplished by either fMRI scans of relevant brain functions or the afferent–efferent reasoning proposed by Dennett (1969); and (2) the evolutionary basis of critical behavior patterns. Nor does super-personal cognitive psychology rule out sub-personal cognitive psychology though this remains a separate line of inquiry that is not subsumed by the former.

Super-personal cognitive psychology nevertheless raises questions that are more than theoretical since they have a bearing on the nature and function of efforts to influence consumer choice such as those of governmental agencies and marketing firms. For instance, since the cognitive processes contained in the theory are derivative of environmentally-contingent behavioral learning, can they be said to be causal? Is the best way to change consumers' behavior to attempt to influence their attitudes directly or to modify the physical and social environments in which they are formed? We shall return to such considerations after considering more closely the application of the three kinds of contextual theory to the explanation of consumer choice. (The aim of the present exposition is establish intentional behaviorism and super-personal cognitive psychology only sufficiently to distinguish teleological behaviorism from picoeconomics, and both from radical behaviorism, in order to pursue their distinct explanations of consumer choice.

Intentional behaviorism

Two sources of explanation cohere in the concept of intentional behaviorism. The first is Dennett's and runs from the neural substrate of cognitive activity to the personal level of intentional ascription. Dennett's account begins, we have seen, with the neural event – specifically its role in an afferent–efferent process – and ascribes content on the basis of the resulting evolutionarily consistent logic. In other words, the direction of ascription is from neurology to intentionality, from the sub-personal level to the personal level of explanation. In the second, the logical sequence of investigation is from the super-personal level to the sub-personal – from the verbal and non-verbal behavior of the participant to the physiological correlate(s) of both that behavior and the personal-level ascriptions of content that may be made in order to fulfill the theoretical imperatives that intentionality enjoins upon extensional behavioral science. The logic of intentional behaviorism requires that the procedure embrace the super-personal level of analysis in which intentional ascription at the personal level is achieved via the observation of operant behavior (environment–behavior relationships) through extensional behavioral science. The purpose of the philosophical exercise that Dennett advances is, as he proposes, to ascertain what intentional content can be ascribed to the findings of neurological science, but the de facto procedure is more likely to entail using physiology and the logic of natural selection as a means of checking whether pre-ordained desires and beliefs can be rationally ascribed at the personal level. The consequent methodology procedure is thus: (*first*) the observation of environmental–behavioral relationships (including self-reports of emotion) at the super-personal level, leading to (*second*) the ascription of emotional content at the personal level, leading to (*third*) the search for the neural correlates of emotion at the sub-personal level. Desires and beliefs, and other mental content, are thus decided upon at the super-personal level as a result of the uncovering of environment–behavior links; their appropriateness to this personal level ascription is further confirmed, however, by reference to the degree to which they can provide an additional heuristic overlay to the theories and findings of neurocognitive research at the sub-personal level on the basis of evolutionarily consistent reasoning.

Evidence of neural substrates of cognition (e.g., from fMRI scans) can show areas of the brain associated with mental activity such as thinking and emoting. However, they cannot reveal the content of these mental events. This can be done only by probing the environment–behavior superstrates of cognition (e.g., by using the contextual stance). Therefore, Dennett's strategy in *Content and Consciousness* logically requires the further incorporation of the super-personal level of explanation through which confirmation that the appropriate content is being ascribed. This requirement is doubtless implicit in his description of his strategy but, if his logical argument is to be completed, it needs to be made explicit in terms of an extensional behavioral science based on the contextual stance. The superordinate framework of conceptualization and analysis presented by intentional behaviorism incorporates both Dennettian and Skinnerian analyses within a single, comprehensive account. Strictly speaking the contextual stance need not be restricted to operant psychology: it is simply a means of suggesting environment–behavior relationships that are consistent with selection-by-consequences, and which can, therefore, act as indicators of the intentional content to be ascribed at the personal level. (See Exhibit 5.1).

The next question that arises is, On what basis is content to be ascribed to theories and findings at the super-personal level in order to arrive at a psychology of the person that takes environment–behavior relationships into consideration? In order to find an answer to this question it is necessary to go back to Dennett's strategy of ascribing content to the sub-personal theories and findings of neuroscience, and it may be worthwhile reviewing its central themes now. At the same time, if the analogy between a sub-personal : personal level linkage and a super-personal : personal level linkage is to be confirmed, it should be possible to show how the reasoning that develops for adding content to the extensional findings on environment–behavior relationships applies to the resolution of the problems of personal level psychology, behavioral continuity, and delimitation.

The required interpretative device is that of content-ascription in terms of the desires and beliefs it would be rational for the individual to have in view of his or her situation defined by the intersection of his or her learning history and the behavior setting he or she faces. Both evolutionary reasoning and the behavioral analysis of matching phenomena suggest that the contingencies with which an individual will have come most obviously into contact in the course of phylogenetic

Exhibit 5.1 Mind

Mind is a theoretical entity that explains and stimulates research. There is an ontological and a linguistic argument for the concept. The underlying reason is that experience does not reduce to physics. This denies neither the materiality of experience and consciousness, nor that experience has a physiological substrate. Since we do not know the mechanisms that link experience to neurology, "agnostic materialism" is inevitable. Neurology may be the only evidence of the existence of mind, when we are asleep or otherwise unconscious, but its dependence on conscious experience means that when we wake our minds are more than our brains. This is the ontological argument for speaking in terms of minds based on the interaction of neurophysiological development and conscious experience. The linguistic case derives from intentional versus extensional language. We understand the content of our own subjective experience in terms of beliefs, desires and other intentions, and we can reconstruct the conscious experience of others to predict or explain only in these terms. Dennett's intentional psychologies are levels on which such heterophenomenology may be undertaken. In speaking of beliefs and desires, we are engaging in a form of expression that is importantly different from those of the extensional neuroscientific and behavioral sciences, in which we ordinarily research. The contextual psychologies and integrated cognitive-behavioral model portray the means by which behavioral experience enters the definition of mind.

and ontogenic histories will be those producing behavior that tends toward optimization of outcome. In any situation, therefore, we can assume beliefs, attitudes, and intentions that are consistent with this objective. As long as the conceptualization and – at the level of empirical research – measurement of these cognitive constructs is in line with those pursued by attitude theorists, there is a convincing rationale for the attribution of content to the findings of extensional behavioral science based on the contextual stance (that is, the location of behavior at the intersection of learning history and behavior setting.) These constructs directly link the elements of the contextual stance with the process of content ascription.

Implementation of the strategy

The strategy that Dennett advocates for the addition of content to physiological research may be followed in the case of operant behavioral science in order to generate a psychology of the person that takes environment–behavior relationships into consideration. How is this to be achieved? In order to find an answer to this question it is necessary to go back to Dennett's strategy of ascribing content to the subpersonal theories and findings of neuroscience, and it may be worthwhile reviewing its central themes now. At the same time, if the analogy between a sub-personal–personal level linkage and a superpersonal– personal level linkage is to be confirmed, it should be possible to show how the reasoning that develops for adding content to the extensional findings on environment–behavior relationships applies to the resolution of the problems of personal level psychology, behavioral continuity, and delimitation.

The strategy of ascribing content to the theories and findings of extensional behavioral science cannot be pursued in the absence of a convincing rationale. Recall that Dennett's strategy is to assume that the sequence of events that are to be intentionally explained are appropriate from an evolutionary perspective; the next step is to propose structures that will account for these appropriate sequences. The environmental significance necessary for the brain to discriminate useful from unuseful neural events is extrinsic to those neural events, the brain's necessary distinctions cannot stem solely from extensional descriptions of extrinsic stimulation and past behavior. The brain has to be able to discriminate and store fortuitously appropriate structures. Some close analogy of natural selection must be sought to provide for the capacity of the brain to do this. The necessary capacity could itself be an outcome of the evolution of species. An intentional system has to be able to discriminate and respond to the environmental factors that impinge upon it and to do this it must be able to "interpret peripheral stimulation." This entails producing within itself not representations but states or events that "co-occur" with the conditions or objects in its perceptual field. Information abstracted from the environment will nevertheless remain non-intelligent unless something else it added to it; what must be added consists in the detection of afferent and efferent links.

The links between the sub-personal–personal and super-personal– personal levels of analysis can in each case be characterized in Skinner's (1981) term "selection by consequences." The first is dependent on an evolutionary history that produced phylogenic consequences which determine the structure of the brain and its functioning, the neural affer-ent–efferent relationships to which content is added in the process of intentional ascription in order to delineate the personal level of analysis. The second depends also, indirectly, on this process since it is through natural selection that the organism's capacity to change as a result of contact with environmental consequences presumably came about. However, in a more direct way, this link is the result of ontogenic con-sequences through which behavior is shaped in the course of a life-time. Again there is a need for intentional ascription, even if (or possibly, especially if) operant behavior instantiates physiological change within the organism. Donahoe et al. (1997, p. 196) state that "In a stable context, control by consequences (as opposed to antecedents) stands as a behavioral law, but we propose (at another level of analysis) that the effects of those consequences are imple-mented by changes in synaptic efficacies," an idea they trace back to Watson. But this argument merely addresses the sub-personal–personal levels of linkage that Dennett proposes, and has no direct bearing on the relationship between the super-personal–personal levels which are proposed here as a function of ontogenic development.

Intentional ascription revisited

An extensionally-based system of radical behaviorist interpretation attempts to account for these necessary linkages by resorting to physio-logical mechanisms, private events, and rules; yet, there is no reason for taking any of these seriously at the explanatory level since they do not provide the necessary continuity even in the terms required by an extensional science of behavior (Foxall, 2004). The required interpreta-tive device is that of content-ascription in terms of the desires and beliefs it would be rational for the individual to have in view of his or her situation defined by the intersection of his or her learning history and the behavior setting he or she faces. Both evolutionary reasoning and the behavioral analysis of matching phenomena suggest that the contingencies with which an individual will have come most obviously into contact in the course of phylogenic and ontogenic histories will be those producing behavior that tends toward optimization of outcome. In any situation, therefore, we can assume beliefs, attitudes and inten-tions that are consistent with this objective. As long as the conceptual-ization and – at the level of empirical research – measurement of these cognitive constructs is in line with those pursued by attitude theorists, there is a convincing rationale for the attribution of content to the findings of extensional behavioral science based on the contextual stance (that is, the location of behavior at the intersection of learning history and behavior setting.) These constructs directly link the elements of the contextual stance with the process of content ascription.

Dennett criticizes "S–R theorists" for being unable to show how a novel stimulus can arrive at or select the appropriate response. (Although behavior analysts are immediately likely to interpret reference to "S–R theorists" as not applying to them, the following argument is just as applicable to operant psychology as to S–R psychology and it is clear that Dennett is including operant and respondent behaviorisms in the same category here.) He continues by pointing out that an animal might detect a stimulus but not "know" what the appropriate response is (the stimulus in question could as well be discriminative stimulus as unconditioned or conditioned.) No afferent can be taken by the brain to have significance A unless it is recognized by the efferent side of the brain has having it, i.e., until the brain has produced the appropriate response. The content of a neural event or state depends not only upon its "normal state of stimulation" but also whatever additional efferent effects it produces. The determination of these factors necessarily takes us beyond the extensional description of stimuli and responses.

Content can be ascribed to a neural event only when it is a link between an afferent and an efferent – and not just that but a link in an *appropriate chain* between afferent and efferent. The content is not something one discovers within this neural event but an extra interpretation. The ultimate justification for such ascription is provided by evolutionary thinking – the intelligent brain must be able to select the appropriate response to a specific stimulus. Why should this be less the case for the link between extensional operant analysis and the personal level of analysis than for that between physiology and that level? A totally biological theory of behavior would still not be able, Dennett claims, to account for *what the person is doing.* Intentional ascription simply describes what a purely extensional theory would describe, nothing more, but in a different way. This different way may be useful to the physiologist, however. Neuroscience that does not view neural events as signals, reports or messages can scarcely function at all. No purely biological logic can tell us why the rat knows which way to go for his food. Nor can any purely contextualistic logic reveal this in the absence of some sort of "Dennettian overlay." In neither case does the proposed intentional ascription detract from the extensional version of events but adds an interpretation that provides greater intuitive understanding of the system.

The import of intentional ascription must, however, in the course of the present argument, go thus far and no further. It retains the a-ontological assumption about cognitive events, states, processes and structures with which, along with Dennett, we began. There is no justification for uncritically accepting the entire apparatus of the information processing account of behavior be this based on cognitive conjecture or neurophysiology. The justification of intentional behavior-ism lies in the necessity of connecting efferent–afferent processes in some way that (a) physiology cannot, (b) behavioral science cannot, and (c) that aids the coherent explanation and prediction of behavior. What Dennett calls a centralist theory, therefore, has two explanatory components. The first is an extensional account of the interaction of functional structures; the second, an intentional characterization of these structures, the events occurring within them, and states of the structures resulting from these. The links between the extensional account and the intentional interpretation consists of a hypothesis or hypotheses describing the evolutionary source of the fortuitously propitious arrangement in virtue of which the system's operation in this instance makes sense. These hypotheses are required in principle to account for the appropriateness which is presupposed by the Intentional interpretation, but which requires a genealogy from the standpoint of the extensional, physical theory. Despite the inevitable imprecision of this approach, the challenge is to make the case that the ascription of content to the theories and findings of behavioral science can be of use to the behavior analyst, and in particular, to the process of radical behaviorist interpretation.

Humans are not simply neurophysiological organisms but also persons who exhibit complex behaviors (as Gunderson, 1972, para-phrases Dennett's argument). Dennett's case for the ascription of content rests on the understanding that because some neural events, states and structures *can be construed as being* about other things, that is, intentional, it is possible to ascribe content to them. The basis of the contextual stance is similarly that humans are persons as well as organisms whose behavior is determined by the contingencies of reinforce-ment. Moreover, some of the environmental elements on which our behavior is contingent *can be construed as being* about things, i.e., are such that it makes sense to attribute content to them, to add an extra layer of interpretation that is relevant to the personal level. Whereas Dennett speaks of only two levels of analysis, however, we have distin-guished three. We have noted his argument for a *personal* level, at which the individual as a whole discriminates such "mental" entities as pain, and a *sub-personal* level of brains and neurons, at which level the physiological correlates of pain behavior can be detected. "…[T]he terms in our mentalistic vocabulary are nonreferring. Rather like 'sakes' or 'miles', [or centers of gravity] mentalistic terms in appropriate contexts tell us something, but succeed in doing so without thereby referring to any entities any more than the words 'sakes' or 'miles' refer to sakes or miles." (Gunderson, 1972, p. 593). At the super-personal level we turn to the environmental contingencies that shape and maintain responding in order to find an extensional basis for the ascription of such content. Several factors distinguish this level from both the personal and the sub-personal level based on neuroscience that Dennett identifies.

First, the super-personal level cannot capture anything of the personal level including some essential components of what it is to be human, such as being able to discriminate pain. No matter how we grimace and howl and hold our painful heads, no matter what consequences these overt actions have by way of producing sympathy or medicine or exemptions from work from others, these superlevel events are entirely separate from the discrimination of pain. Second, the super-personal level constitutes an extensional approach to the science of behavior, one which can explain much behavior at that level but which is incapable of dealing with the things that can only be discriminated at the personal level: pain, that it is time to go home, and other intentional matters. Only by the addition of a heuristic overlay of interpretation can these personal level matters be accommodated. Third, even though neither level reduces to the other, it is incumbent upon us to show how they are linked if we are to make legitimate and convincing interpretive ascriptions. The link, moreover, must be consistent with evolutionary reasoning. There are several strands to be considered here. (a) The capacity for operant reinforcement is bestowed by natural selection. What Skinner (1981) calls "selection by consequences" is the analogy/homology that links the two processes at least at the level of phylogenic and ontogenic consistency. (b) In the case of linking the personal and sub-personal levels, the links must supervene (i.e., add appropriate interpretation) between the afferent and efferent processes of the brain. The corresponding processes in operant conditioning are stimuli and responses: the heuristic overlay of intentionality must link these in ways that an extensional account cannot. There are three such ways: (i) to elucidate the personal level, (ii) to demonstrate continuity of behavior from setting to setting, (iii) to solve problems of equifinality by delimiting operant interpretations that (attempt to) proceed solely at the extensional level. These considerations bring the interpretation within the scope of an evolutionarily consistent framework of conceptualization and analysis. How? The animal that is to be successful in negotiating its environment must be able to discriminate discriminative and other setting stimuli in order to act appropriately (with behavior that will be reinforced).

There is no more reason to believe that a physiological account will eventually be available to show how this occurs any more than there is a possibility that a physiological account will be able to demonstrate an individual's discrimination of pain. The discrimination of appropriate behavior occurs at the personal level. The recognition of appropriate inaugurating stimuli is a similar process. At the very least, the intentional mode of explanation cannot be abandoned until the physiological link is demonstrated: to trust in eventual physiology is superstitious in a way in which the ascription of intentionality is not if the latter strategy results in more effective predictions of behavior. Physicists who shun the concept of center of gravity in favor of a belief in some distant more physical explanation would be showing a similar level of superstition. That physicists are not embarrassed to include centers of gravity in their predictive work should be an example to the psychologist.

Intentional behaviorist interpretation

The alternative to an extensional system of radical behaviorist interpretation, then, is the amalgamation of extensional operant behavioral science and Dennett's intensional stance by which content would be ascribed to its theories and findings in order to provide a basis for radical behaviorist interpretation. The reality of this may be closer to us than we have imagined. The point is sometimes made that radical behaviorists often incorporate the language of intentionality in their popular accounts of behavior, the implication being that the extensional operant account is thereby diminished, perhaps incapable of adequately describing the events that are the subject of the accounts in question. Skinner (e.g., 1974) argues that in order to communicate to a non-specialist audience, it is useful to adopt everyday language, as does the professional astronomer speaks of the sun "rising" and "setting" when addressing children. Many behaviorists have taken this at face value and not concerned themselves further with the charge that the use of such language necessarily invokes a theoretical stance which is inevitable in the explanation of behavior. In view of the import of the current argument, this is a serious matter that behavior analysts ought not to ignore so easily.

The accounts in question are generally interpretations rather than reports of experimental work and this suggests that at least at the level of interpretation intentional language is inevitable not only to communicate to pedestrians but to express the ideas involved in accounting for complex activity in operant terms. "Thinking" and "feeling," the very stuff of private events, are almost always spoken of in intentional language: we do not just think, we think *about* or think *that*; we do not just feel, we feel *that*; and so on. We can treat such events as stimuli and responses that do not differ in kind from those that are publicly available – though this is to make an enormous ontological leap that can never be the subject of a scientific analysis – but to insist that thoughts and feelings are simply discriminative stimuli (or establishing operations, or other source of antecedent stimulation), associating them in the process with a physiological level of extensional analysis, is to leave out entirely the personal level to which Dennett draws attention, the level without which no psychological explanation can be complete.

The suggested program is not a call for the use of mediating events or the kinds of theory that Skinner repudiated. Even less is it a regurgitation of the sometimes argued notion that the intentional and contextual stances might be conjoined or a synthesis generated that would combine "the best of each." This is not possible in practice because their respective intentional and extensional bases are incommensurable (Foxall, 1999). But the adding of content to an extensional account is not a synthesis or amalgamation. It is not adding anything to the findings and theories derived from the experimental analysis of behavior. Rather, it is the derivation of another level of interpretation in order to facilitate understanding and prediction by taking the personal level of experience into account.

In order to advance the debate between cognitivists and behaviorists, this account takes Dennett's thesis about the relationship between extensional science and intensional psychology at face value. To do this is to share, again for the sake of argument, (a) his assessment of the (literal) shortcomings of purely extensional science as a means to understand behavior: such science simply does not go far enough in the quest to explain all behavior, and (b) his judgment that the link between the two is found in the imperatives of behavioral science is, like physiology, an autonomous approach to knowledge in its own right but it is incapable of explaining all human behavior within its own theoretical and methodological purview, nor even that it can engender plausible interpretations (that is expressed in non-convoluted language) of all behavior. It is here that an important parallel with Dennett's analysis leads to a major conclusion: the extensional science of physiology is to Dennett's intensional physical psychology what an extensional behavioral science is to the intensional psychology of social cognition. In other words, the extensional science provides the evolutionary basis for understanding behavior biologically to which intensional cognitive interpretation verbally ascribes an a-ontological, initially non-empirical dimension which yields predictions of certain behaviors that the extensional approach of itself can neither explain nor predict. What is true for the piece-piece of social cognitive psychology – attitude research – is likely to be generally the case.

The strategy of ascribing optimality (rationality) to systems in order to predict their behavior is a methodological simplification that involves further ascription – of posited entities such as beliefs, attitudes and intentions which, as we have seen, have the function of fine-tuning the prediction by linking it to the system's environmental history and behavior setting. The three stages of the intentional strategy make its dependency on the prior application of the contextual strategy clear. Dennett takes pains to avoid this conclusion. He denigrates (radical) behaviorism by, first, casting it as a simplistic S-R paradigm, and, secondly, by asserting, in the absence of any adduced evidence, that it has proved unsuccessful in predicting behavior. The first of these caricatures fails to engage with the operant behavior analysis of the last thirty years, especially the analysis of behavior at the molar level, the post-Skinnerian analysis of the verbal behavior of the listener, etc. The second ignores a mass of empirical evidence. Both overlook the possibility of radical behaviorist interpretation, that is, the use of the contextual stance to account for the behavior that is not amenable to an experimental analysis. Indeed, the use of the intentional stance is advocated here only in the context of radical behaviorist interpretation. It is important that the extensional science of operant behavior analysis continue its program for two reasons: first, to provide an evolving and expanding base for the content ascription to which content can be ascribed in the process of interpretation; secondly, to provide alternative, competing and challenging explanations. Insofar as the growth of knowledge depends on "the active interplay of competing theories" (Feyerabend, 1975), it is essential to have (i) a thriving experimental analysis of behavior, (ii) operant interpretations which themselves attempt to function on an extensional level only, and (iii) operant interpretations that contain the intentional overlays necessary to provide accounts of behavior at the personal level. Their interaction is, indeed, a *sine qua non* of intellectual progress. Hence, what characterizes the intentional behaviorist approach is the incorporation of both the contextual and the intentional stances into a single framework of analysis. Social cognitivists must reconstruct desires and beliefs in the context of the individual's rationality by considering its situation. The contextual stance facilitates this reconstruction by *de*constructing the notion of situation in terms of (a) a learning history, (b) the current behavior setting, and (c) their interaction. This is both consistent with and a means of operationalizing Dennett's view that the organism will have those desires and beliefs that are appropriate to it given its situation.

Intentional behaviorism differs from the other systems of explanation in its comprehensive inclusion of the various elements of the contextual and intentional stances, as well as in the understanding that the ascription of intentionality reinforces rather than detracts from the prior existence of an extensional behavioral science. It follows Dennett's subtle recognition that the addition of an intentional layer of interpretation does not discover anything new but tells another story about the theories and findings produced by operant psychology. The result is not just an extra story that maps on to the original in a one on one fashion: rather it extends the scope and relevance of the interpretation. Moreover, intentional behaviorism recognizes that social cognitive psychology proceeds in a similar manner, and raises the possibility that psychology will find a platform on which it might unite.

6
Contextual Psychology (2): Super-Personal Cognitive Psychology

> In essence, we should expect an organism to have evolved a psychological solution to some problem when the problem requires the organism to have more information about a feature of its environment than cues in its environment provide. When the information an organism can mindlessly detect falls short of the information the organism actually possesses, it is because psychological processes are present to span the gap. (Shapiro, 1999, p. 97).

Theories that deal only in identifying the necessary intentional idioms to explain behavior, such as the Bolles–Bindra–Toates expectancy theory (Exhibit 2.2), function at the level of intentional behaviorism. They are competence models and as such seek semantic understanding. Super-personal cognitive psychology, like Dennett's sub-personal cognitive psychology, seeks to uncover the syntax of the brain, but in contrast to Dennett, by relating environment–behavior consistencies to physiological structures and functions. It is more extensive than Dennett's sub-personal cognitive psychology which validates its intentional interpretation on the basis of the findings of neuroscience. Super-personal cognitive psychology is, like intentional behaviorism, involved in the ascription of content not only basis of neuropsychology but, initially at least, turns to molar patterns of behavior to make such attributions. To the extent that sub-personal psychology takes behavior into consideration, it is in far more ad hoc a manner than that required of a fully extensional behavioral science that relates patterns of behavior to sequences of environmental consequences. Super-personal cognitive psychology thus attempts to provide a more comprehensive account of behavior in which the ascription of intentionality and cognitive functioning takes place only at the personal level but on the basis of additional sources of extensional information.

But the strategy of super-personal cognitive psychology is more complicated than that of intentional behaviorism in that it requires that a case be made not simply for intentional ascriptions that are designed to cover the deficiencies of a purely behavioral theory, but to uncover the putative cognitive reasoning behavior within the individual that would be consistent with his or her molar patterns of behavior. Given the view of cognition adopted here, however, it is uncertain how far this can be entirely a performance theory since much of it revolves around making a case for the kinds of mental functioning that would be required to account for the behavior in question rather than providing an ontologically realist account of cognition. This would involve the identification of the neural substrates correlated with molar patterns of behavior and thus transcends super-personal cognitive psychology. However, super-personal cognitive psychology leads the way to a more comprehensive cognitive-behavioral psychology that is capable of developing into a full-blown performance theory.

The strategy of super-personal cognitive psychology itself involves the postulation of what is required of an information processing psychology that would be consistent with the behavior patterns observed. Much has been said of the structure of such a theory (see Foxall, 2005, Chapter 2). The more comprehensive, integrated psychology to which this may lead on brings our enterprise closer still to that of Dennett's quest for a sub-personal cognitive psychology while retaining the by now essential features of a behavioral account – the avoidance of the mereological fallacy and the incorporation of molar patterns of behavior as a major criterion variable for the ascription of intentionality.

Why cognition?

The first question that requires an answer in the context of a research program that has been concerned with the efficacy of a radical behaviorist exposition of consumer choice is: why introduce cognition? Before we can answer this, however, there is a more fundamental one: what is cognition? The standard psychological dictionary is well-exemplified by Reber (1985, p. 128) who speaks of cognition as "A broad (almost unspecifiably so) term which has been traditionally used to refer to such activities as thinking, conceiving, reasoning, etc. Most psychologists have used it to refer to any class of mental 'behaviors' (using that term very loosely) where the underlying characteristics are of an abstract nature and involve symbolizing, insight, expectancy, complex rule use, imagery, belief, intentionality, problem-solving, and so forth." This is a very basic answer but it is sufficient for present purposes.

The cognitive imperative

The cognitive imperative is the need to use cognitive concepts in the explanation of behavior, i.e., mental (or private) activities as causal in their own right, rather than just relying on intentionality to fill a gap in behavioral explanation. We move then from intentional behaviorism which is a-ontological to cognitive psychology which has definite ontological overtones even though it is theoretical. Dennett's sub-personal cognitive psychology approach is not sufficient to capture the full determination of cognition. The move is therefore to a framework which employs also super-personal cognitive psychology.

The cognitive imperative actually arises out of radical behaviorism. Rule-governed behavior can reflect contingencies but some rules (e.g., religious myths) have no contact whatever at any time in any place with any contingencies that could govern the behavior to which they refer. Yet they affect behavior in the most profound and dramatic manner: e.g., that of suicide bombers, as well as in more everyday ways: that involved in the fundamental decision-making involved in solving a task. Radical behaviorist research into the role of humans' verbal instructions in determining their more overt motor behaviors invokes the ontological separateness of operant behaviorism from other (e.g. cognitive) systems. Horne and Lowe (1993, pp. 56–7) state that "when performing on … concurrent schedules, adult humans will generally attempt to assess the reinforcement schedules in operation and will construct explicit rules for responding that are fairly easily recalled in postexperimental questionnaires". As radical behaviorists, of course, it is not their intentional to stray into intentional explanation: "In attempting to draw attention to the fact that verbal cues and rules have a role to play in studies of this kind, we do not wish to assert that they are the only, or even the most important, determinants of schedule performance; verbal behavior itself clearly has its origins in environmental consequences and is maintained by them." But we are left wondering where such rules come from. And whether the language of assessment and rule formulation does not commit its authors to an intentional explanation whatever their intentions. As we begin to wonder how such rules, once they travel from one person's private behavior to that of another person, can be said to be accepted, elaborated, modified, combined, dismissed, are we not inevitably adopting the terminology of cognitive information processing? The behavior in question cannot be said to be environmentally determined in any way. To say that the rule is accepted only from someone with whom one has a positive learning history of rule-acceptance is non-empirical; moreover, it is subject to the same need for a cognitive link between the rule and whatever gives it credence i.e., one's learning history of rule-following.

Cognition as a personal level phenomenon

It is important to maintain the original personal/sub-personal distinction because cognition, whatever else it might be, appears to be a phenomenon of the personal level; this location is, moreover, crucial to our ideas of what cognition is, what determines it, and whether it is behaviorally causal. It is argued here that (1) the definition of cognition is such that it cannot be other than a personal level occurrence, and (2) what is normally understood as cognition overlaps sufficiently with Elton's understanding of consciousness, which he argues is a personal level phenomenon, to make cognition locatable only at that level.

First consider what cognition is. Among many definitions from which we might select, Heyes (2000, p. 20) portrays it in terms of "theoretical entities providing a functional characterization of the operations of the central nervous system, which may or may not be objects of conscious awareness, and that are distinct from perceptual and motor processes." Theoretical entities are ascribed entities and ascription belongs at the personal level. Cognitive terms are intentional and belong at the personal level. Sub-personal cognitive psychology attempts to link the intentional and the neurological: best if they are kept distinct conceptually for the reasons given in Part I. They refer to functions of the central and peripheral nervous systems which of course makes them material but because they are entities of the kind exemplified by parallelograms of forces they are not physical in the sense that tables and neurons are. They are both invented entities and intentional objects; hence, they belong at the personal rather than sub-personal level. They are not part of an extensional science, since they cannot be tested or verified in the same way as physically measurable entities. Therefore, they do not belong at the sub-personal level, which is characterized by extensional science.

Second, consider Elton's argument that a distinction is in order between the intentional stance and the personal level/stance, both of which belong to the overarching category of rationalizing stances. The personal level arises when an individual can give reasons for his or her actions and when such reasons can be adjudged good or bad reasons. We can ask a consumer "Why did you buy the more expensive brand?" and receive the reply that "It will last longer" or "My friends expect me to." It does not follow that the behavior was actually motivated or caused by these reasons, only that they can be given in explanation. Some systems cannot give such reasons – animals and computers, for instance. We can use the intentional stance to predict their behaviors, but the personal stance can be taken only by humans. Elton's point is that consciousness is a property only of systems capable of providing the narrative accounts of their behavior that require the ability to take the personal stance, i.e., people. Only such can reason, decide, deduce, and so on: or at least only such can describe their doing so. This can I think be tied into the personal phenomenology of thinking and knowing, feeling and emoting that is part and parcel of what is generally called personal experience or consciousness.

An integrated cognitive-behavioral psychology

Super-personal cognitive psychology expands naturally into a framework of psychology that integrates both the contextual psychologies we have considered and the initial proposals of Dennett for a psychology that attributes intentionality on the basis of neuroscience. Such a comprehensive understanding of psychology must incorporate the various strands of explanation represented by sub- and super-personal cognitive psychologies, and this requires an account of how the two levels of explanation are related. There are two sources of relationship: the evolutionary consistency of the accounts involved, and the relationship of the operant conditioning that is inherent in the molar patterns of behavior to the sub-personal level of neuroscience.

The first involves the identification of afferent–efferent linkages at the sub-personal level links for sequences of molar operant behavior at the super-personal. Two examples of this are given next: the relationship of the intensity of felt (or at least reported) pain to operant contingencies, and the role of operant verbal behavior in the experience of fetal pain. Of these, the question of the intensity of experienced pain addresses clearly the relationship between neurology, private (or mental) events, and operant conditioning, though behaviorists may be more convinced by the welter of work on behavioral psychology and neuroscience that was recently featured in a special issue of the *Journal of the Experimental Analysis of Behavior* (2005, Volume 84, Number 3). The other example is more controversial and is presented not because I wish to take sides in the debate but to illustrate the kinds of considera- tion – (a) physiological development and readiness for the experience of pain, and (b) the role of a verbal community in producing a con- sciousness of pain – that are being employed in it.

The second concerns the principle of selection by consequences as an overarching paradigm for evolution: while Dennett's strategy for the reli- able ascription of content advanced in *Content and Consciousness* (Dennett, 1969) relies on natural selection, operant behaviorism turns to the process whereby contingencies of reinforcement during the lifetime of the individual contribute to a repertoire of environmentally-selected behaviors. Should a comprehensive cognitive-behavioral psychology turn to an even broader paradigm such as evolutionary psychology?

The neurological basis of operant behavior

A familiar component of research in behavioral neuropsychology is the attempt to relate environment–behavior relationships to dopamine release; if this can be shown to be evolutionarily consistent, it justifies the ascription of the appropriate intentional content at the personal level. Similarly, research that shows that pain is a personal level phe- nomenon that can be systematically related to operant conditioning (Flor, Knost and Birbaumer, 2002) as well as neural substrates comes into this category. This is more than establishing that operant condi- tioning leads to dopamine release, or the differential locations of neurons that fire when alternative brands of soft drinks are presented, or when different kinds of decision-making are occurring – though all of these are relevant. It means establishing relationships between sequences of environmentally-maintained behavior (operant condi- tioning) and neurological activity, a link between the super-personal and the sub-personal, from the whole complex of which an inference can be made about what the organism is doing at the personal level. Pain, for instance, would not be inferred from either a sub-personal physiological pattern of afferent–efferent linkages or a super-personal relationship between certain verbal and non-verbal behaviors like screaming or holding ones thumb after hitting with a hammer, but from evidence that connected the two. Flor and her colleagues (Flor et al., 2002) have demonstrated, for instance, that the reports of pain made by back-pain sufferers are susceptible to operant control. The solicitous behavior of a spouse, or their mere presence in the same room, provides reinforcement of the pain sufferer's verbal reports of pain; brain wave activity associated with pain has been identified only when the spouse was present to complete the operant training. More generally, such mental ascriptions as depression depend upon a knowledge of both the patient's past history and his or her current environment (Kagan, 2006; see also Exhibit 6.1).

Exhibit 6.1   Fetal Pain

A debate within the medical literature that bears on this relates to the requirements that both physiological development and verbal consciousness be present in order to account for fetal pain. This debate centers on whether pain can be ascribed simply as a result of a reaction to a stimulus by an organism that has reached a particular stage of physiological development or whether such ascription must also take into consideration the opportunity for some level of social conditioning derived from an operant analysis of the organism's behavior. Pain is a matter of subjective experience; fetal pain is such that those who may be suffering it cannot report it verbally; and we lack objective means of registering pain directly (Glover and Fisk, 1999). The problem of when to ascribe pain is of central practical significance to medical practitioners and ethicists in the context of abortion and operations within the womb, but the outcome of the debate is not as pertinent here as the theoretical assumptions and modes of reasoning made by the various protagonists.

The argument that fetuses can and do feel pain dismisses the claim that a fetus withdraws from noxious stimulation only as a reflex response rather than as a genuine experience of pain: such an inference is said to be "naïve unless one can confidently exclude suffering" (McCullagh, 1997, p. 302). The ascription of pain rests on the development of the requisite physiological structures, though what these precisely are is still a subject of dispute. McCullagh argues that it is not obvious why experiential and emotional elements need enter into the definition of pain: "Aborted fetuses respond to trigeminal stimulation by seven weeks' gestation, and the relevant thalamic nucleus approaches maturity by 12 weeks' gestation. How sound are claims that motor responses in the first trimester are totally reflex?" (ibid.) Saunders (1997) proposes that consciousness of pain might be "a purely cortical sensation" and cites the suggestion of the Commission of Inquiry into

---

Exhibit 6.1 – *continued*

Fetal Sentience (1996) that a fetus as young as six weeks of age might experience pain. The argument here is that, whatever the physiological mechanisms turn out to be, they alone are sufficient for the attribution of pain to a fetus. All protagonists would agree that consciousness has a biological basis, but the implication here is that biological development provides sufficient grounds for the ascription of pain. The thalamus is known to be implicated in pain in patients in a persistent vegetative state or with hydrocephalus, as well as in anencephalic infants. For exponents of this point of view, even young fetuses show sufficient thalamic development for the attribution of pain. "Who would make the parallel claim that patients with Alzheimer's disease cannot feel pain, simply because they are incapable of remembering it later?" (Saunders, 1997, p. 302). Glover and Fisk (1999) conclude that an early limit of sixteen weeks can be placed on the fetus's capacity for bodily awareness, based on anatomical developments known to be the requirement for the experience of pain, and that physiological development supports the view that pain experience might occur from weeks 24–26 of gestation onwards. In addition, they cite the behavioral evidence that preterm babies, born after 23 weeks' or more gestation, respond to noxious stimuli by screwing up their eyes, opening their mouths, clenching hands and withdrawing limbs, "which in an older baby would show itself in pain" (p. 882).

Note that no-one denies the necessity of some form of "consciousness" to have developed in order for pain to be experienced. The question is whether neuronal developments are sufficient for consciousness. Dennett (1991b), too, assumes that reasoning experience is necessary for consciousness, which must therefore be confined to more complex animals. Although Dennett's sub-personal cognitive psychology has some role for behavior, it does not make explicit how an extensional behavioral science could enter into explanation; rather, it is generally scathing about any role for behaviorism in psychology. Dennett (1991b), however, makes very clear the role of language in consciousness. In the more restricted context of the debate about fetal pain, a much more specific role for behavior and experience has been proposed.

Derbyshire (2006), for instance, presents a sophisticated argument which questions whether neurobiology can ever support the notion

Exhibit 6.1 – *continued*

of fetal pain which concludes that "The subjective experience of pain cannot be inferred from anatomical developments because these developments do not account for subjectivity and the conscious contents of pain" (p. 909). While acknowledging that the biological requirements for pain are available from about twenty-six weeks' gestation, Derbyshire claims that to the extent that pain requires content from beyond the brain, fetuses are incapable of feeling pain no matter what their state of neural advance. "Without this content, there is the response to noxious events, otherwise known as nociception, but no pain... By this definition, pain is not merely the response to noxious stimuli or disease but is a conscious experience.... [C]onscious function can only emerge if the proper psychological content and environment has been provided. Before infants can think about objects or events, or experience sensations and emotions, the contents of thought must have an independent existence in their mind.

This is something that is achieved through continued brain development in conjunction with discoveries made in action and in patterns of mutual adjustment and interactions with a caregiver." (Derbyshire, 2006, p. 911). In words reminiscent of Skinner's (1945) argument with respect to the learning of verbal behavior that describes one's subjective experience, Derbyshire claims that "When a caregiver points to a spot on the body and asks 'does that hurt?' he or she is providing content and enabling an internal discrimination and with it experience." (ibid; see also Derbyshire 1999, 2003; Derbyshire and Furedi, 1996).

Precisely because we are not here concerned with the rights and wrongs of this debate, we can dispassionately formalize the models that underpin the arguments on each side. The fact that the debate may well remain inconclusive for a very long time yet is, moreover, consistent with the pluralistic methodology advocated here. The "neuro-physiology is enough" argument is akin to a very strict sub-personal cognitive psychology in that it claims that the formation of certain evolutionarily-consistent afferent–efferent linkages is sufficient for the ascription of mentality, in this case the experience of pain at the personal level. Putting it this way, it seems that Dennett's original (1969) argument for the ascription of intentional content, based on what I have called the "categorical

Exhibit 6.1 – *continued*

distinction" between the person and sub-personal levels, is actually closely allied to his sub-personal cognitive psychology (Dennett, 1981) and, particularly to this the rather extreme for it takes for the "neuro-physiology is enough" campaign. Personally, I am happy to retain this model in our armory, for two reasons. First, the day that the capacity to experience subjective pain is determined by armchair philosophizing, no matter how well-informed by positive extensional science, is the time to relocate extra-terrestrially. Second, there is a great deal that such an approach can contribute to the prediction and control of behaviors such as reflex responding to noxious stimuli. We are dealing here, however, with an extensional neuroscience, one which is concerned with the positivistic description of behavior and its physical correlates, rather than with a science that is able to go beyond this point by explaining. There is still room for a super-personal approach which formally incorporates an extensional behavioral science, i.e., for intentional behaviorism and super-personal cognitive psychology.

Selection by consequences

Part of the genius of Dennett's (1969) original scheme for the ascription of intentional content is his insistence that the leap from the sub-personal to the personal level of explanation be bounded by the consistency of the afferent–efferent links found at the former with natural selection. How is this methodological principle to be incorporated into the more comprehensive cognitive-behavioral psychology to which intentional behaviorism and super-personal cognitive psychology have led us?

The principle of selection by environmental consequences is the basis of a range of explanatory mechanisms in the biological, social and psychological sciences (Skinner, 1981). Common to all is that the inferred selective operation of the environment is held to determine the continuity of an organism, practice or organization and the class or species to which it belongs. In the neo-Darwinist synthesis, a predisposing genotype contains the potential of an organism to develop and behave, adapt and survive; but, it is, ultimately, the adaptation of the phenotype to the environment that decides it biological fitness, or capacity to reproduce, and – thereby – that of the genetic material to replicate (Dawkins, 1986). The evolutionary explanation of behavior in social science, has been identified by van Parijs (1981) as operant conditioning, the procedure in which the rate of a response is determined by the prior consequences of similar behavior (Skinner, 1974). Selection by consequences thus applies both to the "contingencies of survival" that determine the course of natural selection, and to the "contingencies of reinforcement" that shape and maintain operant behavior. Cultural evolution is a subset of the latter: practices that result in the wellbeing and survival of social groups or organizations are thereby selected and transmitted from generation to generation (Skinner, 1981). Dawkins (1988, p. 33) points out that, whereas in natural selection "the replicators are the genes, and the consequences by which they are selected are their phenotypic effects," in operant conditioning "the replicators are the habits in the animal's repertoire, originally spontaneously produced (the equivalent of mutation). The consequences are reinforcement, positive and negative [and punishment]."

The limitation of this approach, however, is that it limits replication within the repertoire of the individual. Memetics (e.g., Dawkins, 1976, 1982; Dennett, 1994) proposes that ideas, skills, responses can be characterized in terms of an non-genetic replicator, the meme, that "jumps from brain to brain" in the process of cultural transmission. Especially if memes are conceptualized as founded upon or even inhering in propositional attitudes, memetics bears some affinity with intentional behaviorism, insofar as it proposes an a-ontological unit that saves an extensional theory that cannot otherwise deal with behavioral continuity, the personal level of explanation, and the delimitation of interpretation. Since intentional behaviorism employs behavior rather than neurology as the primary criterion of intentionality, the more embracing idea of selection by consequences encompasses a more appropriate evolutionary framework than natural selection alone. Cognitive evolutionary psychology would then seem to offer an appropriate framework for super-personal cognitive psychology (Barrett, Dunbar and Lycett, 2002; Buss, 1995, 2004, 2005; Crawford and Krebs, 1997; Dunbar and Barrett, 2007).

Evolutionary psychology emphasizes the content of cognition rather than the process. (This is not to say that the process is unimportant but that it is context dependent.) This is consistent with the evolutionary psychological view of Tooby and Cosmides (1992) that the mind is modular, consisting of information processing capabilities that evolved in the course of natural selection in ancestral environments (Duchaine,

Cosmides and Tooby, 2001; cf. Buller and Hardcastle, 2000). These capabilities cannot be context-independent: they evolved as specific responses to particular adaptive problems that early humans faced: the need to attract a mate, acquire a language, detect cheaters in social exchange, and avoid predators. These mental mechanisms were shaped according to the specific social and physical vicissitudes present during the Pleistocene era and have not evolved further in the meantime. The modules that evolved to help solve particular problems are character-ized as algorithms (decision rules) with today retain the specificity of function that brought them into being and honed them. Mental capabilities do not therefore take the form of the domain-general content-independent mechanisms often assumed in general cognitive psychology. Both the task to be solved and the current social and phys-ical environment are involved in eliciting the appropriate mental mechanism for the problem solving of the moment (Janicki and Krebs, 1998).

Hence, and we shall return to this point in the next chapter, people do not enter the world with minds that resemble blank slates (Pinker, 2002); nor can they learn skills, behaviors or attitudes with equal ease. Contra the notion of the relationship between culture and human behavior prevailing in social anthropology (e.g., Geertz, 1973), humans are not passive recipients of the culture in which they happen to have been born. Rather, the components of culture, including behaviors, symbols, and cognitions, are the product of the evolved mental pro-grams within the mind which also influence how the individual responds to cultural elements.

The evolutionary psychological approach is not the only means of accounting for the biological nature of culture. We have already encountered the notion of the meme and argue that it is germane to the IST or intentional behaviorism level of explanation. The current exposition concentrates on evolutionary psychology, however, because it provides the clearest foundational level integration of the various components of super-personal cognitive psychology. Where alternative approaches are relevant this will be noted in what follows but there is not attempt here to review the entire corpus of theory in this area (Foxall, in preparation). Rather, as in other chapters, the emphasis is on identifying factors that enter into the explanation of the findings of research in consumer behavior analysis. In particular, we are concerned first with results within this program for the relationship of consumers' responses in terms of pleasure, arousal, and dominance purchase and consumption environments, and second results of a long-standing empirical program of research on the relationship between cognitive style and early adoption. What is the evidence that these might be cognitive characteristics that evolved as part of human ancestral history?

Before answering this question, it may be useful to take note of the ways in which cognitive evolutionary psychology differs from traditional cognitive psychology. First, evolutionary psychologists refuse to treat cognition as a process regardless of its content. This is consistent with the primary argument of the evolutionary psychologists Tooby and Cosmides (1992) to the effect that information is processed by means of independent, domain-specific modules rather than general cognitive processes. Second, evolutionary psychologists argue that these modules evolved through a need not for cool rationality but for "hot cognition" – i.e., to respond emotionally to critical events in ways that would promote survival and fitness. There are thus natural links between cognition and affect. The tendency in evolutionary psychology is, therefore, to concentrate on how cognitive modules would have been designed to solve real problems posed by objective reality.

An example of this is provided by our research on pleasure, arousal, and dominance that was discussed in Chapter 1. Models of consumer cognition and the model of innovation adoption proposed by Rogers (2003) are generally arranged in the traditional form assumed by consumer behavior texts and cognitive psychology texts: a sequence of processes such as attention, encoding, retrieval, and complex problem solving. The assumption has been, at least in cognitive psychology where such things are more likely to be made explicit, that the same processes apply in general across content domains – from letter recognition to person perception. However, there is evidence that similar stimuli are processed differently depending on their content. As a result, we are now in a position to answer the question and in the process to elucidate the results of our work on consumers' cognitive/affective responses to environments, which have been discussed in depth in Foxall (2005). A case was made there for considering these elements of consumers response as fundamental within environmental psychology, but cognitive evolutionary psychology is even more illuminating.

Kendrick, Sadalla and Keefe (1998) summarize the fundamental assumptions of evolutionary psychology as follows. First, natural selection has shaped both humans' physical bodies and the behavioral and cognitive programs that operate them; second, natural and sexual selection processes have encouraged the development of universal species-typical solutions to the social and physical problems presented to our ancestors; and third, these processes have also encouraged the sexes to develop different behavioral and cognitive strategies (females are, for instance, more selective in the selection of mates; such behavioral differences are, it is assumed, related to underlying cognitive differences. These must be tempered by an understanding of the domain-specificity of human cognitive functions, and of the functions that cognitive developed to perform in the evolutionary contexts encountered by our ancestors. So what cognitive structures would those ancestors have required to cope with this "environment of evolutionary adaptedness"?

These authors pinpoint the essential problems as: face recognition, language learning, the perception and understanding of dominance in status hierarchies, and the perception and understanding of agreeableness of others. Face recognition is closely related to the need to recognize others as part of the social group or as alien to it, but also to read the emotional states of others so that appropriate approach or avoidance behaviors can be enacted. Perhaps this would better be called person recognition since it encompasses more than the face: body language, voice recognition, attribution of friendliness to the tone of voice, etc. matter a great deal. Moreover, the essential factor in this seems to be perception by exception: the identification of the degree of discrepancy presented by these stimuli from a norm that is adjudged safe. If so, this ability is a facet of what Mehrabian and Russell (1974) refer to as *arousal*.

Humans can be expected to think about their relative positions in status groups as these reflect *dominance* and submissiveness (of themselves and others). Dominance is, furthermore, another of the fundamental human emotions studied by Mehrabian and Russell (1974). As far as the detection of agreeableness or pleasantness is concerned, this ability would surely apply not only to the social but to the physical environment, and is as such close to what Mehrabian and Russell (1974) argued for as a basic human emotional phenomenon: moreover, as they pointed out, the pleasantness of environments is measured by the construct *pleasure*.

Kendrick, Sadalla and Keefe (1998) note that agreeableness and dominance emerge from factor analytical studies as "the main axes of a circumplex of interpersonal terms" (citing Wiggins and Broughton, 1985; see also Foxall, 2005); that cross-cultural research also implicates the prevalence of words relating to these concepts in language across cultures (White, 1980). White's argument is that hominid development designed human minds to be especially sensitive to issues arising from the dominance and agreeableness of others. It seem obvious that people's everyday problems with other people involve these dimensions

(Gurtman, 1992). Kendrick, Sadalla and Keefe (1998, p. 488) conclude that "From an evolutionary perspective, the tendency to think about other people in terms of dominance and agreeableness is thus funda-mental to human cognition." Closely connected with this is the neces-sity of humans' having means of evaluating and responding to potential mates, which rely also on notions of agreeableness/pleasant-ness and dominance. Specific mechanisms detect anger and hostility in others. Angry faces are detectable on the basis of their being discrepant from happy faces. This ties in well with the argument that pleasure, arousal, and dominance are fundamental human emotional responses. These three basic emotional reactions to consumer environments must, it emerges, be central also to a cognitive evolutionary psycho-logy. Moreover, a strong argument can be put that psychological hedo-nism, the avoidance of pain and enhancement of pleasure, constitutes an ultimate human motive (Sober and Wilson, 1998).

The dominance theory devised by Cummins (1998) is based on the observation that struggle for survival is often characterized by conflicts between the dominant and those who were trying to outwit the domi-nant. She traces the evolution of mind to this strategic arms race in which the weaponry is mental capacity to represent and manipulate internal representations of the minds of others. This in turn explains the emergence of ToM. It is the necessity of solving problems that arise form social conflict and competition that impels the growth of cogni-tive capacity. Finding solutions to these problems is essential since they impinge so much on survival and fitness. As a result of finding such solutions, social structure became characterized by dominance hierarchies, and the more complex these have become, the greater the neocortical development of the primates included within them. Cummins's argument is that the need to reason accurately about the nature of dominance hierarchies guided the development of primates' cognitive architectures. The sort of reasoning required of members of a status hierarchy includes (a) the ability to make discriminations among ranks, (b) the recognition of what is permitted and what forbidden given one's rank, and (c) the decision to engage in or deviate from activities prescribed by the group to ensure one's upward social mobil-ity (Cummins, 1998).

A strategy for an integrated psychology

The tentative strategy of this integrated psychology has four stages. It begins with the intentional idioms found to be useful at the level of intentional behaviorism, but, additionally and wherever possible, those that have been supported by empirical test. An example of the intentional behaviorism phase of this stage is incorporation of the S–S* and R–S* links proposed by Bolles's syllogism. Dickinson's (1997) program to substantiate these proposed links comprises an empirical program. Indeed, in the absence of empirical evidence for the at least epistemological usefulness of the content introduced in the process of intentional behaviorism, one would have to rethink the program before proceeding to this stage.

The second stage is to employ the psychological structures further by enquiring how they are implemented in the brain. The necessary sequence in super-personal cognitive psychology is that followed by Dickinson: "Whereas in the theoretical vacuum of the 1960s I had hoped that the pattern of behavioral dysfunction produced by neural interventions would reveal the psychological structures and processes of instrumental action, I now have sufficient confidence in the present psychological understanding to reverse the research strategy and ask how the brain implements these processes and structures." (Dickinson, 1997, p. 361)

The third stage involves relating the brain processes to specific afferent–efferent linkages and their evolution in the process of natural selection. This reinforces the original ascription of intentionality made in intentional behaviorism at the personal level. That level is, of course, where they remain. Finally, it is necessary to relate the behavior–environment relationships on the basis of which the intentional behaviorism ascriptions were made to the evolution of such behaviors in the process of evolutionary psychology. This procedure is not a prescribed route for empirical science but reflects how some scientists have worked and how as a result science has progressed in the direction of what I have called super-personal cognitive psychology. Above all, it is iterative and corrigible.

Contextual psychology: A summing-up

Of the various kinds of contextual psychology discussed, intentional behaviorism and super-personal cognitive psychology are both behavioral/behaviorist and intentional. Here, I will simplify by referring to them just as *contextual psychology*. What is their nature? In particular, why should we think of them as behavioral, intentionalistic, and contextualistic?

Intentional behaviorism is behavioral in that it takes the explanation of behavior to be its primary aim: behavior is the dependent variable.

In this it eschews a strong influence in cognitive psychology in which, in Chomsky's words, "Behavior is evidence. It's not what you are studying: what you are studying is competence, capacity. If you study man's insight you want to know what is going on in his brain: behavior gives the evidence for that. But the study of behavior is like calling physics 'meter-readings science' because meter readings are the data. But in a serious field, you wouldn't identify the subject with the data." (quoted in Virués-Ortega, 2006, p. 245). The point is that nature does not tell us what our dependent and independent variables should be: we are as much at liberty to study behavior and its causation as to study brain functioning but confine our interest in behavior to its role as an index of what we are really interested in. (See also Moore, 1999).

It is intentional in that it appreciates that certain gaps in behavior theory can be filled only the ascription of content at the personal level of explanation. As such, it tends toward the competence theory pole of the competence–performance theory continuum. It makes no ontological claims with regard to these other than that they are "real" in the sense that theories cannot do without assuming them to be present and responsible for the continuity of behavior: not necessarily causative in their own right, therefore, but necessary to posit in order that we can give enduring causal status to the environmental variables that control behavior. To some extent it is Rylean in its approach to higher order dispositions such as attitudes and intentions (Ryle, 1949), but it is concerned principally with those dispositions that can/must be expressed in the language of intentionality. It insists, however, that content is always to be attributed at the personal level of explanation and has no place in the sub-personal or super-personal. These levels provide the extensional neuro- and behavioral sciences on the basis of which intentional ascriptions are made.

And it is contextual in two ways. First, its chief criterion for the ascription of content is behavior, specifically the molar patterns of behavior that can be reasonably understood as operant insofar as they are maintained by (or at least correlated with corresponding patterns of environmental consequences: this may be inferred from experimental data or from radical behaviorist interpretation; see Foxall, 2004.) Second, in addition to this ontogenic basis for ascription, it retains Dennett's (1969) phylogenic criterion for the evolutionarily consistent ascription of content based on afferent–efferent linkages at the sub-personal (neurophysiological) level of analysis. It may be difficult in practice to fulfill both of these criteria in every instance; in such eventualities, the behavioral criterion remains sacrosanct, else Dennett's (1969) formulation would suffice.)

Super-personal cognitive psychology is behavioral on the same grounds as intentional behaviorism. It is intentional in that it seeks to identify and relate the cognitive components of a system that could undertake the functions specified by a competence theory such as intentional behaviorism. How are beliefs, attitudes, intentions, etc. formed? How are they related? How are they implicated in the generation or maintenance of behavior? To this extent, it tends toward the performance end of the competence-performance theory continuum. Cognition is understood as theoretical, a series of interrelated constructs derived from first-personal reports of private events that correlate with sub-personal neural substrates and super-personal operant superstrates.

Finally, it is contextual in three ways. First, its chief criterion for the ascription of cognitive functioning is behavior, specifically the molar patterns of behavior that can be reasonably understood as operant insofar as they are maintained by (or at least correlated with corresponding patterns of environmental consequences: this may be inferred from experimental data or from radical behaviorist interpretation; see Foxall, 2004.) Second, it seeks to establish the relevance of the behavior patterns on the basis of which it ascribes cognitive functioning by reference to the possible evolution of those patterns – in this it turns critically to evolutionary psychology. And, third, it seeks patterns of afferent–efferent linkage as proposed by Dennett (1969) that are consistent with both its ascription of content on the basis of molar behavior and its inferences from evolutionary psychology.

Part III
Behavioral Economics

7
Herrnstein: Matching and Melioration

> My own view… is that *akrasia* in rational beings is as common
> as wine in France. (Searle, 2001, p. 10)

This chapter and the two that follow compare and contrast the three
varieties of behaviorism that have proved most effective in understanding consumer behavior: radical behaviorism, teleological behaviorism,
and picoeconomics. In the case of radical behaviorism, which has
been extensively examined in earlier chapters, only a relatively brief
overview is given, followed by an account of how this extensional
behavioral science has contributed to behavioral economics. This provides material by which the contribution of teleological behaviorism
and picoeconomics to the analysis of everyday consumer choice can be
evaluated in succeeding chapters. In the case of teleological behaviorism and picoeconomics, a more general account is provided of their
nature as modern behaviorisms, and their contributions to the analysis
of more extreme consumer behaviors, those in which consumers forfeit
self-control in the pursuit of their consumption goals, are considered.
In addition, this chapter classifies radical behaviorism, teleological
behaviorism and picoeconomics on a continuum of behaviorisms from
extensional behavioral science to intentional behavioristic to super-
personal cognitive psychology.

Radical behaviorism

Radical behaviorism's claim to be considered the paradigm extensional
behavioral science rests upon its demonstrated capacity to predict and
control behavior in the closed settings of the animal laboratory and its
impressive ability to do likewise with respect to human behavior in the

relatively closed settings of the experimental situation and those in which applied behavior analysis projects typically take place. In these respects the experimental analysis of behavior succeeds admirably on its own terms as an extensional behavioral science. Its language is scrupulously extensional and Skinner for one went to enormous lengths to avoid intentional usages (except at times in popular accounts). Indeed, of the behaviorisms that are particularly relevant to the analysis of economic behavior, radical behaviorism is the clearest candidate for the required extensional behavioral science since it generally avoids intentional terms, successfully predicting and controlling behavior without their use – at least within the relatively closed settings of the experimental space. Teleological behaviorism neither avoids intentional terms, nor can it. Picoeconomics openly embraces them. In order to explore further the differences among these three behaviorisms, I should like to develop a framework that both derives from and extends Dennett's work which illustrates how extensional behavioral science, intentional behaviorism, and a super-personal cognitive psychology are defined and related.

Radical behaviorism is the most extensional but radical behaviorists use intentional terms in popular expositions *and* interpretations of complex behavior. It may need far more intentionality in order to explain: Taylor (1964) has shown that stimulus and response are terms that rely intrinsically on intentionalistic assumptions, for instance, and I have argued that there are three remaining reasons why an explanation based on extensional behavioral science would need to be supplemented explicitly by the incorporation of intentionality. Taking it, however, as a science of behavior, we must admit that it predicts behavior exceedingly well – especially in relatively closed settings – and assists their influence/control. I would place it on the continuum from extensional behavioral science to cognitive psychology – just beyond the former pole in the cognitive direction.

The behavioral economics of consumer choice

Contributions to consumer research by behavioral economists working in the traditions of the experimental analysis of behavior and experimental economics (e.g., Alhadeff, 1982; Kagel, Battalio and Green, 1995) have not in general aroused interest among marketing scientists. Small exceptions have arisen where the subjects of behavioral economics research have been human rather than non-human animals as for instance in the case of the token economy (Foxall, 2002). The approach taken toward experimental economics by these authors nevertheless suggests avenues of experimental and non-experimental research for those whose primary interest is the study of consumer choice in the context of modern marketing systems. In this article, we show how techniques developed by behavioral economists can be transferred from the animal laboratory to the analysis of patterns of consumer choice occurring in the natural environments provided by supermarkets and other retail outlets. In the process, we present evidence that this form of analysis can be invaluable to marketing researchers and executives as a means of understanding the factors that motivate and control familiar patterns of consumers' brand and product choice, the substitutability, complementarity and independence of competing brands and products, and the structure of markets for consumer goods. We draw particular attention to the roles of product functionality versus branding in the maintenance of consumers' buying patterns, the extent to which consumers can be said to maximize, and the explanation of their decision processes for frequently-purchased goods.

Although "behavioral economics" refers to several lines of inquiry, including perhaps most famously the work of Herbert Simon (1979), we employ it here specifically to denote the amalgam of behavior analysis, experimental economics and behavioral biology that has been pioneered by such authors as Herrnstein, Rachlin, Ainslie, Kagel and Green. Drawing on the behaviorist tradition in which the rate of behavior is held to be determined by the nature of the reinforcing consequences that follow it (Skinner, 1938, 1974), they have resolved the psychological variables that compose the operant paradigm into economic analogues such as price, quantity demanded and payment in order to test hypotheses derived from economic theory in the context of animal experiments (Kagel et al., 1995). Some of the methods employed in this research can be applied to the analysis of consumer choice in naturalistic marketing settings.

An important debate in the evolution of behavioral economics has been – and to some extent remains – the question whether consumers maximize in some sense or follow some other decision rule such as satisficing. Controversy has long surrounded economists' assumption that consumer behavior maximizes utility (or the satisfactions obtained from owning and using economic products and services). While distinguished economists such as Friedman (1953) argued that maximization was a feasible assumption as long as it contributed to predictive accuracy, equally distinguished behavioral scientists such as Simon (1959) decried the lack of empirical support for the assumption and argued that consumers, like other economic actors, are content to achieve a satisfactory rather than maximal level of return for their efforts, i.e. to *satisfice*. The advent of experimental economics brought empirical data to bear on the question of maximization through controlled studies of animal behavior in which responses (key pecking or bar pressing) are analogous to *money*, food pellets, or other items of reward to *goods*, and the ratio of responses to rewards to *price*. Two intellectual communities have grown up around this research, each associated with its own set of conclusions: the behavioral economists, exemplified by Kagel et al. (1995), whose experiments satisfy them of maximization, and the behavioral psychologists, exemplified by Herrnstein (1997), whose work provides them with evidence for an alternative decision process, *melioration*, in which the consumer selects at each choice point the more rewarding option without necessarily maximizing overall returns. A more precise formulation than satisficing, melioration refers to the choice of whatever option (e.g., one of a number of products) provides the consumer with the greater/greatest immediate satisfaction; while he or she can be said to maximize returns at each choice point in a sequence of purchase decisions, there is no reason to expect that the behavior involved will maximize overall return as economic theory predicts. Despite protracted debate, no solution to the problem has been found which satisfies both camps. But, as marketing scientists, we can safely leave the protagonists, as Guthrie characterized Tolman's rats, "lost in thought."

Failure to generate definitive experimental data has not deterred these behavioral scientists from suggesting, in the absence of any direct evidence, how the behavior of human consumers is related to the system of rewards that ostensibly maintains it. The application has, however, devised and tested a method of obtaining data on consumers' purchase choices over time which have direct relevance to our understanding more clearly how consumer choice is distributed over a sequence of purchase occasions, and when such behavior can be said to maximize.

Much of the experimental work mentioned above takes the form of studies of *matching*, which refers to the tendency of animals and humans to distribute their responses between two choices in proportion to the patterns of reward programmed to be contingent on each choice. Herrnstein (1961, 1970, 1997) discovered, defined and built upon this phenomenon. Defining choice not as an internal deliberative process but as a *rate* of intersubjectively observable events that are temporally distributed, Herrnstein's dependent variable was not the single response that needed contextual explication in terms of a single contingent reinforcer: it was the relative frequency of responding, which he explained by reference to the relative rate of reinforcement obtained from the behavior. Animals presented with two opportunities to respond (pecking key A or key B), each of which delivers reinforcers (food pellets) on its own variable interval (VI) schedule, allocate their responses on A and B in proportion to the rates of reward they obtain from A and B. This phenomenon, known as "matching," has been replicated in numerous species including humans and has found applications in behavior modification and organizational behavior management, to name but two relevant fields. In particular, it provides a framework for the behavioral analysis of consumption (Rachlin, 1989, 2000a). The phenomenon is particularly well researched in contexts that require an individual to allocate a limited period of time between two choices, each scheduled to produce reward at a different rate.

Most choices for human consumers are rather different, requiring the allocation of a fixed income between alternative choices, each of which exacts a different monetary sacrifice. In this case, responses take the form of surrendering money in varying amounts, while the reward is the receipt of a fixed amount of the good in question. Price is the ratio of units of money that must be exchanged for units of the good. Both matching and maximizing theories make a similar prediction of behavior on such schedules: the individual will maximize by exclusively selecting the schedule that provides the higher return. Studies of animal choice confirm this prediction.

The reason is that, given the parameters of matching in the context of consumer choice, where the schedules that govern performance are close analogues of the ratio schedules imposed in the operant laboratory, both maximization and matching theories predict a similar pattern of choice, one that eventuates in maximization *and* matching by virtue of the expectation that consumers will always select the cheapest alternative when selecting among brands. The expected behavior pattern is, therefore, exclusive choice of the more favorable schedule. Although there is some evidence that this is generally the case, there are frequent exceptions in that consumers sometimes buy the most expensive option or, on the same shopping trip, purchase both cheaper and dearer versions of the same product, something that animal experiments, which demand discrete choices in each time frame, does not permit its subjects. In other words, the marketing system adds complications to the analysis that cannot be anticipated within the original context of the behavioral economics research program. Even behavioral economics research with human consumers in real time situations of purchase and consumption (token economies and field experiments) have not been able to incorporate such influences on choice as a dynamic bilateral *market* system of competing producers who seek mutually satisfying exchanges with consumers whose high levels of discretionary income make their selection suppliers not only routine but also relatively cost-free. Behavioral economics experiments with human consumers have at best been able to incorporate only a portion of the full marketing mix influence on consumer choice. It has typically been possible to employ price as a marketing variable but not the full panoply of product differentiation, advertising and other promotional activities, and competing distribution strategies which are the dominant features of the modern consumer-oriented economy. Moreover, because it is the marketing mix, rather than any of its elements acting in isolation from the rest, that influences consumer choice, such experiments have been unable to capture the effect of this multiplex stimulus on purchasing and consumption.

Matching, maximizing, and melioration

Matching, the tendency of individual organisms to allocate responses among alternatives in proportion to the reinforcement obtained from each, is a well-documented phenomenon of both non-human and human responding in experimental contexts (Davison and McCarthy, 1988). The matching relationship is represented by the Generalized Matching Law (Baum, 1974):

$$\log (B_1/B_2) = s \log (R_1/R_2) + \log b \qquad (1)$$

where B_1 and B_2 are the allocations of behavior to choices 1 and 2 respectively, R_1 and R_2 are the rates of reinforcement derived from choices 1 and 2 respectively, b is a measure of bias in favor of either B_1 or B_2 that stems from factors other than the schedules of reinforcement in operation, and s is the sensitivity of the behavior ratio (B_1/B_2) to the reinforcement ratio (R_1/R_2).

The parameter $\log b$ or *bias* constitutes the intercept of the linear log-log formulation of the law. Deviations of this parameter from unity are interpreted as indicating a consistent preference for one option independently of its reinforcement rate schedule. Such bias is generally a result of experimental artifacts that could make one response less costly than the other. The exponent s constitutes the slope of the linear log-log formulation, and corresponds to a deviation from ideal matching ($s = 1$), indicating that the individual favors the richer ($s > 1$, over-matching) or the poorer ($s < 1$, under-matching) schedule of reinforcement more than predicted by the matching law (Baum, 1974, 1979). Furthermore, research using matching analysis with qualitatively different reinforcers (e.g. food and water) has shown to be an exception to the predictions of matching law. When using qualitatively different commodities, as gross complements (i.e. when an increase on the consumption of one product requires the increase of the consumption of a second product, as is the case with food and water), it has been found that choice ratio has an inverse relationship with the reinforcement ratio, showing the exact opposite of what the matching law predicts (Huish, 1978; see Kagel, Battalio and Green, 1995 for a review). Hence, this particular effect has been named *anti-matching*, and in operational terms it consists of a result of $s < 0$ in the generalized matching equation (Kagel et al., 1995).

Matching, as has been said, is concerned with the relationship of *frequency* of responding to *frequency* of reinforcement: on this basis it is said to be a molar process, and the alternative level of analysis is the molecular which is based upon single behavior–reinforcer incidents (Baum, 1973). Molar patterns are discernible from a comparison of the *rates* at which responses are emitted and reinforcement obtained. One source of explanations for what is happening at the molar level is a consistent molecular level theory. An epidemiologist might seek an explanation for the correlation of rates of cigarette smoking and rates of lung cancer in the general population (a molar level of analysis) in the effects of smoke-borne carcinogens on tumor development and growth (a molecular level of analysis in the terminology employed here). Similarly, Herrnstein (1979) sought an explanation of matching in terms of the molecular process (i.e., concerned with explaining an individual response) he called *melioration*, in which the behavioral option offering the higher local rate of reinforcement is chosen at any time, and equilibrium is reached when responses are allocated so as to equalize the average reinforcement rates. We shall return to melioration in a moment since its import is easier to grasp after considering why matching is relevant to consumer choice.

The extension of matching to the interpretation of non-experimental consumer behavior in humans is commonplace (e.g., Herrnstein, 1997). Its further extension to the interpretation of consumers' distributed brand choices within a product category appears, on the face of it, a straightforward matter. (A product category is the set of functionally equivalent brands, each member of which embodies all of the essential functional characteristics of the category; indeed, it must do so in order to hope to compete with established brands. Branding is the differentiation of brands within a product category by means of managerial action). Brand choices within a product category, such as the selection of either the Heinz or the Crosse and Blackwell brand from a range of baked beans products on a supermarket shelf, follow well-documented patterns (Ehrenberg, 1972/1988). The impulse to interpret consumers' sequential brand purchasing in terms of matching underlain by melioration is, therefore, compelling.

Moreover, the clearest evidence for the matching law comes from experiments in which the alternative reinforcers are direct substitutes for one another (Davison and McCarthy, 1988); Heyman (1996) argues that both perfect substitutability and confidence that the nominal reinforcement frequencies exclusively control behavior are required for matching to occur. Green and Freed (1993) argue that substitutability inheres in the similarity of the functional attributes of the reinforcers (goods or commodities). Yet in affluent consumer markets, manufacturers and retailers annually incur large expenditures not only on production systems and quality controls to ensure that the physical formulation of their brand is standard for the product category, but also on branding and promotional efforts to differentiate their brand(s) from those of other manufacturers and retailers. While the former expenditure is fully explicable in terms of Green and Freed's understanding of the substitutability of reinforcers as consequences of purchase that provide a set of functional benefits, the latter expenditure can be understood in behavior analytic terms only be an extension of the meaning of reinforcement. These considerations illustrate the kinds of assumption and procedure that a behavioral interpretation of consumer choice needs to adopt.

Green and Freed (1993, p. 151) point out that work on the matching law generally has used reinforcers that are qualitatively similar (actually, identical) reinforcers. They also note that "in choices between qualitatively different reinforcers (such as between orange juice and grapefruit juice), relative obtained reinforcement value would not equal relative amount consumed; yet if one assumes the matching relation to be true, then some other factor must be incorporated to preserve the relation between relative obtained reinforcement value and relative amount consumer for qualitatively different reinforcers" (Green and Freed, 1993, p. 151). Rachlin et al. (1980) go so far as to claim that substitutability inheres in the measure of sensitivity, s, of the generalized matching law (equation (1)); $s = 1$ would, therefore, imply perfect substitutability. They adduce empirical evidence for this view, showing that in the case of pigeons', rats' and monkeys' choices of food versus water, $s \approx -10$, indicating complementary products, whereas for these animals' choices of food versus food and water versus water, $s \approx 1$. Although this is not a universally accepted view, there is general agreement even among its critics that s represents qualitatively different reinforcers (Baum and Nevin, 1981). While economists have generally studied non-substitutes, psychologists have concentrated on substitutes. The assumption of both has been that highly branded versions of a product category (Coca Cola and Pepsi Cola, for instance) are substitutes. The integration of matching research and behavioral economics is desirable in order to combine their ideas of substitutability. A marketing analysis raises additional questions such as, What is the relationship between brands of this sort and those less-differentiated by marketing activity (such as own-label colas).

On the assumption that s is a measure of the substitutability of the choice alternatives available, under- or over-matching and anti-matching presumably indicate some level of the independence or complementarity of these options. Another assumption of our empirical work was that the price structures faced by consumers resemble the ratio schedules. As predicted in the case of behavior on such schedules, consumers should both match and maximize by always selecting the most favorable option, the cheapest alternative. By and large, our analyses found both patterns. Brand competition was generally marked by ideal matching (Foxall and James, 2001, 2003; Foxall and Schrezenmaier, 2003; Foxall, Oliveira-Castro and Schrezenmaier, 2004), product choices by some degree of under-, over- or anti-matching (Romero, Foxall, Oliveira-Castro and Schrezenmaier, 2006). Similarly, though again with some exceptions, consumers maximized by purchasing the least expensive of the brands composing their considerations sets (Foxall and James, 2001, 2003; Foxall and Schrezenmaier, 2003; Foxall, Oliveira-Castro and Schrezenmaier, 2004).

The exceptions occurred, first, because the composition of consumers' consideration sets often meant that their selections were among premium priced, higher quality brands, or at least those more highly differentiated through promotional activity, rather than among all of the brands that made up the product category. As a result, their selecting the least expensive brand refers only to their choosing within the limitations of this subset of available product versions. A second source of exception was that some consumers bought more than one brand on a single shopping trip, often adding a rather more expensive brand to the cheapest within their consideration set. No doubt the different brands were intended for distinct situations of usage, as when a standard and less expensive fruit juice is purchased for consumption by children of the household in the course of the day and a more expensive version is obtained for the family's use at breakfast. The sheer desire for variety sometimes led consumers to select a more expensive brand on occasion, either in addition to or instead of the cheapest alternative. In the qualitative phase of the research one respondent reported that she "just had to" buy a distinctively-flavored brand of butter from time to time; another, that she would purchase a cheaper store brand sometimes even though this was not part of her regular repertoire simply as a result of the convenience of shopping at a different supermarket (Foxall and James, 2001, 2003). But, apart from these predictable exceptions, the predictions of both matching and maximization theories were fulfilled. Although matching is a truism in the case of consumer choice – the more one buys, the more one spends, and at more or less constant prices the relative amount spent on one brand will be proportionally similar to the relative amount of it that is bought – these studies have clarified a number of matters in marketing and consumer research.

The empirical findings on matching have been extrapolated from the laboratory to provide an interpretation of complex human economic behavior in terms of *melioration*, "the process in which a difference between local rates of reinforcement leads to a continuous change in the distribution of behavior in the direction of an equality of local reinforcer rates" (Davison and McCarthy, 1988, p. 136). An everyday example of melioration involves the way in which drivers on a major highway frequently switch lanes, selecting the clearest and fastest way forward, returning to the original lane or a third when that becomes the most advantageous. Overall, the driver may or may not reach the final destination more quickly than had he/she remained in a one lane for the entire journey, but immediate advantage (the local rate of reinforcement) leads to an averaging of the rates of reinforcement over all choices. An equilibrium is finally reached when the average reinforcement rates of each lane are equalized. Where T_1 and T_2 are the times allocated to the two responses, the local difference in reinforcer rates, R_d, is:

$$R_d = (R_1/T_1) - (R_2/T_2) \tag{2}$$

As a result of the sensitivity of behavior to local rates of reinforcement, time allocation changes; stabilization is achieved when $R_d = 0$.

Melioration, in which the behavior offering the immediately higher or highest rate of reinforcement is chosen, may result in particular circumstances in overall maximization of reinforcement, but usually leads to a suboptimal outcome. Melioration thus provides a molecular level mechanism to explain the behaviors to which matching refers (Herrnstein and Vaughan, 1980). Our empirical work was inspired by the possibility that "consumers who practice 'repertoire buying' might be said to show matching, since they apparently select among brands according to some principle of melioration – perhaps responding locally to small price differentials or non-price deals. But there is no direct evidence of this on the present assumptions" (Foxall, 1999).

Broader implications of matching

Matching has been mentioned thus far solely in terms of its implications for explaining routine consumer behavior. But matching has implications for a more extreme form of consumer behavior, namely the consumption of addictive substances and engaging in addictive practices. These are central in themselves to the explanation of consumer behavior since they are part of it, but they will prove also to be highly relevant to the explanation of routine consumer choice and the development of consumer theory to embrace wider aspects of consumer behavior analysis within the same framework of conceptualization and analysis. This section introduces the main theoretical developments of matching as a means of understanding and of treating addictive behaviors, developments that are due to the work of Herrnstein, Rachlin, and Ainslie. In particular, the theoretical bases of the systems proposed by Rachlin (teleological behaviorism) and Ainslie (picoeconomics) are, in addition, relevant to the study of routine consumer behavior. The theoretical developments that derive from this analysis make it possible to bring other aspects of research in the consumer behavior analysis framework into the explanatory system, namely consumers' affective reactions to consumption environments, saving versus spending, and "green" consumer behavior.

Research based on the matching law indicates that "irrationality, in the strict sense of the economist, is in fact normal!" (Ross et al., 2005, p. 48). People naturally entertain inconsistent preferences for future rewards as the delivery of those rewards extends in time. At time t they prefer a larger reward that will not be forthcoming for a longer time; at $t+1$ they prefer a smaller, sooner reward. After consuming this shorter, sooner reward (SSR), they may wish they had waited for the larger, later reward (LLR). Such temporal discounting of reward value is better described by a hyperbolic function than an exponential. Herrnstein's melioration theory and Rachlin's relative theory of addition differ from Ainslie's (1992) theory by introducing, in addition to hyperbolic discounting, the tendency of the consumption of addictive commodities in one time period to diminish the utility derived both from the addictive substance itself and from other activities (Ross et al., 2005, pp. 64–5). The incidence of tolerance means that the addict has to take more of a drug in succeeding time periods to receive the same level of utility. Also, because drug consumption disrupts one's ability to engage in and enjoy other activities consumption of the former in time period t reduces the utility obtained/obtainable from consuming the latter during $t+1$. Finally, note that both theories distinguish local utility from global utility. "Local utility refers to the utility one gets immediately from an action, while global utility refers to the utility one gets form a given sequence of actions." (Ross et al., 2005, p. 66).

The finding of matching research that the individual tends to discount hyperbolically indicates that his or her consumption choices are responsive not to the global utility presumed by economics but to relative local utilities (Herrnstein, 1961; de Villiers and Herrnstein, 1976). The consumer does not maximize in the sense required by economic theory but "meliorates" by selecting the immediately more profitable alternative on a series of choices; such local maximization is not always compatible with overall optimality (Herrnstein, 1981; Herrnstein and Prelec, 1991). As a result the consumer may be inclined toward addiction for the following reasons. First, there is a tendency of substance use to reduce subsequent utility from the substance and from other activities; second, melioration involves choosing the alternative that delivers the higher/highest local utility. Although local and global utilities are reduced by substance use, the addictive commodity is consumed because melioration is such that by consuming more of that commodity local utility is always higher than not consuming it. The only means of overcoming addiction, Ross et al. (2005) argue, is to broaden the time horizon that is embraced by "local" so that the hangover is included as well as the drinking. This may mean that the average utility of the whole night-before-and-morning-after period is reduced or that the hangover's negative utility reduces the utility of the excess drinking so that it becomes more likely. They amount to the same thing really but the main point is that this process, (which, as we shall see, is described by Ainslie as "bundling"), has considerable significance for understanding extreme consumer behaviors involving compulsivity and addiction (Herrnstein and Prelec, 1992).

8
Rachlin: Teleological Behaviorism

Skinner's [1953] radical behaviorism accepts inner causes [Zuriff, 1979] and rejects mental terms, whereas teleological behaviorism does the reverse. (Rachlin, 1995, p. 110)

In summary, a problem of self-control arises where we find a pattern in behavior, particular components of which are *dispreferred* relative to alternatives that are inconsistent with that pattern (Rachlin, 1995, p. 116, italics added).

Much depends on what you understand by "dispreferred." We have already encountered teleological behaviorism in the context of the requirement that behaviorist explanations and interpretations should be capable to delimiting the range of consequences that can realistically be causally employed in accounting for behavior. This chapter examines more closely the epistemological status of teleological behaviorism and its contribution to the explanation of consumer choice. In formulating teleological behaviorism as a philosophy of behavioral science, Rachlin follows Aristotle in distinguishing efficient from final causes. Efficient causes precede their effects and consist in the set of internal nervous discharges giving rise to particular movements; they would include internal physiological and cognitive precedents of activity. The analysis of efficient causes yields a mechanism that answer the question *"How* does this or that movement occur?" Final causes are consequences of behavior. Final causes may inclusively fit into one another as the causal web extends outward from the individual who behaves: "eating an appetizer fits into eating a meal, which fits into a good diet, which fits into a healthy life, which in turn fits into a generally good life. The wider the category, the more embracing, the 'more final' the cause." (Rachlin, 1994, p. 21). The analysis of final causes is an attempt to answer the question "*Why* does this or that movement occur – for what reason?" (p. 22). The process of finding the causes of behavior is one of fitting the behavior into an ever-increasing molar pattern of response and consequences. The dependent variable in Rachlin's scheme is not a single response, however, but a temporally extended pattern of behavior. Similarly, the causes of behavior are extended, a series of consequences nested within one another from the closest to the most remote. We have seen that, from these extended patterns of behavior and consequence, can be discerned emotional and "cognitive" behaviors: indeed, the emotion or thinking or believing or knowing *is* the pattern of extended behavior. Rachlin's work in behavioral economics is highly relevant here because an important cause of behavior is the utility function that describes the entire sequence of extended behavior of the individual (Rachlin, Battalio, Kagel and Green, 1981).

For Rachlin, the causes of behavior are to be found in the network of contingencies that control the pattern of behavior of which an observed response (say, drinking or abstaining from alcohol) is a part. Taking a molar view of environment–behavior relationships (Baum, 1973, 2002, 2004), he assumes such patterns, rather than single responses, as his unit of analysis. These patterns over time are what give rise to the ascription of mental language to behavior. Patterning is the key according to Rachlin to both understanding and modifying behavior (cf. Fantino, 1995, p. 118). The capacity to embed a desired behavior in a pattern of ongoing behavior is the key to its success. The more long term a pattern of behavior is, the more costly it is to the individual to interrupt it. Hence the primrose path is avoidable if the environment can be appropriately structured to "increase the salience of temporally extended patterns of behavior and their consequences" (Fantino, 1995, p. 119). The problem presented by the shorter term (molecular) option's providing greater immediate reward is, he claims, capable of being overcome or ameliorated by embedding that response in a pattern of responses that are extended through time.

A mental event cannot, then, be identified with a single act: it is a pattern of behavior. It is that very pattern of behavior that is the mental event. Moreover, the pattern must be publicly available before it denotes mentality. If nobody sees you for a time holding your head, grimacing, nobody hears you say "Oh, my brain hurts" or "That's the last time I'll take a drink, God, if you just let me feel better this time," then the teleological behaviorist view is that you do not have a headache. It's as simple as that. No public evidence, no mentation. The mental event, the pain in this case, *is* those sustained behaviors. The causation of a behavior lies in the pattern of consequential events that ensue from it; in the case of economic behavior (all behavior, perhaps, though the possibility of accurate measurement recedes the further one strays from market exchange) the ultimate cause of behavior is the utility function that describes its outcomes. (See Exhibit 8.1).

Exhibit 8.1   Teleological Behaviorism

Because teleological behaviorism purports to be a much broader explanation of human behavior than does either of the other schools of behavioral economics with which we are concerned, it deserves closer inspection at the theoretical level.

The value of Rachlin's position is twofold: first, it avoids unnecessary mentalism of the speculative kind; second, it forces us to articulate the causes (consequences) of behavior as tightly as we can in order to relate them causally to the behavior itself. But I would depart at three points from Rachlin's teleological behaviorism. First, note that while his teleological approach may be useful, it leaves us with the problem of *delimitation (equifinality)*. What do we include in the utility function of the person whose behavior we are trying to interpret behaviorally? The problem is that numerous consequences follow from the behavior under interpretation. This is the problem of equifinality that Lee (1988) identified as an inescapable component of radical behaviorist interpretation. If the categorization of teleological behaviorism in terms of intentional behaviorism which I intend now to argue for is accepted, this in itself suggests a solution to the problem. Second is the problem of the *personal level* of analysis. It is essential in the interpretation of complex behavior to reconstruct at the 3rd personal level the personal level that the person had. (Dennett's heterophenomenology). The terms in which we do this can only be derived from our first-personal knowledge. Now it can be argued that Rachlin does not need this level of analysis: in constructing an interpretation it would be sufficient to deduce the emotions (and other intentions) from the behavior of the individual. We might then retort, why bother using this language at all? The first-personal level is essential to the interpretation of your behavior, described above, as a headache: only because when I have done those things have I also

Exhibit 8.1 – *continued*

felt a private sensation of pain in my head can I interpret your behavior as a headache rather than the pre-match ritual of a New Zealand rugby player or candidacy for the funny farm. I also know that on occasion I have had the private sensation without doing any of those things which, had someone else been there, would have been public behaviors. Third, there is the inevitable use of intentionalistic language when describing the elements of mind. Whether these are seen as causal does not matter. It is a departure form the extensional behaviorism of Skinner (*qua* scientist rather than public expositor) and also from the extensional behavioral science that is required for intentional behaviorism and cognitive behaviorism. They are especially apparent when Rachlin speaks of the first occasion on which a person who has been following one pattern of behavior (e.g., excessive drinking of alcohol) changes this pattern by performing an act that may initiate a pattern with alternative consequences.

This third is serious. It involves a personal level of analysis and cannot be understood fully without taking account of the first-personal. Why does Rachlin use mental terms to redescribe behavior? Why not just describe the behavior in behaviorist terms and ignore the mental vocabulary? The reason is that certain behaviors such as shouting ouch, jumping up and down, throwing down the hammer are associated with an interior feeling of pain by the individual who has just hit his thumb instead of the nail. We say that such a person is in pain. But we do not do so because the verbal community has trained us to associate the word pain with such behavior. In regard to such behavior, it has trained us to say or think "You are jumping about" or "Why are you shouting like that?" and to discern that the person doing these things may be experiencing similar discomfort to that which we have felt when we have done similar things and that the word pain might be appropriate, so that we might also say "does it hurt much?" This is because it has previously taught us to use the word pain in connection with certain inner feelings we have. Sometimes these feelings are accompanied by our just having hit our thumb with a hammer, jumped up and down, and so on. That is our sole justification for saying another person is in pain when we see him do these things. But the ultimate criterion for using the word pain

Exhibit 8.1 – *continued*

is derived from our having been trained by the verbal community when we ourselves feel certain sensations within our bodies. That is why Rachlin uses it to describe overt behaviors. Sometimes we collide with the world such that people say "Gosh, that must hurt!" or act as though we must be in great pain; even we may cringe if we shut our finger in a car door. But sometimes we simply do not feel any internal pain and can say, despite having felt ourselves cringe No it does not hurt.

In sum, teleological behaviorism undoubtedly begins as an extensional behavioral science insofar as it attempts to account for behavior in terms of its consequences, particularly by locating behaviors within a structure of behavioral patterns. It is intensional, however, insofar as it attempts to define mental events by reference to those patterns of behavior. Admittedly, it does not seek the converse, i.e., to explain behavior by reference to mental events. It seems we can define a corresponding fallacy to that of mereology in which the properties that properly belong only to the person are attributed to his or her behavior. The thinking, knowing, feeling etc. are said to inhere entirely within the behavior. It is the ascription to one's behavior of things, events, actions that can be ascribed only to the person, and that includes all that we call mental and emotional. Let us call this the contextual fallacy: it consists in attributing to the super-personal level of analysis properties and behaviors that can only be ascribed at the personal level. This, I submit, is the fallacy of teleological behaviorism; perhaps we could call it the "periological" fallacy!

Rachlin argues that psychological reality inheres in patterns of behavior over time, as his parable of deaf Eve and hearing Adam exemplifies (see Rachlin, 2000a, pp. 19ff.) "Although there must be differences between the internal auditory mechanisms of Adam and Eve – physiological differences, underlying the psychological differences between them – the *psychological* difference itself (hearing versus not hearing) rests in Adam's actual behavior over time (his discrimination) and Eve's actual behavior over time (her failure to discriminate)." (p. 21). *Teleological behaviorism* involves "suspension of an *inner life* as distinct from *life*." Life is what is acted out, overt behavior. Teleological behaviorism requires third-person observation to establish our mentality on the basis of our overt behavior. If there is no-one to see the results of our thoughts, we have not thought them. Our mental life... is our pattern of behavior extending into our pasts and futures. "Mental events are... perceptible patterns in our overt behavior." (p. 19) "A thought is one theme within the pattern, a wish is another, a hope is another" (ibid.). Note that while Rachlin accepts a priori that the use of mentalistic terms is legitimate, he speaks of their relationship to behavior in inten- tionalistic language. This is another dimension to his acceptance of mentality.

Teleological behaviorism and intentional behaviorism

The value of this position is twofold: first, it avoids unnecessary men- talism of the speculative kind; second, it forces us to articulate the causes (consequences) of behavior as tightly as we can in order to relate them causally to the behavior itself. But Rachlin's teleological behav- iorism is not an extensional behavioral science. It incorporates inten- tionality in three ways: (i) to designate patterns of behavior, (ii) to achieve a basic exposition of teleological behaviorism, and (iii) to account for changes in the pattern of behavior.

To designate patterns of behavior

Emotionality and cognition consist according to teleological behavior- ism in patterns of behavior that are observable by third parties. The emotion/cognition inheres in, is coterminous with the sequence of behavior. Teleological behaviorism provides a means of linking envir- onment–behavior relationships, that occur at the super-personal level of analysis, to the ascription of intentionality at the personal level. It thus has much in common with intentional behaviorism, though it does not treat intentionality either a-ontologically or causally.

To achieve a basic exposition of teleological behaviorism

Rachlin speaks openly of *information,* in the form of CSs and discrimi- native stimuli, that *signals* respondent or operant contingencies. The "whole process," he says, including presumably the signaling , is part of operant or respondent conditioning. This cannot be a form of words made necessary by a popular exposition because *Mind and Behavior* (Rachlin, 1994) is a technical book, and intentionalistic language is not in any case translatable into extensional. Moreover, the book speaks of verbal reports as being of representations and decisions, which are operations that can be described only in intentional terms. Very clearly, in describing how the behaviorist explores this diagram form left to right, he says that "Behavioral inferences and models are inferences and models about respondent and operant contingencies that may not be present at the moment but serve as the *context* for current actions (Staddon, 1973)." (p. 33) He clarifies this by speaking of the apparently generous behavior of a shopkeeper whose actions might be explicable not in terms of his generosity but by there being a sales promotion in force at the time of his act. The grocer's personal motives cannot be ascertained from his single act but only from the pattern of behavior into which it fits, its context. Now if we are going to make *inferences* and to build *models* about behavior and its mental meanings, we are in very non-behaviorist territory. We have even gone beyond merely redescribing behavior in mentalistic terms; an inference or model involves something over and above the observation of behavior; it is exactly what Dennett says we do when we ascribe content on the basis of observations made at the sub-personal level of physiology – except that in the case of teleological behaviorism they are being made at the level of super-personal observation: they are inferences from patterns of environment–behavior relationship. Why, after all, are we inferring anything about the motive of the grocer if we cannot do this without knowing his behavior which *is* the motive? Why use this term at all? If the term is simply a redescription, we do not need it; if its function is to provide behavioral continuity or to delimit interpretation or to provide a personal level account, we are in the realm of intentional behaviorism. However, this would change the nature of teleological behaviorism in the process since it would be to acknowledge that something real is required to account for behavior, albeit not in the tables and chairs reality sphere, and that this is intentional since it can only be expressed in intentional language.

To account for changes in behavioral patterns

This arises from Rachlin's treatment of the breaking of patterns in the process or self-control. His explanation of behavior cannot proceed without the ascription to the individual of intentionality or even cognitive processing. Hence, on the first occasion of one's ceasing the pattern of overeating – i.e., the next time one eats – there is no pattern of reduced/healthy/responsible eating. The initial lone act must be accompanied by the intentionally construed procedure of changing one's attitude or intention, or the attribution of cognitive processing with respect to one's future, novel behavior. This is the kind of explanation we have called super-personal cognitive psychology. The point is well put by Kane in his response to Rachlin's (1995) exposition of self-control. Kane (1995, pp. 131–2) argues that the word "Pattern" is ambiguous, referring to either (1) a customary form of behavior, or (2) an internal plan or intention to act in a customary way. Rachlin thinks he is talking exclusively about (1), not an internal state but an overt sequence of acts. Kane believes any theory of self-control must include both (1) and (2). A person who has habitually drunk 4 beers every night may, on sight of his midriff, determine to reduce this to two. After two he is tempted to a third but goes home instead. According to Rachlin, exercising self-control is continuing a pattern that is costly to interrupt. The man's exercise of self-control on the first day after his resolution must involve a pattern-as-internal-cognitive-plan for at that point there is no actual pattern-as-overt-behavior to continue through the exercise of self-control. The only overt pattern in force on that day-after-resolution is the four-beer a day pattern and it is this that must be interrupted by the exercise of self-control, not continued. "It seems that Rachlin must make a concession to cognitive theorists on this point or else find some behavioral substitutes for internal plans newly formed by resolutions or choices." (Kane, 1995, p. 113). This covers a larger point. Rachlin talks a lot about a person faced with changing a habit as making a choice. This is of course intentionalistic language and would bring his theory into the realm of intentional behaviorism. but how is the choosing to be ascribed? Teleological behaviorism claims that choosing is a mental act that is coterminous with a pattern of overt behavior, but at this point the person has committed only one act, an act of thought, that cannot be called a pattern at all, still less a pattern of overt behavior. Intentional behaviorism would ascribe such a choice to him on the basis of his suddenly changed behavior on the first night of post-resolution drinking, but the ascribed intentional behavior would be a theoretical device rather than an observed *pattern* of behavior. Hence, in order to delimit its interpretations of complex behavior, teleological behaviorism cannot avoid the assumption of intentionality, not necessarily ontologically but certainly linguistically. (Exhibit 8.2).

In moving towards the question of behavior modification, Rachlin notes that the individual perceives his own motives more accurately and clearly as he gains more information about the context in which his actions occur, the context provided by the "wide-scale" behavior patterns into which his acts fit. How are these wide-scale patterns best described? For Skinner, the notion of the operant was sufficient. This is

Exhibit 8.2   Self-Control

Rachlin's treatment of self-control deserves further exposition. He argues that (1) we intend to act in obedience to learned social rules as long as the actual act of obedience is in the future (Rachlin, 2000a, p. 3) but that (2) we can only act in the present. I.e. we want to do X now and Y in the future where X and Y are mutually exclusive (having a drink, staying sober). As the future becomes the present, however, and since the present is the only time at which we *can* act, we always prefer X. In Ainslie's (2001) terms, this is showing a preference for smaller-sooner over larger-later. Rachlin's approach, however, avoids resort to internal events. In Rachlin's approach, it is patterns of behavior that lead to self-control, not the outcome of internal strategies of will.

Rachlin (1995) notes that behavioral accounts of self-control has been conceptualized in terms of control of behavior by events that are delayed rather than immediate, e.g., choice of a delayed reinforcer of higher value in favor of an more immediate reinforcer of lower value. Since the discount functions facing humans and animals are often non-exponential, we observe the discount reversal effect: failure of self-control. So how is self-control to be achieved in these circumstances? He considers first *external commitment* – "self-imposed severe punishment". Control by physical constraint (having your stomach wired to reduce or prevent obesity) does not work because the problematic behavior returns when the constraint is removed. Moreover, this method does not adapt to changing circumstances. Also, many behavioral changes occur without such dire commitments – e.g., people give up smoking without aversion treatment. But, as Rachlin points out, there are many instances in consumer behavior with less dire consequences than overeating or smoking where self-imposed constraint works: taking out concert subscriptions, joining a health club, etc. These are precisely the kinds of choice that consumer behavior analysis has concerned itself with, and the various behaviors that fit into the eightfold way of the BPM contingency matrix can be explained in these terms (see Chapter 10). We could add the things he does: interpersonal agreements such as marriage, adoption: each of these provides for punishment for defection (and perhaps reward for adherence) over and above the rewards and punishers that are intrinsic to the activities. He moves on to

Exhibit 8.2 – *continued*

internal commitment, to which he refers as an odd sort of cognitive concept since it does not involve information processing. External commitment is observable but internal must be deduced from behavioral cues. He argues that, since external commitment involves either self-imposed physical restraint or self-imposed punishment, internal commitment must consist in internal self-imposed physical restraint or internal self-imposed punishment. These are logically impossible, however. But are these the only options? Rachlin's answer is to posit another form that self-control takes: the understanding that it is externally characterized. The first step is to see that the SS/LL dichotomy does not describe most choices in everyday life. E.g., the extra dessert vs being thin. Most real life choices are not mutually exclusive. Any particular extra dessert can be eaten without the consumer being fat or socially disapproved or unhealthy as long as such consumption is not the norm. While the reward for eating the second dessert arrives soon but the reward for forgoing it does not truly arrive later. We will not wake up thinner and healthier a couple of weeks after refusing a dessert. These consequences do not arrive at any particular date.

the crux of Rachlin's method of explanation: a complex behavior such as building a house or loving one's spouse or being a butcher can be described in Skinner's operant terms only with some difficulty since each includes a variety of acts that might differ from person to person: "The defining characteristic of building a house or loving your spouse is that they each constitute *a perceptible behavioral pattern. Perception is in turn defined as a discriminative pattern of movement of an observer, including the householder or lover (or butcher) as observers of their own behavior. The behavioral definition in each case rests on common consequences of the behavior – common contingencies.*" (Rachlin, 1995, p. 116, emphasis added). Since perception is intentional (Chisholm, 1957), however, this method of ascribing mentality on the basis of observation of behavior is similar to the method characterized in an earlier chapter as intentional behaviorism. There are differences, of course: intentional behaviorism first takes an a-ontological view of ascribed mentality whereas Rachlin sees it as behavior; moreover, intentional behaviorism uses ascribed mentality to fill the gaps in an extensional explanation in order to account for the continuity of behavior and the personal level as well as to delimit the scope of a behavioral interpretation. However, there is an essential point of confluence here.

The point is more forcefully made as Rachlin goes on to contrast his system with cognitive and physiological theories. These, he notes, posit common efficient causes – be they internal representations, mechanisms, intentional systems – *"rather than common overt discriminatory acts of an observer".* (Rachlin, 1995, p. 116, emphasis added). Now the intentionality that intentional behaviorism ascribes is not internal, nor even ontological, but a theoretical device. It is not ascribed on the basis of claims about what is happening within the organism but on the basis of the use of language: perception is a term that is unequivocally intentionalistic and therefore belongs to a quite different kind of explanatory mode from that of extensional behavioral science. The intentional language which Rachlin now uses to describe how to approach the problem of impulsive behavior confirms this interpretation. For he designates the problem of self-control as a conflict between particular acts and patterns of acts: When the particular act firs into the pattern – when we *like* what we *believe* is good for us – self-control does not apply. The squirrel saving nuts is not controlling itself because the particular acts it performs are exactly what it momentarily *prefers* to do: the squirrel engages in nut saving for its own sake and not for any larger good (providing food for the winter). We know this not from the squirrel's verbal report or by empathy with the squirrel but by observing the squirrel's behavior under various controlled conditions... For instance, a squirrel will continue to save nuts even when they are systematically removed from its cache (Hinde, 1970). When there is a conflict between an act and a pattern, however, – when we *like* what we *believe* is not good for us or do not *like* what is – then our behavior is either self-controlled or impulsive, dependent on our choice." (ibid.; italics added). In the passage already quoted at the head of this chapter, Rachlin makes clear that, "In summary, a problem of self-control arises where we find a pattern in behavior, particular components of which are *dispreferred* relative to alternatives that are inconsistent with that pattern" (ibid., italics added). A person's eating the ingredients of a healthy breakfast, all of which he *"prefers,"* is not exercising self-control, but if he *prefers* another food to each of these ingredients and nevertheless eats the healthy breakfast he is controlling himself. (Rachlin, 1995, pp. 116–17)

Note here the use of intentionalistic language (which I have italicized): this matters not just because it is different language per se but because such sentences are not capable of translation into extensional.

It is indicative of a wholly different means of explanation from that required of an extensional behavioral science. If that language is used on the grounds that it refers to a pattern of behavior – the sort of pattern that teleological behaviorism says *is* the mental event – why use it unless one is prepared to depart from an extensional account? Moreover, Rachlin's explication of the means by which a larger pattern is to be inferred from a single act (or pattern of acts in the case of the squirrel) rests on an arbitrary criterion. The nut saving still fits into the larger patterns of surviving the sinter, reproducing, being a sensible squirrel, etc. notwithstanding the experiment. His approach to the squirrel's wants and beliefs has no analogue in the determination of whether the complex behavior (not subject to experimentation) is to be seen as part of a larger pattern or not.

In addition, the term *prefers* as used in the last of these quotations must refer to a pattern of behavior in which, for instance, the eater has consistently chosen breakfast item A over breakfast item B in a long series of trials. This is far removed from the behavioral definition of preference in the case of consumer choice. How are we to designate the preferences of consumers in terms of teleological behaviorism? There is nothing so clearcut as the kind of experimentally-determined preference that Rachlin assumes. At best, for most consumers, we have a pattern of relative behavioral preferences for three or more brands over time. The brands in question are functionally equivalent as shown by our matching analyses (Foxall and Schrezenmaier, 2003; Foxall et al., 2004; Romero et al., 2006). Consumers do not purchase the cheapest available brand, however, but the cheapest within their limited consideration set (presumably consisting of tried and tested brands on the basis of learning history). All brands within this set may well be priced at a premium over and above the price of the cheapest brand within the produce category. Consumers appear to be maximizing a combination of utilitarian (functional) and informational (symbolic) benefits, the latter resulting from non-product elements of the marketing mix and firms' efforts at branding and corporate image building. The only conflict must be between those brands that are priced very low and which provide relatively little informational benefit (when these are not chosen) and those that *are* chosen: the higher-priced, higher utility/higher information brands. There is a conflict in other words between maximization (or satisficing) of utilitarian reinforcement and maximization (or satisficing) of informational reinforcement. Rachlin's next move is to argue that if internal and external commitment are unlikely to account for the overcoming of impulsivity, what can is the establishment of patterns of behavior into which particular acts fit such that the interruption (external) of such a pattern is costly. Actually, what he is advocating is the closure of the behavior setting. We have found that behavior setting closure is important in the maintenance of consumer behavior (Foxall and Yani-de-Soriano, 2005) in much more mundane situations than he described with respect to addiction: this again strengthens the view that the principles he promotes apply much more in settings where genuine matching (i.e., of substitutes) obtains than when the choices are not mutually exclusive; hence, that there is a continuum from everyday consumer behavior to impulsive (unplanned) consumer behavior to compulsive (additive) consumer behavior. Rather than being an extensional behavioral science, teleological behaviorism appears to belong to the classification we have called intentional behaviorism. Although, basing his argument on Dennett (1978, p. 154fn), Rachlin (1995, p. 110) describes teleological behaviorism as a personal level theory, it actually strives to function as an extensional behavioral science that performs at the super-personal level. As Rachlin (ibid.) says of teleological behaviorism: it "looks for order in the relationships between organisms and environment rather than for mechanisms within the organism". However, its incorporation of intentionalistic vocabulary shifts it toward intentional behaviorism.

There are two reasons for placing teleological behaviorism in this area of the continuum and a third interesting consideration. First, Rachlin seems unable to provide an exposition of teleological behaviorism without recourse to intentional idioms. Second, the breaking of a pattern requires the assumption of perception and decision. These cannot be interpreted behaviorally since they are not patterns of behavior but one-off actions. In addition, there is the use of intentionality in the redescription of patterns of behavior.

Rachlin (1995, p. 110) summarizes the difference between radical behaviorism and teleological behaviorism in the passage quoted at the head of this chapter: "Skinner's [1953] radical behaviorism accepts inner causes [Zuriff, 1979] and rejects mental terms, whereas teleological behaviorism does the reverse." By doing this, radical behaviorism must accept the criticism that it employs theoretical terms but it avoids the argument that it has departed from its extensional program by embracing intentional explanation. Teleological behaviorism, however, lies open to this charge, not because that is the intention of its author but because of the language it uses. We have seen that Rachlin (1995, p. 116) defines the mental as a pattern of behavior: e.g., loving one's spouse. The patterns of behaviors is the love/loving. Now here we have the opposite of defining emotion as the neurological events (sub-personal) that may be associated with it: instead we call the overt behavior (super-personal) the emotion.

Let us summarize the position of teleological behaviorism on the continuum of behaviorisms. The patterns into which particular acts are fitted are perceived not so much by the actor as by the investigator. Indeed, the man swinging a hammer may not perceive at all the pattern of cathedral building into which this act ultimately fits but if he is thinking about its broader consequences at all may perceive it as part of a pattern of earning a living. Many of the patterns we observe in daily life are unpredictable unless we can ascribe to the individual (in a third personal manner, what else?) what he intends to do, hopes to achieve, etc. Few people build more than one cathedral in their life-times (how many cathedral builders have managed to see one through to completion?) Apart from banal predictions such as that he will con-tinue to swing the hammer, we can say little about this man without having the information to ascribe intentionality to him. And for this, if it is possible at all, we need something akin to Dennett's heterophe-nomenological method. If we are to search for still wider patterns of consequence in order to explain behavior, we cannot sensibly delimit our interpretations without recourse to the ascription of intentionality. How can we reckon the causes of the scientific behavior that led to the splitting of the atom without ascribing delimiting intentions to the participants rather than citing the ultimate pattern of the bombing of civilians into which their particular acts finally fitted? It seems to me there are only three ways to overcome this problem: find a limited pattern into which the act fits, invent a learning history which "explains" the act, or ascribe intentionality heterophenomenologically. The first option is Rachlin's solution. Even a rat's pressing a bar fits into a pattern, he argues, of seeing the bar, receiving food as a result of pressing, and eating the food. The difficulty here is deciding how to delineate the pattern which we need to take into consideration: we are back to our hammer swinger – can he even be said to be building a cathedral let alone producing interminable boredom for Grand-tourists of the future; perhaps he is only putting bread on the table on that par-ticular day. The second, conjecturing a learning history, is something Rachlin specifically rejects for it harks back to the efficient causation of Skinner's radical behaviorism. The third, reasoned intentional ascrip-tion, is exactly the same process that would be involved in inventing a learning history for the hammerer or the scientists involved and using that as the efficient cause of their behaviors but (a) it explicitly draws attention to the actual nature of such conjectures, drawing honest attention to the fact that we are proposing an untestable hypothesis here, and (b) is expressed in the language of intentional idiom.

Perhaps Rachlin is searching for the limited pattern (option 1) when he speaks of the alcoholic whose behavior changes from nightly binge drinking to having just three drinks before going home as a function of his *deciding* or *determining* to make the change. But on the first occasion of his putting the new pattern into action, there is no pattern of restrained drinking. Teleological behaviorism requires, nonetheless, that the new relative abstemiousness fit into some pattern or other if it is to be explained, and tries to make it intelligible by locating it within a process of self-perception, decision-making and resolution on the part of the convert. But this is actually option 3, that of reasoned intentional ascription, as the language used makes clear. Option 2 remains the method of extensional behavioral science, represented by radical behaviorism, confined to the attempt to predict and control, requiring intentionality only if it seeks to explain further which it does not. The actually strategy adopted by Rachlin locates teleological behaviorism close to the intentional behaviorism point on the continuum. Although teleological behaviorism is consistent with Herrnstein's theory, the particular alternative to substance consumption considered by Rachlin (2000a) is *social interaction*. This is, first, because social interaction is a close economic substitute for addictive substances such as smoking, drinking, and drug use. (Though one might argue that such social interaction is a complement of much addictive behavior.)

Second, while the marginal utility of substance consumption decreases over time, that of social interaction increases. Having a beer tonight will provide more utility if one has not imbibed for a while, but speaking to a neighbor on the telephone has higher utility if one has previously been socializing. (This must surely depend, however, on individual differences whether these are conceived of as based on physical inheritance or learning history. For instance, what Rachlin says here is true of extraverts: introverts who are exposed to too much socialization may well clam up for a week.) These changes in utility are dubbed by Rachlin the *price habituation* of substance consumption and the *price sensitization* of social interaction. The tendency toward melioration means that a consumer always selects the choice that yields the higher/highest utility when the selection is made. A person may be in equilibrium as far as social interaction and drinking are concerned but a traumatic event like divorce could reduce his social interaction (by making it more expensive and scarcer to obtain). Since drinking is a substitute for social interaction he drinks more to make up for the loss of social interaction. As a result of the price habituation of alcohol consumption and the price sensitization of social interaction, drinking more and socializing less will reduce his utility from both drinking and socializing. But the person is likely to drink more since the utility of drinking exceeds that of the (now far more expensive) social interaction. Addiction is a predictable consequence.

9
Ainslie: Picoeconomics

> *Public* side bets – of reputation, for instance, or good will – have long been known as ways you can commit yourself to behave… What I'm describing are *personal* side bets, commitments made in your mind, where the stake is nothing but your credibility with yourself. They wouldn't be possible without hyperbolic discount curves, nor would they be of any use. (Ainslie, 2001, p. 94).

Just as I argued earlier that the distinction between extensional behavioral science and intentional behaviorism was one of complements rather than rivals, so I would now like to suggest that the distinction between teleological behaviorism and picoeconomics lies in the various functions they fulfill rather than in their competing for the same explanatory ground. For, if I have placed teleological behaviorism in the region of intentional behaviorism and super-personal cognitive psychology, I should propose that picoeconomics comes closest to the rounded cognitive psychology that embraces both the sub-personal and super-personal in addition to the personal level where cognition occurs.

Rachlin's view is that self-control results from the perception of enduring patterns of behavior rather than the individual acts that compose them, i.e., the adoption of a molar rather than a molecular view of one's own activities. Rather than seeing the immediate choice to be made, the self-controller sees the sequence of established actions. Ainslie points out that this leaves unresolved the question of how the patterns of behavior arise. His answer is that "hyperbolic discount curves make self-control a matter of self-prediction." This is explicitly intentionalistic if not cognitive. Ainslie's approach rests on the fact that people not only mistrust their own future preferences but "sometimes engage in strategic planning to outsmart the future selves that will have these preferences." He proposes that people maximize their prospective rewards by discounting hyperbolically. Ainslie uses the concept of intrapersonal "interests" to account for the conflict between behaviors that are presented by intertemporal rewards. These interests are conceived of as the "mental operations selected by a particular kind of reward." This is surely a cognitive interpretation of what is happening, though one that derives its explanatory variables from neuroscience, intentionality, and behavior. A more complete cognitive psychology than even an extreme critique of teleological behaviorism could accuse that system of. "The ultimate determinant of a person's choice is not her simple preference, any more than the determinant of whether a closely contested piece of legislation becomes law is simple voting strength in the legislature; in both processes, strategy is all."

A good starting point to understand picoeconomics is to compare and contrast it with teleological behaviorism. Both teleological behaviorism and picoeconomics agree on the tendency to discount temporally distant rewards hyperbolically. "One desire is generally preferred over the other but there is a region of time during which the preferences are reversed" (Kent Bach: Review of *Picoeconomics*) "people's inchoate appreciation of their changing temporal preferences leads them to adopt various strategies of impulse-control and self-reward." (ibid.).

An essential difference is Rachlin's view that self-control results from the perception of enduring patterns of behavior rather than the individual acts that compose them, i.e., the adoption of a molar rather than a molecular view of one's own activities. Rather than seeing the immediate choice to be made, the self-controller sees the sequence of established actions. Ainslie points out that this leaves unresolved the question of how the patterns of behavior arise. Ainslie takes Bratman's example of the pianist who wants to perform well at the evening concert but drinks too much wine at dinner. He speaks of him "preferring" to give a good performance even when he sits down to dinner but this preferring can only be cognitive: there is no behavioral sequence from which it can be inferred. Even if the pianist says this is his preference he can only be referring here to an internal choice, a cognitive act. This language suits Ainslie's picoeconomics which is cognitive but not Rachlin's teleological behaviorism.

For Ainslie "hyperbolic discount curves make self-control a matter of self-prediction". This is explicitly intentionalistic if not cognitive. Rachlin always claims his uses of such language are behavioral. Ainslie's approach rests on the fact that people not only mistrust their own future preferences but "sometimes engage in strategic planning to outsmart the future selves that will have these preferences." He proposes that people maximize their prospective rewards by discounting hyperbolically.

Ainslie uses the concept of intrapersonal "interests" to account for the conflict between behaviors that are presented by intertemporal rewards. These interests are conceived of as the "mental operations selected by a particular kind of reward". This is very much an intentional behaviorist interpretation of what is happening, though it lacks the a-ontological basis of intentional behaviorism. Indeed, what he writes is that the contingencies select the mentality, but unlike Skinner's formulation in which the mentality is merely a "collateral response," in Ainslie's system the interests are active in formulating – or at least explaining – behavior.

Nevertheless, the point here is that, in accordance with both intentional behaviorism and cognitive behaviorism, Ainslie is ascribing mental events (intentional idioms) on the basis of the contingencies apparently governing overt choice behavior. One criterion he uses for the ascription of mental content is that the interest in question involves conflict: presumably because two sets of contingencies are in operation, each leading to a particular outcome (reward) that is incompatible with that offered by the other set. Eating ice cream and losing weight. Eating vanilla ice cream or eating chocolate ice cream does not (necessarily) involve conflict so is not assumed to lead to an interest. No mental ascription is needed. The matter of ascribing content is governed au fond by the contingencies however: the point is that the person does not increase the value of his reward by deferring the choice of chocolate in case he later switches to ice cream. Only where there is conflict (based on the differential rewards available at different times) does conflict arise and thus warring interests. "When alternative rewards are available at different times, each will build its own interest, and an interest will be able to forestall the other only if it can leave some enduring commitment that will prevent the other reward form becoming dominant." "The ultimate determinant of a person's choice is not her simple preference, any more than the determinant of whether a closely contested piece of legislation becomes law is simple voting strength in the legislature; in both processes, strategy is all." The resulting power-bargaining is made necessary by limited means of expression: no-one can do everything.

The consumer who has a private rule "Only have a few drinks on Friday evenings and bank holidays" is, if she follows it, going to give in to the SSR on these occasions but otherwise let the LLR predominate. According to Ainslie there is nothing in the physical or social environment that prevents her choosing the first SSR: only the difference between the summed LLR and SSR values can influence the decision because the giving in to SSR at this initial stage predicts that there will be further surrenders. This predictive value is moreover the reward the consumer gets now for behaving one way or another. (Ross et al., 2005, p. 61). (Note that this puts the causal influence strictly within the consumer's cognitive processes rather than the environmental contingencies). What influences choice is the "intrapsychic free-for-all of successive motivation states attached to short-range, mid-range, and long-range interests" (ibid., p. 63). But how does choice come about in these circumstances? Ainslie uses the concept of the repeated prisoner's dilemma game to represent the nature of the intrapersonal bargaining that his model presupposes. Although the prisoner's dilemma is an interpersonal game, Ainslie redraws it as representing the intrapersonal conflicts between the individual's interests. The single self considers at different times what is the best outcome the present self or what would be best for the present self and a future self as a duo (ibid.). The best thing for the present self to do when considering a SSR-LLR pair of rewards is to select the SSR because only this is currently available. But the present self an the future self would optimally select the LLR because over time they stand to receive greater benefits in this way as they accrue from the sequence of LLRs. Ainslie points out that addicts as well as others are open, in the course of such bargaining, to evasions, distortions, and other forms of self-deception.

Intertemporal bargaining

Ainslie's picoeconomics emphasizes the distinction between exponential and hyperbolic discounting. Exponential discounting means "subtracting a constant proportion of the utility there would be at any given delay for every additional unit of delay." (Ainslie, 2001, p. 28) Assume a new car delivered to me today is worth £10,000 and my discount rate is 20% a year. Then the guaranteed value of the car to me, delivered today but paid for a year ago, would (a year ago) have been £8,000). Two years ago, I would have paid only £6,400. Exponential discounting means that the difference in the utility of an action such as drinking gradually reduces without ever reaching zero or becoming negative. If I would choose to drink now, I would always choose to drink when the drink was delayed. If I would not drink when there was

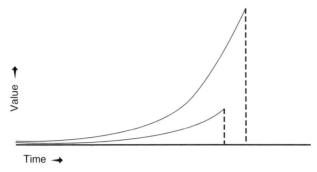

Figure 9.1 Exponential Discount Curves from Two Differently-sized Rewards Available at Different Times

a delay, I would also not choose to drink when it was at hand. Only exponential discounting produces consistent preferences (larger-later is always more highly valued than smaller-sooner). Figure 9.1 shows exponential discount curves from two differently-sized rewards available at different times: not only is the larger-later reward always valued more highly than the sooner-smaller, but their values remain constantly proportional to their objective sizes. It could be then that only exponential discounting is consistent with rationality and that people who have a tendency to discount hyperbolically should learn to keep their impulses in check. (Ainslie, 2001, p. 35). However, such adjustments occur infrequently if at all and where they do only with the greatest exercise of "willpower."

Exponential discounting is invaluable in banking and certain other contexts. However, Ainslie proposes that people often discount hyperbolically – i.e. in such a way as to have inconsistent preferences over time. When individuals discount hyperbolically, conflict is likely to arise between two differently-sized rewards available at different times: the individual shows a marked preference for the sooner-available reward. This is consistent with the findings of matching research. Figure 9.2 compares exponential and hyperbolic discount curves for the same reward. The hyperbolic is the more bowed curve B. As Ainslie points out, "As time passes (rightward along the horizontal axis), the motivational impact – the *value* – of the goal gets closer to its undiscounted size, which is depicted by the vertical line."

Figure 9.3 clarifies the conflict that may arise when individuals discount hyperbolically by presenting curves for two differently-sized rewards available at different times. Unlike the exponential discount

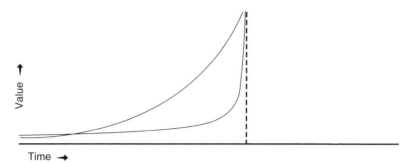

Figure 9.2 Comparison of Exponential and Hyperbolic Discount Curves for the Same Reward

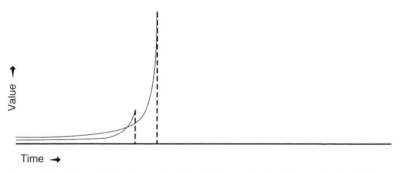

Figure 9.3 Hyperbolic Curves for Two Differently-sized Rewards Available at Different Times

curves depicted in Figure 9.3, these hyperbolic curves can cross. The portion of the curve for the smaller reward that projects above the curve for the larger-later reward, indicates a preference for the sooner-available reward for the duration of the cross-over.

Picoeconomics and super-personal cognitive psychology

The essence of Ainslie's system is not appreciated until one considers the ways he proposes people overcome their addictions. Choices that are regretted can be described in terms of hyperbolic discounting and the strategies that individuals employ in order to make the LLR more probable than the SSR are of four kinds. The first, *precommitment* involves using external commitments to preclude the irrational choice. Ulysses's chosen strategy in binding himself to the mast before he met the Sirens, the addict's use of a substance that will cause her physically unpleasant feelings such as nausea if she imbibes alcohol or drugs, the student's arranging that friends will arrive to give him a lift to the library when his favorite TV show begins – are all means of manipulating the material environment in order to make the SSR less probable or impossible. The second and third, *control of attention* and *preparation of emotion*, are means of internal commitment. Control of attention restricts information processing with respect to the SSR, not dissimilar to Freud's ideas of suppression and repression, though in Ainslie's scheme the process can be conscious as well as unconscious. Taking a route home from the office that avoids bars or restaurants is one example; thinking about the car one can buy if one does not ask for a carton of cigarettes, is another. Preparation of emotion is a form of avoidance or displacement through which one inhibits emotions usually associated with the SSR or to increase incompatible emotions. Reminding oneself of the health risks of smoking or drinking to excess, day-dreaming about that car, thinking of the wrath of others one will incur if one indulges in deleterious habits – all refocus or escape the emotional rewards of addiction through cognitive control.

It is the fourth strategy, however, that involving personal rules (what we have elsewhere referred to as self-rules) to which Ainslie devotes most attention. This is actually an account of how *willpower* operates though it is cast in terms of behavioral economics. Ainslie's account is in any case redolent of intentionality and is a theory of cognitive functioning, thereby placing picoeconomics in the super-personal cognitive psychology camp. Personal rules arise in the context of how an individual perceives the SS and LL choices available to her: on one hand, each separate occasion of two such choices may be seen as isolated in time and space from other choice conflicts; on the other, the individual may perceive a grosser choice, that between a whole sequence of SSRs and a whole sequence of LLRs. If she adopts the latter strategy, she is said to be engaged in *reward bundling* which is a means of self-control. In the absence of such bundling, the consumer will exhibit repeated preference reversals. But if she viewed the choice as that between two streams of behaviors and outcomes, then self-control becomes possible. Self-control results from the consumer perceiving a single choice between an aggregation of LLRs and a competing aggregation of SSRs. The sum of the LLRs is always greater than that of the SSRs. The decision-making is a matter of bringing the LLRs forward in time (in imagination). Ainslie argues that the form taken by the personal rules necessary to ensure this self-control is that of private side-bets in which the current choice predicts future choices. The important point in viewing the reward sequences in this way is that the LLR is *at all times* superior to the SSR even when an SSR is immediately available: preference reversal is therefore not predictable from this model of consumer behavior. "To avoid a reversal of preference, a person can *bundle* a whole series of choices together in anticipation of the higher aggregate reward that would be obtained from preferring the LLRs. She does this by adopting *personal rules* that dictate the choice to be made in a whole class of conflict situations involving the need to delay gratification. These rules take the form of side bets such that he current choice serves as a predictor of future choices. She wins the bet by resisting the current SSR and the expectation of future reward is thereby strengthened and the consumer stands a better chance of resisting similar temptations in the future. She loses the bet, however, if she selects the SSR, some element of her self-image is weakened as is her expectation of being able to resist SS temptations in the future. "Because of the predictive value of current choices for later choices, *which is the reward the chooser gets right now as she makes the choice*, personal rules can bring into the present time the value of rewards in the future, and thus allow people to overcome the effects of the natural hyperbolic discounting." (Ross et al., 2005, p. 61).

Picoeconomics and integrated cognitive-behavioral psychology

Picoeconomics lends itself to the project of the more comprehensive psychology envisioned earlier as a concomitant of super-personal cognitive psychology on account of very recent developments in the neuropsychology and neuroeconomics of addiction (Ross et al., 2005). Ainslie's theory proposes that intrapersonal bargaining between interests representing rewards at various times lies at the center of the cognitive operations involved in strategies of choice. The sub-personal link with this activity is the subject matter of neuroeconomics which "studies the behaviour of the brain as a calculator of the relative values of different possible and actual rewards that a person or other animal could pursue" (Ross et al., 2005, p. 3; see also Glimcher, 2004; Camerer, Loewenstein and Prelec, 2004). Participants in the experiments that comprise this research program undertake decision-making tasks while their brain activity is monitored through magnetic functional resonance imaging (fMRI) techniques. fMRI indicates changes in the blood supply of the brain (which provides oxygen and thus nutrition to the brain) during the performance of such behavioral tasks and thereby suggests where associated brain activity is occurring.

Functional Magnetic Resonance Imaging (fMRI). Neural activity within the brain has associated with it a measurable blood flow that provides the basis of functional magnetic resonance imaging (fMRI). By tracking the blood flow to the vasculature implicated in neural activity, the technique indicates the functional significance of parts of the brain but not the content of any cognitive activity that may be associated with it. The great advantage of the technique is that it permits the brain activity associated with a particular motor or cognitive task or sensory process to be monitored.

The link with neurophysiology derives from the finding that the changes in brain chemistry associated with substance addictions (such as to alcohol and stimulant drugs) is identical to that found in gambling and other "extreme consumer behaviors." An important indicator of this is the finding by McClure, Laibson, Loewenstein and Cohen (2004) that the rewards indicated in decision situations as either immediate or delayed are valued by different neural systems. Their study is an example of the recently emerged science of neuroeconomics in which studies the brain is conceptualized as a calculator of the relative values of different the various rewards available to the individual (Glimcher, 2004; Glimcher and Rustichini, 2004; Ross et al., 2005, p. 3; cf., however, Ainslie and Monterosso, 2004). Two parts of the brain, the limbic system of the midbrain and the prefrontal cortex, are especially important in this process of valuation. The reward system that they compose learns which environmental cues predict reward and the comparative values of different rewards, causes attention to be focused on the cues that predict rewards, and motivates the system to act on these rewards. (It is important to be aware of the mereological problem here with respect to the idea that brain systems "learn," but this is surely a manner of speaking and such learning can be easily specified as adaptive change: to describe such change as learning is hardly to use the intentional stance at a sub-personal level as Dennett's sub-personal cognitive psychology invites; rather, it is simply an extensional account of subsystem behavior couched a little metaphorically).

Neurons communicate with one another chemically when the axon of one neuron (the pre-synaptic or sending" cell) comes close to the dendrite of another (the post-synaptic or "receiving" cell (Figure 9.4); the electrical signal or action potential that travels along the axon releases a chemical known as a neurotransmitter across the gap between itself and the dendrite (the synaptic cleft). Although there are many neurotransmitters, three are particularly relevant to the present context: dopamine, seratonin, and Gamma-aminobutyric acid (GABA).

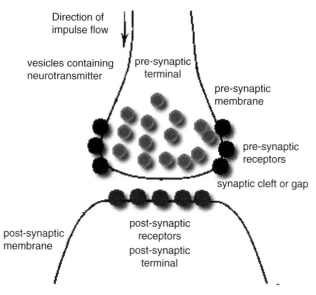

Figure 9.4   The Synaptic Junction between Neurons

As it diffuses across the synaptic cleft, a neurotransmitter encounters a specialized receptor chemical, a protein embedded in the post-synaptic membrane of the dendrite. These receptors generate neural pathways through which the computational processes mentioned above are conducted and integrated.

Drugs cause dopamine to flood one or other part of the reward system; however, it is not pleasure that this dopamine flood creates: pleasure, it, is now apparent, is indirectly related to reward and is a relatively weak motivator of behavior compared to the prospects for positive surprise. As a result of the dopamine flood, therefore, the system focuses on the environmental cues that predict this flood. These cues are provided in the course of the self-administration of the drug and consist in the addict's acquisition of the substance, his or her preparation of it, and all the physical equipment and physical movements that lead to its ingestion. It is the inauguration of this predictive role that is the major function of dopamine in the present context. At the same time, the usually inhibitory function of the prefrontal cortex over the older limbic system is modified by an increase in Glutamate levels. The outcome is that behavior becomes more impulsive and the overall reward system ignores other sources of reward. The system is reacting not to the drug itself but to the cues that predict it (Berridge and

Drugs of abuse and excessive behaviours seem to trigger a similar rise in dopamine release in the reward circuits of the brain–
a crucial step on the way to addiction

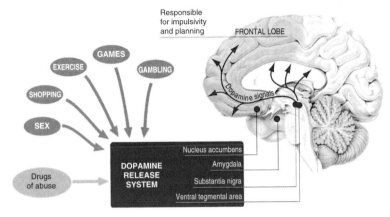

Figure 9.5   The Many Triggers of Addiction

Robinson, 1998; Robinson and Berridge, 2003; Berridge, 2004). This does not diminish the importance of pleasure: it magnifies it, for the drug and the dopamine flood for which it is responsible motivates be because it is a signal of impending pleasure.

Learning systems respond primarily to anomaly, deviation from a norm. surprising events, and the brain's reward system is no exception. This is why addicts come to consumer ever larger amounts of a drug and why the amounts of it are increasingly concentrated. It is also why alternative rewards are excluded from consideration. Entirely consistent with the neuroeconomics model, gambling has the same effect (Figure 9.5). Gambling is designed to produce surprising rewards: "The gambler is buying a maximally convenient, direct manipulation of her mesolimbic reward system." (Ross et al., 2005, p. 5)

Linking the sub-personal and super-personal levels

It is important to keep in mind that super-personal cognitive psychology involves not only the identification of the neural substrates of behavior on the basis of which an intentional or cognitive account of that behavior might be based but also the environmental contingencies that account for molar patterns of behavior which again provide a basis for the ascription of content. The link is the neuroanatomy not just of neurotransmitter release and reception but that of reward, a theoretical entity that accounts for the rate of repetition of a response. In a paper that strives for balance, Winger, Woods, Galuska and Wade-Galuska (2005) draw attention to both sources of theory.

Information from the environment is neuronally transmitted to the brain where it is processed and stored and from which it can be retrieved. The brain's motivational system involves as we have seen the release of dopamine and this takes place in the ventral striatum which includes the nucleus accumbens. "Dopamine release in this area," they summarize, "has been considered a critical mediator of the reinforcing effects of stimuli including drugs of abuse" (Winger et al., 2005, p. 669). These authors not only seek to separate biological and behavioral explanations of addiction at the conceptual level but, interestingly, suggest how the various subsystems might be thought to interrelate in the process of treatment. Hence, they identify "a cortical-striatal-pallidal-cortical circuit in the emotional areas brain" (see Figure 9.6) that explains motivation but argue that what is absent from this neurophysiological account is "how the various circuits are interconnected to integrate the sensory input with the motor output" (Winger et al., 2005, p. 669; see also Cardinal, Parkinson, Hall and Everitt, 2002). The top of Figure 9.6 identifies structures that are related to the reward pathway visible on midline of brain, while the dark lines indicate dopamine pathways. The bottom shows the relation of thalamus (with lateral thalamic nuclei) to the more lateral caudate nucleus and globus pallidus.

Whilst neuroscientists have generally sought addiction in this reward circuitry, Winger et al. claim that a behavior-centered approach provides a more accurate representation of the nature of addiction and the basis for its treatment. Their understanding of drugs is as "reinforcing stimuli that may come to dominate the behavioral repertoire..." because of the relative efficacy of drug reinforcers compared with other sources of reinforcement in the individual's life. Therefore, drug addiction is a behavioral disorder. Addictions are excessive behaviors that occur when alternative behaviors are expected and appropriate. This is a general definition of addiction that applies not only to drug addictions but to overeating and excessive gambling. The common thread is that after exposure to the reinforcer (euphoria, food, money) there ensues an escalation of the behavior on which the reinforcer is contingent. Winger et al. claim that the tendency of the individual to allow the pursuit of such reinforcement to dominate his or her behavioral repertoire is more likely to result from learning historical factors than genetics though the latter may play some part. They also argue that

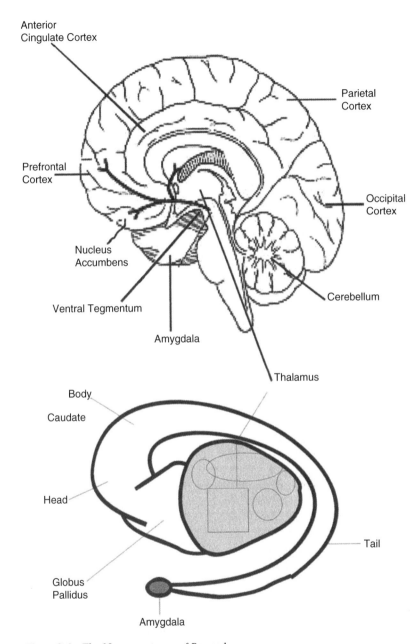

Figure 9.6 The Neuroanatomy of Reward

their approach accounts for individuals' maturing out of addictions as they enter a stage of life that offers alternative sources of reinforcement.

The very difficulties that urge us to avoid simplistic assumptions about the biological bases of addiction bear out the intentional behaviorist and super-personal cognitive psychological models with which we have been concerned. In a review of recent research, Nestler (2000) points out the difficulty of determining precise genetic influences on addiction, first, because of the complexity of the link – many genes may individually contribute marginally to addiction and genetic effects are in any case difficult to establish experimentally; moreover, socio-economic factors such as poverty, crime, and delinquency are among the many non-genetic influences on addiction; in addition, environmental factors such as stress can affect the genotype in ways that influence an organism's response to drugs. A second set of problems stems from the difficulties inherent in quantifying behavioral outcomes such as addiction which show considerable variance and are highly susceptible to environmental modification. I draw upon this source in order to illustrate the obstacles to the establishment of even simple empirical relationships with which a behavioral science approach to super-personal cognitive psychology must contend.

First, it is notoriously difficult to ascertain the precise genetic effects on addiction because of the complexities involved in addiction: each gene may make only a small contribution to addiction which is difficult to ascertain experimentally; non-genetic factors such as poverty, crime, delinquency may contribute to addiction; environmental factors such as stress can affect the genotype in ways that influence an organism's response to drugs. Second, difficulty arises in quantifying behavioral endpoints which show greater variance and are more susceptible to environmental influence than are non-behavioral genotypes. Establishing with precision and reliability the behavioral endpoints of addiction is therefore an important aim of research, but insofar as the connections suggested by empirical research are all measures of endpoints that cannot be unequivocally related to drug addiction the quest for unambiguous measures remains unfulfilled. Because most drugs increase activity, for instance, measures of locomotor activity have been proposed for this purpose since locomotor responses are mediated by the mesolimbic dopamine system which is implicated in reward and addiction, but this remains a controversial connection. A closer measure in non-humans is the measurement of conditioned place preference, the conditioning of the animal to a location that is paired with exposure to drugs. (Note that the behavioral conception and measurement involved here accord with Rachlin's ascription of such terminology on the basis of molar patterns of contingency-shaped behavior.) Such conditioning is mediated to some extent by the mesolimbic dopamine system and resembles some of the powerful conditioning effects of drugs found in humans. However, neither of these tests measures directly the core features of human addiction which inhere in behavioral abnormalities like compulsive drug-seeking and -taking). Abnormalities of behavior such as these may be more clearly ascertained and delineated through the use of operant tests that refer to self-administration of drugs and conditioned reinforcement. The difficulties involved in using these intricate tests mean they have not been widely employed but the point I am making is that logically patterns of operant behavior prove the clearest criteria of addiction. Nestler's view is that in order to obtain close knowledge of the behavioral abnormalities that are at the center of this kind of investigation "operant tests must be applied, including self-administration, intracranial self-stimulation and conditioned reinforcement paradigms" (p. 278).

Addiction itself, I would argue, emerges as best defined and understood as a mental construct to be ascribed at the personal level on the basis of its sub- and super-personal correlates. Addiction belongs therefore to intentional behaviorism (and, through it, super-personal cognitive psychology); indeed, its treatment and attempts to overcome it may involve super-personal cognitive psychology. Although there is undoubtedly a sub-personal neural substrate of addictive behaviors, these are identifiable and definable only through the empirical establishment of patterns of operant behavior at the super-personal level. "Addiction" is then a theoretical device, an intentional element ascribed at the personal level in order to explain behavioral continuity.

Part IV
Explaining Consumer Choice

10
Everyday Consumer Choice

The world is too much with us; late and soon,
Getting and spending, we lay waste our powers;
Little we see in Nature that is ours;
We have given our hearts away, a sordid boon!
(William Wordsworth)

Everyday choices, apparently shaped by unexamined cultural norms
and motivated by emotional rather than rational outcomes, are systematic, even lawlike, and certainly amenable to scientific understanding. And, despite their differences, each of the three behaviorisms we
have considered makes a unique contribution to the explanation of
consumer choice in light of the three reasons why we need an intentional account once we leave the realms of prediction and control
(Table 10.1). The main purpose of this chapter is to explicate the recent
findings of consumer behavior analysis outlined earlier in terms of
radical behaviorism, teleological behaviorism, and picoeconomics.

Teleological behaviorism

Teleological behaviorism, on the understanding accorded it here, provides a means of relating the ascription of content to patterns of
behavior and thereby helps resolve the problems of behavioral continuity, the personal level of analysis, and the delimitation of interpretation. In the case of brand choice, it draws attention to the replacement
of one pattern by another which is the essence of brand switching,
especially when a *new* brand is incorporated into the consumer's consideration set for the first time, and then, if adopted, into her choice
set. It is questionable, however, whether the familiar substitution of

Table 10.1   Theories of Consumer Choice

	Incidence	Behavioral Continuity	Personal Level	Delimitation
Brand/product choice Brand switching New brand purchasing	Matching and deviations therefrom Multibrand purchasing	*Teleological Behaviorism*	*Teleological Behaviorism*	*Intentional Behaviorism*
Patterns of reinforcement	Group differences in demand elasticity	*Teleological Behaviorism*	*Teleological Behaviorism*	*Intentional Behaviorism*
Behavior setting scope	Differences in VB for emotionality	*Teleological Behaviorism*	*Picoeconomics*	*Intentional Behaviorism*
Attitudinal – behavioral consistency/ inconsistency	Patterns of verbal and non-verbal behavior	*Teleological Behaviorism*	*Picoeconomics*	*Intentional Behaviorism*

one brand for another on sequential shopping trips can be thought of in terms of a change in the *pattern* of purchasing: the very substitutability of the commodities suggests that they fit the same pattern at least as far as utilitarian reinforcement is concerned; if there is any functional change in the buying pattern it is because a different level or quality or informational reinforcement is selected. Even so, given the frequency of interchange of brands by the typical multibrand purchaser, talk of pattern change is perhaps exaggerated here. In any case, since multibrand purchasers tend to buy brands they have bought at some time in the past even if long ago, they can be said to be buying within already-existing patterns – interesting but not engrossing. In the case of a multibrand buyer who embraces a *new* brand, however, whether trial or adoption, some change in patterning is legitimately spoken of. Moreover, when a sole purchaser enlarges her consideration and or choice set by the inclusion of a *different* brand *not previously purchased or adopted* there is a genuine switch from one pattern to another, indeed to a *new* one. This is interesting in Rachlin's terms. In the case of broader patterns of consumer choice, it is especially useful in its treatment of behavior that is switched from one contingency category to another by the consumer's apparent closing of the behavior setting.

Rachlin suggests some ways in which this occurs in the case of compulsive behaviors but it can also be seen in the case of more mundane consumer behavior (Table 10.2). However, the cost Rachlin identifies as the barrier to the interruption of an ongoing behavior pattern is usually a forfeit of accumulated informational reinforcement. Moreover, this informational reinforcement sometimes takes the form of self-reinforcement. This all moves us toward super-personal cognitive psychology and picoeconomics.

Everyday consumer behavior and that studied by Rachlin differ in degree rather than kind. Rachlin claims self-control does not arise unless there is a conflict between two behaviors one of which is dispreferred. This seems not to be the case for brand choice since brands are identical in terms of utilitarian reinforcement. Preferences for brands

Table 10.2 Self-control through Closure of the Consumer Behavior Setting

	Closed setting	*Open setting*
Accomplishment (High utilitarian reinforcement + high informational reinforcement)	Interpersonal contracts such as marriages, adoptions, membership agreements, that involve punishment for defection extrinsic to the rewards and punishments contingent on the actions themselves	Living together, casual use of organizations such as health clubs
Hedonism (High utilitarian reinforcement + low informational reinforcement)	Commitment to a course of treatment	Seeking ad hoc treatment
Accumulation (Low utilitarian reinforcement + high informational reinforcement)	Negatively reinforced by the interruption of an ongoing behavior pattern; therefore, taking out of subscriptions, joining health club, etc.	Negatively reinforced by the interruption of an ongoing behavior pattern; but reinforcers (especially informational) either maintain or behavior or fail to
Maintenance (Low utilitarian reinforcement + low informational reinforcement)	Paying bills by standing order or direct debit on a monthly basis	Payment of utilities bills quarterly, semi-annually or annually (with risk of default)

arise at the level of their providing more utilitarian reinforcement or better informational reinforcement. Although it seems unlikely that brands within the consumer's consideration set are unlikely to engender behavior preferred/dispreferred in anything but the most trivial way, the kind of patterning teleological behaviorism draws attention to is present in everyday consumer behavior and that it rests on a deliberate choice by the consumer to consider only a subset of all available brands – those she has direct use-knowledge of and which provide the greatest quantity of the characteristics of the product category consistent with her spending power. Conflict has been avoided by the adoption of this consideration set and by the consumer's general adherence to it as a guide to shopping behavior. The problems of overspending on other items, of inappropriate brand purchases, of time budgeting, etc have all been resolved by the adoption of a pattern that obviates deviation from limited consideration and choice. This is precisely how impulsive (unplanned) buying is avoided and it accounts for the resistance many consumers feel toward even the trial of a new brand introduced innovatively into an existing product category. It means breaking the pattern, incurring costs, perhaps new costs of readjustment as the new brand is trailed, examined, evaluated and included in the consideration set. The patterns of multibrand purchasing we have observed for the majority of consumers and the sole purchasing pattern we have observed for the relatively few are means of self-control. This (a) confirms the idea of a continuum of consumer choice from the mundane to the impulsive to the compulsive, (b) supports Rachlin's contentions about self-control in a context to which he has not generally applied it, (c) raises important questions of explanation which make a version of teleological behaviorism that is classified as intentional behaviorism most appropriate for consumer behavior analysis; for it is only by positing intentionality that we can explain the behavior of the everyday consumer. The incorporation of a new brand into the considerations set requires decision-making and this cannot be understood except intentionally: there is no existing pattern of behavior to account for it. Moreover, it is impossible to describe the consumer's decision-making and subsequent change of behavior without alluding to her concluding that, thinking that, believing that, and so on.

To say that someone has switched from one behavior pattern to another is not to explain either why a new pattern comes into existence or why switching from one preexisting pattern to another takes place at a particular time. *Why* does this discontinuity occur and why does it happen when it does? Rachlin provides an answer when he speaks of the person who changes as perceiving situations and making a decision. This intentionalistic language carries no ontological implications – indeed, it is not even intended by its author to imply intentional content, but his very usage of these terms as we have noted necessarily implicates him in the use of intentional explanation. And this is essential to account for the continuity/discontinuity of consumer behavior. It is an invaluable advance in the behaviorist account of complex choice. For, at the very best, it provides us with a vocabulary in terms of which we highlight the need of a theory of behavior for a means of coping with behavioral continuity and discontinuity. Adopting the vocabulary of intentional content we do not incur any particular theories about what is going on in the consumer's brain or mind, but we can no longer ignore the requirement that we address the necessity of accounting for continuity as a matter of theoretical necessity.

Teleological behaviorism also points to a means of understanding better how the personal level of explanation may be invoked to understand consumer behavior. Indeed, a great strength of this theory inheres in its emphasis on molar patterns of behavior which are sustained by consequential environmental regularities. These are employed to derive intellectual and emotional dispositions, which are said to be coterminous with the behavior patterns themselves; to this extent, teleological behaviorism is consistent with the need for an extensional behavioral science that facilitates the ascription of content at the personal level based on the observation of environment-behavior regularities at the super-personal level. However, the further assumption of teleological behaviorism that changes in behavior are inaugurated by changes in intentionality (decision-making, perception, etc.) takes teleological behaviorism one step closer to intentional behaviorism in which explanation of observed behavior is provided by the ascription of personal level activity. It employs, therefore, a legitimate means of ascribing the intentionality that belongs only at the personal level of analysis, particularly when one pattern of behavior gives way to an apparently anomalous but certainly fledgling act which may be the beginning or continuation of a different pattern of behavior. Since most brand "switching" in consumer behavior is not a resolute and irrevocable move from one brand to another but the continuation of a sequence of brand choices begun much earlier (Ehrenberg, 1972/1988), Rachlin's teleological behaviorism has, in line with the intentional behaviorism with which it is argued here it shares an affinity, drawn attention to the necessity of employing mental language of beliefs and desires, intentions and attitudes to account for what is going on when consumers switch behavior patterns, and hence to invoke an intentional explanation thereof. What is important in placing teleological behaviorism in the intentional behaviorism camp is that some of the mental terms derived from molar behavior analysis are intentional in nature. Here both teleological behaviorism and intentional behaviorism differ from Ryle's (1949) ordinary language account in which terms such as "strength of will" and "character" are interpreted simply as linguistically-based reorganizations of observed behavior. Ryle is unconcerned with the phenomenon of "intentionality" but insofar as it marks out such mental ascriptions as attitudes, motives, beliefs, desires, and intentions it provides means of accounting for the three theoretical deficiencies of a purely extensional behavioral science which we have identified. Moreover, it provides again a vocabulary that permits explanation rather than mere description.

This is also important in that it is only by showing how intentionality can be reliably ascribed at the personal level that a behaviorist interpretation of complex behavior can be delimited. The portrayal of teleological behaviorism advocated here makes possible the required delimitation. For, instead of multiplying the causes of a (pattern of) behavior by endlessly rehearsing its putative consequences down the ages, we are forced to circumvent our interpretations as soon as the possibly of ascribing beliefs and desires presents that would have been present at the inauguration of the pattern becomes practicable. Rather than invoking global warming as a cause of a consumer's buying a sixth SUV, behaviorists can keep their feet closer to the ground by acknowledging that her desires to buy the most economic means of transportation for her business and to impress the neighbors she meets on the school run are the more likely causal factors inferable from the sequence of choices in question.

This recognition that consumer behavior is shaped and maintained by the pattern of utilitarian and informational reinforcement to which it gives rise opens the possibility of another source of conflict that may lead to intertemporal switches in preference. In the case of the everyday consumer behavior with which we are concerned, this conflict will be measured and manageable. The conflict is at the most superficial level between utilitarian reinforcement and informational reinforcement, but, since virtually all products and services lead in some degree to both kinds of consequence, it is between different combinations of utilitarian reinforcement and it, which differ sometimes very subtly.

The conflict may arise, in the case of maintenance in open setting (CC7 of Table 1.2) between somewhat similar brand versions of a standardized product each of which offers a slight variation in price or quality. Here the conflict arises within the contingency category. Or, in the case of less everyday consumption such as a vacation (which might belong in the functional categorization shown in that figure to CC1 or CC3) or a long haul airplane trip (CC4 or CC1), between marked differences in comfort (first class or economy, say), the conflict is between different patterns of reinforcement that define distinct operant consumer behaviors. Teleological behaviorism is especially relevant to the explanation of behavioral continuity, the understanding of the personal level, and the delimitation of behavioral interpretation in such instances, though the particular patterns of consumption involved may be more difficult to delineate than in the case of everyday brand choice; their beginnings and endings are not so obvious. There remains the fairly easy-to-make assumption that a person whose vacations are normally spent racing pigeons from her own yard but who chooses this year to visit the Galapagos Islands instead has "made a decision," "changed her perception of reward," or whatever other intentional idiom fulfills this theoretical imperative. But there are more complicated comparisons to be made and explained when the decision is to sell the birds and take up martial arts. Each choice on the part of the consumer entails its own opportunity costs in terms of the expenditure available for future consumption. At base, therefore, the conflict resolves into a choice between spending and saving (Alhadeff, 1982), but the determinants of he choice have become more complex and the consequences more far-reaching. While Alhadeffian choice proposes that the choice made results from the conflict between learning histories of reinforcement and punishment for similar consumer behaviors in the past, in which social as well as functional product benefits and disbenefits feature (Foxall, 1990/2004), the proposal that current selection of a pattern of reinforcement might be later regretted, allied to the finding that consumer behavior is determined by combinations of utilitarian reinforcement and informational reinforcement, opens up the analysis to considerations arising from the work of behavioral economists such as Rachlin and Ainslie.

Another dimension to the contingencies that impinge on consumer choice is addressed by the inclusion of the scope of the consumer behavior setting to produce the eight categories shown in Table 1.2. Conflict now arises at a still more subtle level. It is this time between subjective experiences of settings that are more or less personally satisfying in terms of directly felt emotional pain or gain. It is possible to portray the continuity of behavior here as imposed by the contingencies of reinforcement alone (as in an extensional radical behaviorist account): the person sits in the lawyer's office for an hour, bored, slightly unnerved, and with much else to do if he is to move home on time, listens to the details of deeds and leases, signs half-read and half understood forms, and so on, because of a history of reinforcement for such conformity to a social system designed and administered by and for others (CC8). His negatively-reinforced behavior is rule-governed, pliant, because he has an appropriate history of rule-following: at least, his history of reinforcement for such radical behaviorism is stronger than his history of punishment. But we suspect that more is going on here than the bare minimum that would allow us, were the situation as closed as the operant laboratory, to predict and control behavioral outcomes. Even in Milgram's (1974) famous experiments on obedience to authority, some few subjects left the situation, and the consumers we have studied in vastly more open settings have always had some freedom to do the same. Why they conform or fail to conform can be attributed to their histories of reinforcement and punishment but we have no means by which to check on this. We can explain the behavior of the house-buyer only by positing that he makes a moment-by-moment decision to remain in the setting, and this interpretation would be endorsed not only by intentional behaviorism but, as portrayed here, by teleological behaviorism. But the personal level activity that we must ascribe in order to account for continuity of this behavior, given that no setting is absolutely closed by the contingencies it contains and presages, has to account in turn by way of desires, beliefs and other intentions, for the consumer's remaining in so aversive a setting. At the same time, this ascription delimits our interpretation of this complex behavior by relating it to the specific intentions that can be ascribed to the consumer *at the time of the behavior's enactment.* None of this seems at odds with teleological behaviorism as this paper has argued it deals with consumer choice.

Preference reversal is a feature of the most routine as well as the most extreme consumer choices insofar as consumers' attitudes frequently fail to predict their behavior (i.e., their evaluative verbal behavior is inconsistent with their subsequent non-verbal behavior). This is readily described in terms of the differing contingencies prevailing at the moment consumers express an opinion and then during the opportunity to purchase or consumer the requisite product or service (Foxall, 2005). Simply to say that the contingencies fail to display "functional equivalence" is, however, to explain nothing. Teleological behaviorism is limited to the statement that a consistent pattern of behavior *is* an attitude; its understanding as a philosophy of psychology akin to intentional behaviorism allows us to use that observation as the basis of an attribution of intentionality at the personal level, something that accounts for the consistency of the behavior, and that delimits its range of causation. But there will always be attitudinal-behavioral consistency under this system. The verbal behavior that may be contrary to it is simply another pattern of behavior, which leads in its turn to the attribution of another attitude to the individual. What we have at the personal level is attitudinal-attitudinal inconsistency and no real way of relating the attitudes involved. At the super-personal level there is behavioral-behavioral inconsistency and it is the reversal of preference inherent in this state of affairs can be explained only as a switch in patterns of behavior.

Picoeconomics

Teleological behaviorism does not provide a complete explanation of consumer behavior, a comprehensive account thereof that satisfies the three imperatives of intentionality. If we want to know why patterns are broken at certain times, etc. we need to delve into the efficient causation of behavior and this requires a (sub- and/or super-personal) cognitive psychology. Picoeconomics is sometimes appropriate for this when intertemporal bargaining can be inferred. This is unlikely to be the case for the selection of one brand over another – at least in the case of the fast moving consumer goods we have considered. But it will matter there to some extent on occasion and as the products considered become more expensive, less frequently bought, the possibility of intertemporal bargaining becomes the greater. The conflict can be seen as one between spending and saving, in which case the conflict of patterns of behavior is most apt and Alhadeff has already mapped out the sort of conflict that arises (albeit in the efficient causation terms of a current choice explained by past contingencies. But it can also be seen as a matter of buying SS (more or better food) now and LL (clothes for the children). Both of these may belong to the same pattern of say being a good parent but the question still arises why one is selected over the other; perhaps why there is a reversal of preferences as the shopper reaches the grocery. However, given the tendency of attitudes (evaluative verbal behaviors) to change frequently with respect to these low involvement products, there is no real evidence of an attitudinal tendency toward brands. We are moving here from teleological behaviorism to picoeconomics. The clearest indicator of the need to do so is provided by consideration of the final sphere of consumer research with which we are concerned: attitudinal-behavioral inconsistency.

Picoeconomics attempts an explanation of the ubiquitous inconsistency of consumers' attitudes and behaviors as a reversal of preferences that involves interpersonal, intertemporal bargaining. Why is this necessary when teleological behaviorism can apparently account for this change in intention as indicated by one behavioral pattern (verbal, "attitudinal") and then another (non-verbal, "overt")? There is a conflict of interests brought about by the differences in situation between the point at which an intention is expressed and that at which the opportunity to behave emerges. One interest is to stay loyal to the pattern established when one predicted one's future behavior via the expression of an attitude/intention ("My word is my bond"); the other is to the expediency of the pattern of (reinforcing and punishing) consequences presented by the current behavior setting ("I am a rational being"). Over and above the ascription of intentionality that teleological behaviorism assumes when it says that a decision is made to switch to another behavior pattern, the picoeconomics approach attempts to elucidate the cognitive decision processes that would be necessary to explain the behavior (and, in particular, the switch from one behavior pattern to another). But this is a search for efficient causation, a quite different mode of explanation from that of teleological behaviorism.

Ainslie's efficient causes reside in the cognitive operations that underlie self-control. This model is valuable for understanding routine consumer choice for, while the conflicts that might lead to overindulgence are less severe than those found in extreme consumer behavior, they are both real and capable of leading past the impulsive behavior that characterizes much everyday consumer choice, the "primrose path," to the compulsive behaviors that can be disabling. Ainslie's fourth strategy for dealing with the present temptations that can lead to dysfunctional consumption – the bundling of future rewards through the formation of and adherence to personal rules – is especially relevant to the consumer behaviors we have described.

The routine instances of consumer choice which we have investigated in the context of behavioral economics do not offer sufficient inter-temporal conflict to require any but the most superficial picoeconomic explanation. While teleological behaviorism is clearly appropriate to the analysis of such choice, picoeconomics requires a much greater degree of intertemporal conflict with the possibility of preference reversal before the insights of its explanatory method become apparent. This is not to say that teleological behaviorism is not relevant to these situations: only that it provides a broader approach to social science than does picoeconomics and thus has greater relevance to the full spectrum of consumer behaviors. There is nothing in the experience of routine shoppers that resembles the Akrasia that Ainslie takes as his starting point. (The "akrasia problem" is that people engage in self-defeating behaviors – e.g., drug consumption, compulsive buying, debt accumulation, failure to carry out plans, procrastination. A poorer payoff is preferred (temporarily), because it is available sooner, to a longer-term better payoff.) The undermatching we found occasionally in the case of brand choice and characteristically for inter-product choices can scarcely be construed as conflict in this sense (it can in any case be shown to be rational in terms of consumer choice in a marketing-oriented economy: Foxall and Schrezenmaier, 2003). Such behavior is hardly self-defeating in the sense that Rachlin and Ainslie are speaking of. There is no question of *delay*: we are talking about very small differences in price for brands that are considered in some important respects identical. Yet we still have to account for one being selected over others. If as Ainslie argues the consumers possesses "*an internal marketplace that disproportionately values immediate rewards*," how does this operate in the case of everyday consumer choice? Can this mechanism disappear? Surely not. The consumer is actually maximizing the totality of reinforcement available, both utilitarian reinforcement and informational reinforcement. Selecting (usually) the least expensive item within her consideration set, she is gaining the informational reinforcement that accrues from being a thrifty consumer, perhaps in relation to a partner or children. She may not be the long-term maximizer of utility theory but she is maximizing on each shopping trip a combination of functional/technical and social reinforcements.

There are three ways in which this is relevant to the consumer behavior analysis of everyday choice. First, it makes clear that the consumer behavior in question is under the control of both utilitarian reinforcement and symbolic reinforcement. Second, as Ross et al. (p. 60) suggest, the picoeconomic analysis of reward bundling can be applied to the routine consumer behavior involved in everyday shopping for groceries as well as to the extreme consumer behavior that involves compulsion and addiction. Persons making such routine choices, Ross et al. suggest, have already made the choice of not engaging in the pursuit of SSRs such as drinking, smoking or gambling. Not having engaged in these SSR activities on the previous day(s), they do not wake up today thinking about them. They are, accordingly, enjoying the larger benefits of the LLRs. Now, I think this still needs a bit of modification before it fits routine consumer behavior as well as it might. The usual LLRs may not be enjoyed because they are inevitably a long way off by their very nature (e.g., better health through not smoking or drinking, peace of mind through not gambling). I think we have to look for other – short to medium term – rewards that are coming in and which sustain this rule-governed abstinence. These are extra money to spend on other activities, the goods that are bought and consumed as a result, the social benefits of replacing say addictive drinking with mixing with friends (Rachlin's solution). These, rather than the usually assumed LLRs are the reinforcers for current rule-following/abstinence. Even more in the case of routine consumer behavior must we look for the immediate payoffs of spending "sensibly", i.e., conducting a predictable life with no financial bad surprises, having sufficient commodities to get through the week/month (meet current needs and those of the immediate future), have sufficient to spend on other goods, peace of mind and social status of doing these things effectively, etc. Third, Ainslie's view that the self is composed of conflicting preferences for rewards that achieve a dominance over each other at different points in time (as a result of hyperbolic discounting) is also of relevance to routine consumer behavior. Such conflict may be between different sources of utilitarian reinforcement, different sources of symbolic reinforcement, or between sources of utilitarian reinforcement versus symbolic reinforcement.

If there is a conflict here it is between utilitarian reinforcement and informational reinforcement. Between maximizing on price by buying the cheapest (event he cheapest in one's consideration set) and providing a socially acceptable level of quality for self and others. The consumer's usual strategy (insofar as we can generalize) is 1. select an appropriate consideration set on the basis of utilitarian reinforcement/informational reinforcement, and experience, 2. select within it (usually) the least expensive option. Conflicts come from the anticipation of alternative consumption situations (buying cheap fruit juice for everyday use and expensive fruit juice for a special occasion). And from a sheer need for variety (buying Lurpak even though it is the most expensive butter). Ainslie says it makes sense to speak of interests only when there is conflict over time as to choice. This applies to our consumer who is weighing future consumption needs (of the higher value juice) against current expenditure). We can see this as either her broader patterns of behavior (providing for the later consumption occasion, being a good consumer, being a good spouse, being a good parent, being a good person, *eudemonia* as Socrates would have said). This is consistent with Rachlin's approach: the successful negotiation of interests differing in their temporal fulfillment but requiring the allocation of resources at the present. Ainslie's solution is undeniably cognitive: *Mental operations are selected for by particular rewards and A proposes that these operations be thought of as the person's interest in that reward.* The resources involved need not be vast to cover the current expenditure – in other words, as far as available income is concerned the consumer could conceivably buy any brand) but, since their disposal eventuates not only in utilitarian reinforcement but also in informational reinforcement (getting the most for one's money, being seen to behavior rational, saving, etc.), there is a conflict. Moreover, the real choice faced by a compulsive at any time is exactly that faced by the brand buyer: to consume (buy) or not to consume (save). It is not realistically between consuming now and being thin, healthy, sober, later. At most, it is between consuming (buying) now and following a rule that says these things will follow abstinence. Our ordinary consumers and our compulsives are not so different after all.

No matter whose theory we adopt, the pattern of choice uncovered by consumer behavior analysis surely are of a piece with the behaviors these authors have investigated. Less dramatic, less crucial to the overall life of the person but of a kind with the impulsive behaviors they have focused on. And what is impulsive buying or compulsive purchasing as we normally understand it other than a conflict between utilitarian reinforcement and informational reinforcement? The situation faced by the consumer (the "consumer situation": i.e., the range of consequences contingent on her behavior in the current setting) is exactly that of the person having to relate a single act (that either belongs to an established pattern or initiates one) rather than to an act that belongs firmly within another pattern. (i.e., spending frugally vs consuming appropriately) in Rachlin's terms, or in Ainslie's terms the choice between dieting (saving) or consumption of ice cream (buying the dearer version). It is not really the conflict between Brand A and Brand B therefore, but between broader behavioral units.

Overall, there seems to be a single set of causes that account for (a) everyday consumer behavior, (b) impulsive consumer behavior, (c) compulsive behavior more generally. The cause is a conflict between utilitarian reinforcement and informational reinforcement over time and its resolution is determined by the consumer's ability to anticipate future consequences rather than discount them. In the case of the everyday consumer, the current consequences of behavior are a mixture of utilitarian reinforcement/informational reinforcement in which each may function at a different level depending on the discretionary income available to the consumer. The future consequences that matter are principally informational, secondarily utilitarian. By and large the future is successfully anticipated either because (a) present acts nest appropriately in larger patterns of long-term behavior (Rachlin), or (b) the consumer does not allow short-term interests (SS) to outweigh longer-term interests (LL) (Ainslie). The first explanation may rest on some intentional terminology in order to explain the continuity of behavior, and the inclusion of new brands in the consideration set. The second is cognitive, relying on the mental balancing of competing interests. We have no reason to believe that everyday consumers differ biologically or fundamentally from impulsive or compulsive consumers; the differences we are looking at arise predominantly from the contingencies. Indeed, occasional drinkers may become everyday "social" drinkers who later find themselves on the primrose path who then become unstoppable topers. They are the same people: we assume that the contingencies have changed in that the consequences of their behaviors are differentially selected.

But where is the conflict, the contradiction? Where would this turn into compulsive buying? What is the consumer protecting her interests from? In Alhadeffian terms from the punishment that even everyday purchasing brings in its wake. In this sense consumer behavior always involves conflict between spending and saving, and this may nest well into the broader patterns of behavior to which Rachlin draws attention such as being a good spouse/parent, being frugal, having money to spend on other things, etc. Can we say anything about this in terms of hyperbolic discounting? In the case of the impulsive buyer, note that most consumers often buy on impulse in the sense that their precise purchases are unplanned; 50% of grocery purchases can be accounted for in this way as can 50% of book sales. Perhaps this is the primrose path, for the immediate consequences may be benign (the ease with which one solves the problem of buying a birthday present), or at least not deleterious ("I guess I needed a book on medieval Greek music; I just had not expected to get it so soon.") Such impulsive buying is apparently dominated by a lack of utilitarian reinforcement.

The immediate consequences are less utilitarian than informational (assuming liquid funds are available or credit can be obtained). The longer-term consequences are both highly utilitarian and highly informational (conspicuous consumption; i.e., status consumption CC1) or principally informational (i.e., hedonism, CC3). *For the compulsive consumer:* the consequences are all utilitarian? This is going to move the pattern of consequences from CC3 to CC7. Moreover, the setting is becoming more closed. This is the continuum assumed by Herrnstein, Rachlin and Ainslie but they have chosen to analyze the compulsion extreme. The results of consumer behavior analysis are primarily concerned with the other extreme of rational decision-making and anticipation of the future. But, why do we need teleological behaviorism and picoeconomics to understand these behavior patterns? Intentional behaviorism (represented here, though not exactly by teleological behaviorism) supplies a rationale for behavioral continuity and a personal level explanation. It also adds to teleological behaviorism a means of delimiting interpretations of the behavioral patterns involved. It is a kind of IST, composed of abstracta but not lending itself entirely to a cognitive model of choice. Picoeconomics is by contrast close to the super-personal cognitive psychology that consists in illata that can become the variables of a testable cognitive model.

All in all, this analysis is unconvincing as a serious attempt to show that Ainslie's work applies – as teleological behaviorism certainly does – to routine consumer behavior. Even though there are temporal considerations in this sort of consumer behavior, they do not conform to the basic model of intertemporal preference reversal. Perhaps there is conflict on some level but it is nothing the consumer cannot deal with and is not the sort that leads to breakdown. Other consumer behaviors, however, are closer to this model. Purchasing on credit, saving-up week-by week or month-by-month for an expensive desired item, buying a cheaper variety of a product today rather than waiting until one has saved enough for a higher-quality version, are all examples of SS>LL in everyday consumer behavior. In all of these cases, teleological behaviorism would point to the change in behavior as the result of the adoption of a novel pattern of behavior. But picoeconomics permits a more thorough examination of the mental event required to account for the continuity of behavior, the personal level of analysis, and the delimitation of behavioral interpretations.

Whereas the ascription of intentionality at the personal level based on extended patterns of environmental-behavioral linkages is like putting down a marker at the personal level, an acknowledgment that behavior theory requires some mechanism or device to account for these elements at a post-descriptive level of analysis, such a competence theory tells us little about what might be capable of entering into a fully scientific theory that can explain as well as predict. Super-personal cognitive psychology is the means of accomplishing this. And, I have argued, picoeconomics falls into this category. The three imperatives of intentionality can be addressed via Ainslie's suggestion that personal rules and bundling of future benefits have a strong effect on behavior. These are cognitive procedures which are selected for on the basis of the rewards redounding to the molar patterns of behavior that take place at the super-personal level. The processes consist according to Ainslie in the interest the individual has in the requisite reward.

Intertemporal bargaining, the placing of side bets with oneself, the bundling of future rewards are all activities than can be understood only at the cognitive level. They are activities that elucidate the three imperatives of intentionality in ways that go beyond the ascription of intentionality. The meeting of present and future in the mentality of the consumer is a cognitive prerequisite of understanding the continuity of behavior; it further elucidates the content of the personal level (which is the only one at which cognitive activity can be ascribed); it delimits, moreover, the behavioral interpretation of complex behavior at the point where a plausible cognitive response to the contingencies of molar behavior can be inferred.

By its very nature, super-personal cognitive psychology requires that the elements of sub-personal behavior be related systematically to an operant account of behavior. The BPM provides a means of achieving this relationship. The neurophysiological account above is entirely consistent with the proposal that gambling (at least organized casino gambling) belongs in the Accomplishment area of the BPM contingency matrix which is an operant behavior predicted to be maintained by increasingly stretched VR schedules of reinforcement (Foxall, 1990/2004); it is, moreover, additional evidence that it belongs in the closed segment of the scope continuum (CC2 in Table 1.2). As Ross et al., 2005, p. 1) put it, "Gamblers both want to win each bet and to participate in an activity that is stimulating because there's a serious probability of losing." Accomplishment, which is the operant class of behaviors maintained by high utilitarian reinforcement and high informational reinforcement, is also consistently related to consumers' verbal reports of high levels of pleasure and arousal, and arousal indicates surprise.

11
Consumer Initiation and Imitation

> [P]eople are selective in the kind of ideas they pursue or adopt; the main argument being that no person ever rejects them all and no person every accepts them all or at the same time... Individuals pursue the ideas and artefacts that appear to be of use to them compared to the perceived cost of acquisition. (Kirton, 2006, p. 301)

In dealing with everyday consumer choice we have said little about what causes it to change, notably the introduction of new brands, new products, new practices. Why do established patterns of behavior exhibit dynamic breaks in continuity from time to time? Why do consumers stop buying within their current brand repertoire, if only temporarily, in order to try a new version of the same product? The topic is usually subsumed under the heading of consumer innovation or innovativeness in the marketing literature. But it is also relevant to the understandings of patterns of behavior and their interruption put forward by Rachlin and Ainslie. Crucially, however, it provides insight into the nature of the quest for evolutionary consistency in the ascription of intentional content on the basis of contingency-shaped molar behavior sequences. In this way, the analysis of consumers' initiating and imitative behaviors becomes a vehicle for discussing the role of evolutionary logic within the framework of exposition for consumer theory worked out in the earlier chapters. The processes should be amenable to analysis in terms of an extensional behavioral science, intentional systems theory, intentional behaviorism and super-personal cognitive psychology. It should be possible also in this context to explore further the evolutionary basis of complex consumer behavior. This chapter relates consumer innovation to the intentional and behavioral components of explanation found in intentional behaviorism and to super-personal cognitive psychology. In particular, this discussion seeks to ascertain whether an account in these terms of the consumer behavior of consumers over the adoption life cycle can adhere to the criteria listed for these frameworks at the close of Chapter 6. This involves, first, understanding the shortcomings of a purely extensional account of the diffusion of innovations and the consequent need to ascribe intentionality at the personal level to account for consumer initiation (the earliest trial and adoption of newness) and imitation (later trial and adoption based on the experience of initiators); it also requires understanding of the extent to which evolutionary logic can account for the neuroanatomy of reward (links between operant conditioning and the sub-personal level of extensional biology, and for the establishment of particular molar patterns of behavior as the result of human ancestral histories. Moreover, it begs an answer to the question of how everyday consumer behavior is to be understood on a similar basis to that proposed for the extreme choice that have been the focus of the work of behavioral economists and the out-of-the-ordinary phenomena of consumer innovation. The overall purpose of this chapter and the next in addressing these concerns is not to examine these themes exhaustively with respect to consumer behavior but to argue that they impinge upon the explanation of choice and that a comprehensive account therefore requires their inclusion.

Adopter categories

The diffusion of newness is usually depicted in terms of a normal distribution of adoption frequencies over time (Rogers, 2003). The speed of diffusion is known to vary directly with the relative advantage of the novel item, its compatibility with current technologies and consumer behaviors, its conspicuousness, and trialability, and indirectly with its complexity and the costs and risks involved in adopting it. Consumers' perceptions of these factors are also known to influence their adoption decisions and the timing of their adoption: indeed, the earliest adopters are identifiable in standard market research investigations of such perceptions. In addition to these differential perceptions of the characteristics of an innovation, such elements of consumers' personalities as their flexibility and self-esteem are known to influence their decisions to adopt it, as do their socio-economic status, communications behavior, previous consumer behavior (e.g., being a heavy or a light user of the product category), and pattern of social involvements. Any basic textbook of consumer behavior describes the processes of adoption in some detail (e.g., Foxall, Goldsmith and Brown, 1998) and yet there has been little progress in the *explanation* of this aspect of consumer choice.

Merely to describe the diffusion of innovations in these terms is inadequate, however, for it fails to identify precisely how these influences act on consumers' decision-making or how products spread through the social system at different rates and with different levels of success. The usual depiction, due in particular to Everett Rogers's pioneering work, is of a cognitive decision procedure in which individuals make up their minds to adopt, and subsequently to confirm or disconfirm their choice. This idea of how adoption takes place is entirely consistent with the prevailing comprehensive models of consumer choice (see, especially, Chapter 2 of Foxall, 2005). Diffusion is expected to occur as different kinds of consumer finds the adoption of the item beneficial, and these categories of adopter are defined in terms of standard deviations from the mean time of adoption: the 2.5% of adopters are termed "innovators" by Rogers; the 13.5% as "early adopters;" followed by 34% he terms "the earlier majority," and an equal proportion who make up the "later majority." Finally come the "laggards" who account for the last 16% of the market. Diffusion is a matter of communication of the benefits of the innovation from one category of adopters to the next (Goldsmith and Foxall, 2003). Rogers's scheme is shown in Figure 11.1.

Despite the variety of adopter categories, the prime area of research interest in this field has been the identification of the characteristics of the first adopters, the so-called "innovators." As a result, more is known about this group than any of the later adopters. I should like to make use, however, of what is known of the characteristics and behavior of all adopter categories from the viewpoint of both the more orthodox cognitive approach and the behaviorist alternative which I introduce later. First, though, let us review a long-term attempt to identify innovators, their features and their behavior. Before doing so, I should like to introduce a change in terminology in order to avoid confusion. Rather than refer to consumer innovators, I should prefer consumer initiators since these are the people who initiate markets. Moreover, I wish to use the term innovator to refer to a specific cognitive style. Later adopters, I shall refer to as consumer imitators, although I shall recognize various categories of imitator.

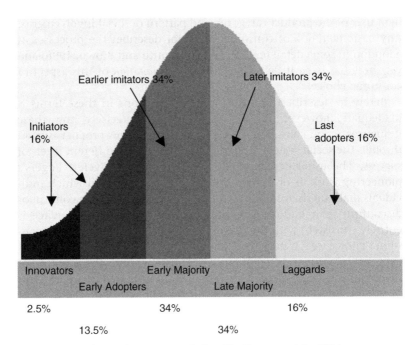

Figure 11.1 Adopter Categories as Defined by Rogers and the BPM

Consumer initiation and imitation as operant behavior

Figure 11.1 also proposes a sequence of the four operant classes of consumer behavior identified by the BPM in terms of which the communication of innovations may be interpreted in a behavioral perspective. The rationale for this sequence is most apparent in considering the differences between the initial and later adopters (cf. Midgley, 1977; Rogers, 2003). The general argument is that initial adopters are drawn from those consumers whose behavior, for the product class/category in question, is described as Accomplishment. This may be a general lifestyle characteristic of this group. They are experienced consumers who have a level of product knowledge and expertise in consumption plus a degree of wealth that allows then to make earlier adoption decisions and to act on them. They are not necessarily older than later adopters but, at least in the product class under consideration, are sufficiently economically socialized to act first. They should, therefore, differ from later adopters on all four explanatory variables posited by the BPM. Initiators, as opposed to later adopters will exhibit differences in the pattern of utilitarian and informational reinforcement that maintains their behavior, a learning history that predisposes them towards earlier adoption, a susceptibility to the motivating effect of behavior setting elements that encourage earlier adoption, and the presence of state variables that facilitate earlier rather than later adoption.

Pattern of reinforcement

By assuming that initiators' consumer behavior is characterized by Accomplishment, the model understands that they are susceptible to relatively high levels of both utilitarian (pleasurable/utilitarian) and informational (social/symbolic) reinforcement. This is consistent with the evidence. Not only incentives, based on relative economic benefit and utility, but also social recognition and status motivate the first buyers of innovations (Bandura, 1986). The rewards of early adoption identified repeatedly in the diffusion literature may be classified as producing primarily economic benefit (utilitarian reinforcement) (Rogers, 2003). Among the sources of economic advantage are some innovation characteristics usually treated separately but which are fundamentally related to the economic, technical and functional benefits that are contingent upon adoption: relative advantage, compatibility, low complexity and low economic risk.

These are elements in the consumer's learning process, which actually refers to a class of economic costs. All are concerned with the costs and benefits of integrating the innovation into an existing physical and social system, particularly with the joint effects (cost reduction and/or the release of synergy) of operating it alongside existing equipment or practices. Economic advantage consists in what has hitherto been described as incentives or utilitarian reinforcement. Social benefit is the conferral of status, usually through he conspicuous use of the innovation, though sometimes through its highly visible purchase. The prestige which accrues from these consumer behaviors may derive from others' admiration of the economic relative advantages conferred by the innovation but, unless the item is additionally amenable to social observation, it cannot deliver the additional social advantages which corresponds to feedback or informational reinforcement. Not only are these sources of economic and social benefit known to be associated with the speedier diffusion of innovations: Initiators perceive greater positive benefit (relative advantage, conspicuousness, compatibility) and lower negative consequences (risk, complexity) than do later adopters.

Learning history

Initiators generally have a shorter decision process than that of later adopters. They are venturesome, impulsive, able and willing to bear risks and make relatively rapid decisions to adopt. The new products they buy are discontinuous innovations, having maximal impact on current consumption patterns. Initiators need less interpersonal influence than later adopters, having, as have noted, less need for others to legitimize their adoption decisions. Moreover, initiators are more self-reliant and inner-directed than later adopters (Midgley and Dowling, 1978). But their behavior is far from spontaneous and innate. Initiators have greater expertise with the relevant product class, possibly deriving from their heavy use of the product and their opinion leadership. Their capacity to recognize atypicality, to think in abstractions, combining product features, to deal with a large number of separate product dimensions, and to examine the environment for new products are also indicative of experience and expertise. Their being less influenced than later adopters by interpersonal communications is the result of experience; like any other behavior, it is the outcome of a situationally-determined learning history, the consolidated outcome of contingency-based learning and vicarious adoption with the product class and exposure to the innovation in question mediated by mass communication.

These initial adopters model the new consumption behavior to the less active sections of the population and thereby initiate the market (Rogers, 2003). The behavior of the initiator group is associated with innovations that confer substantial relative advantage over currently-used products and methods, both economic and social. In the terms of the BPM, such innovative adoption is maintained by high levels of both utilitarian and informational reinforcement. These consumers can afford to acquire the tangible benefits of innovative products; it he process of consuming them, they enhance their status and prestige (Bandura, 1986). Moreover, they can afford to undertake the early adoption of some innovations that fail: event his conveys to others that the adopter has the economic means and socials standing to disregard the occasional loss. They have positive attitudes towards newness and progress, and are more likely than others to be offered credit and, if required, to accept it (Rogers, 2003).

State and setting variables

Initiators are affluent relative to members of the later adopter categories, risk takers who are eager to try the innovation for its own sake.

There is no unequivocal evidence of their being older than other adopters. But they have higher social status, greater upward social mobility, and a more favorable attitude towards credit than later adopters. They also show more extensive social participation, are "cosmopolitan", have greater knowledge about innovations and display more opinion leadership (Rogers, 2003), all of which are likely to be the result of more extensive consumer experience. Most crucially of all, and true of a wide range of product classes including food, personal care items, domestic appliances, computers and computer services is that initiators are already established and heavier users of the product category in question. They are experienced users with a high level of product field expertise, which may account for the absence of communicated experience in their innovative decision-making. Moreover, they are likely to have established relationships with retailers or other suppliers and to be able to arrange trial of the new product; the effect is to enlarge their learning history and enable quicker comparisons and decisions to be made.

Categories of later adopters

"People who strive to distinguish themselves from the common and the ordinary adopt new styles in clothing, grooming, recreational activities, and conduct, thereby achieving distinctive status" (Bandura, 1986, p. 150). But the capacity of an innovation to confer status is closely linked to its exclusivity: as it diffuses, it becomes commonplace. When the product is approaching the end of its life cycle, it has become a routine acquisition, appealing only to those who are tradition bound, economically limited, and so conservative as to try new (to them) products that have been severely tried and tested by preceding adopters. By the time these consumers (the Last Adopters) adopt it, the product has ceased to be an innovation in any radical sense: it may embody continuous improvements of a minor kind but its adoption is unlikely to have an extensive impact on consumption. These consumers, to whom Rogers refers as "the Laggards," are depicted in the diffusion literature as having no capacity for leadership, including opinion leadership: they are not, therefore, reinforced by high levels of informational reinforcement. What utilitarian reinforcement maintains their behavior is similarly of low intensity: only products that cannot fail are assumed.

Between the initiators and the Last Adopters are the Earlier Imitators (Rogers's "deliberate" Early Majority), and the Later Imitators (Rogers's "skeptical" Later Majority). The assignment of these adopter groups respectively to the contingencies maintaining consumer lifestyles marked by Hedonism/Utility and Accumulation is not quite as clear-cut as that of the first and last adopter categories to Accomplishment and Maintenance. But the characterizations are supported by the diffusion literature. The Earlier Imitators are not leaders despite their fairly high level of social interaction: they are not reinforced primarily by informational consequences of their actions. Moreover, their interest is in "getting it right" when they try new products: they are cautious, taking time to deliberate before deciding. These actions suggest a high level of functional utility, utilitarian reinforcement. The behavior of the Later Imitators is negatively motivated. This group adopts an innovation only when it has become economically essential to do so – its members are not seeking utilitarian reinforcement, however. When they do adopt the item, it is principally for reasons of social pressure: they must finally adopt in order not to lose the honor or esteem of their fellows. Their adoptive behavior is thus negatively reinforced but by considerations of informational reinforcement. Products adopted by these adopter categories are dynamically-continuous; they embody improvements incorporated by manufacturers who by this time have experience of the market's requirements and may represent considerable extensions of the functional attributes of the innovation. They impact on consumption patterns and are purchased by groups seeking price and utility advantages.

Sources of contingency patterns

The principal influence on the changing contingencies that bring each of these adopter categories successively into the market are the marketing activities of firms and industries which inaugurate and modify a life cycle for the new product through a series of marketing mixes that provide, one after the other, the functional and social benefits that motivate each of the adopter groups to purchase. This life cycle of the product class has been described in terms of four stages: introduction, growth, maturity and decline/attenuation (Foxall, Goldsmith and Brown, 1998). The decision processes of consumers at each broad stage in the product life cycle have been described in terms of the cognitive model which pervades consumer psychology. By contrast, this section describes the environmental factors that maintain consumer behavior at each stage. Hence, a classification of the behaviors of the adopter categories associated with each of the product types delineated above derived from the BPM analysis proposes four corresponding adopter groups, defined on the basis of the contingencies likely to determine their overall operant pattern of purchasing and consumption responses. This alternative depiction of the changes inherent in the process of diffusion relies on the different forms in which a product appears as it traverses its life cycle. Changes in a commercially successful product over this sequence of life cycle stages, supported by the non-product elements of the marketing mix and social communication, reflect (and partly comprise) the environmental context within which appropriate classes of consumer behavior are sequentially reinforced (Foxall, 1993b).

The product that initiates a life cycle is, by definition, a radical innovation, the first brand in its product class. Such products are often supported by heavy media communication and bear a high, "skimming" price. They are frequently distributed through exclusive outlets. These *discontinuous innovations* have far-reaching disruptive effects on the consumption behavior of their adopters. They possess substantial relative advantage over existing products which perform a similar function; moreover, adopters at this initial stage of the product life cycle perceive low levels of risk and complexity in the innovation. Discontinuous innovations are also usually conspicuous and likely to enhance the status of those who consume them publicly. Only those who have reached the Accomplishment stage of the consumer life cycle (at least in the relevant product class) are likely to purchase such products rather than to re-use current products or to save. Such consumers uniquely possess the product experience, income and social position which make acquisition of these sources of high utilitarian and informational reinforcement a probability.

These initial adopters of a new product are predisposed by the positively reinforcing consequences of previous innovative consumer behavior to try new products, stores and programs early in the life cycles of such items. At the beginning of the diffusion process, the innovative buyers are experienced consumers at a relatively advanced stage of their consumer life cycle. This does not imply that they are necessarily older than most consumers; their propensity to purchase innovations is a function of their accumulated or inherited wealth as well as their current level of income. Moreover, we have defined the Accomplishment lifestyle in terms of advanced consumer behavior, a function of consumer socialization, rather than by extraneous variables such as age. Nor, in the case of truly discontinuous innovations, can they have direct experience of the new product class. But they do have empirical knowledge of the product class it replaces and are aware of the need which it satisfies.

Subsequent adopters are seeking, by contrast, clear product benefits which may become apparent to them from observation of the experience of the earliest users. As the product progresses through its life cycle, relatively major changes are likely to be made to it, to overcome teething troubles and accommodate it to the requirements of different market segments. These changes, which result in *dynamically-continuous* new products do not alter the product fundamentally but adapt it, more or less, whilst sustaining or increasing its high level of economic relative advantage. At first, such changes are likely to be relatively major modifications of the product type: the result is to maintain the newness, the innovativeness of the product. Its adoption still has major impact on the consumption pattern of users, though not as far-reaching as that experienced by the Innovators. Later dynamically-continuous changes are likely to decline in magnitude. The product still has a degree of disruptive impact on the consumption behaviors of its adopters but this is severely declining.

Dynamically-continuous products, bought by the Earlier Imitators, are supported by a marketing mix that includes falling price levels, limited promotion which stresses the functional improvements that have been incorporated, and an expanding range of retail outlets. They still offer very high relative advantage in their functional performance, high compatibility with current products and practices and a low level of perceived complexity. They also act to confirm the status of the buyer. The high utilitarian and low informational consequences of adoption suggest that the consumers who buy dynamically-continuous items have lifestyles characterized by Hedonism, i.e. those seeking direct and proven utility rather than a strong need to demonstrate social standing.

This group of Earlier Imitators, whose behavior is reinforced principally by utilitarian reinforcement, is more conservative than the initiators, having waited to see the economic and functional benefits of adoption demonstrated before assuming the risks of earlier-than-average adoption; these consumers are not as affluent as the Innovators but are of above average income or wealth and can, therefore, be fairly early adopters of status-conferring innovations. Interested primarily in their own welfare, both economic and social, they are reinforced principally by considerations of utility or hedonism rather than status. Such utility may arise from falling prices and from step changes in product development, leading to relatively major dynamically-continuous product changes, each of which accommodates the innovation to the peculiar demands of emergent market segments. These might even be segments defined temporally. These consumers are also likely to be attracted to fashion items and fads.

When the product approaches the last phases of its cycle, change in both product and non-product marketing mix elements is more incremental; the product can be best described as *continuous* and its adoption has minimal impact on the consumption patterns of the consumers who use it. As more suppliers enter the market, numerous brand versions, each showing minor improvements, appear. Distribution becomes widespread and promotional appeals stress the social necessity of owning the item. These market-dominated variables are further supported by vicarious learning and word-of-mouth from satisfied users. The Later Imitators, select the continuous innovation in order to avoid the relative disadvantage of the old product or method; they also seek to avoid the low status associated with retaining outmoded practices and may encounter substantial social pressures to conform. The operant class of relevance to the adoption of products offering low utilitarian or functional advantages and entailing high informational or status considerations is Accumulation.

The last adopters of all purchase when the product is ubiquitous, brands have proliferated and product development takes the form of line extensions, low prices, minimal promotional appeals. Such steady-state markets are characterized by an abundance of impersonal communication among consumers. Purchasing and using the product is now a matter of economic necessity, the avoidance of self-evident demerits of failure to adopt, and social conformity, escape from ridicule. The consumer behavior involved here is clearly Maintenance (see Table 11.1).

Table 11.1 Adopter Categories Defined by Pattern of Reinforcement and Product Type

Initiators	ACCOMPLISHMENT	Discontinuous Products	First 16% of adopters
Earlier Adopters	HEDONISM	Dynamically Continuous Products	Next 34% of adopters
Later Adopters	ACCUMULATION	Continuous Products	Next 34% of adopters
Last Adopters	MAINTENANCE	Ubiquitous Products	Last 16% of adopters

Intentional behaviorism

An extensional account such as this links external stimuli to the timing of the adoption of innovations but it does not explain why an individual continues in his or her behavior while certain contingencies persist only to modify that behavior in response to novel contingencies. There may be neural correlates of such continuity and change; there certainly are changes in the external environment associated with them. But, while these factors allow the behavior in question to be contextualized, predicted and perhaps controlled, they do not provide an explanation of the individual psychology involved in the process of continuity and change. We cannot account for such behaviors without resort to intentional idioms. To say that the consumer simply "discriminates behaviorally" in the presence of new contingencies is not sufficient to account for the changes that are occurring: as Rachlin's account of the adoption of a new act (whether this becomes a novel pattern of behavior is immaterial) shows, it is necessary to speak of the consumer's perceiving and deciding in order to complete the picture of what is happening. This is intentional terminology: it accounts for the change in behavior and it constitutes an (admittedly embryonic) account in heterophenomenological terms of what has brought about the change. As I have said more than once, there is no reason not to halt inquiry at the point of having provided an extensional description, and this level of analysis is essential to the research program and theory development with which this book is concerned. But a more complete explanation eventuating in the generation of a greater variety of propositions for empirical investigation can be obtained by the development of an overtly intentional account. Moreover, without an account of the consumer's intentions at the point of adoption, it is impossible to produce a definitive listing of the behavioral consequences to which the behavior can be attributed.

Although they have not used the terminology employed here, several marketing authors have suggested frameworks for the study of innovativeness which belong essentially to the intentional behaviorism model. They account for innovative behavior by posting a purely hypothetical construct, *innate* or *inherent innovativeness,* present in everyone to some extent; the degree of innovative behavior a consumer instances (from the purchase of a single innovation through purchasing innovations within a specific product category or groups of related categories to purchasing innovations over a wide spectrum of product categories) is explained by the ascription to him or her of

higher or lower amounts of this trait. Positing this trait carries no ontological implications, for, following Bunge (1967), it is said to exist only
in the mind of the investigator. These are competence theories in that
they are seeking to specify the necessary functions of an intentional
system that would account for its behavior.

Midgely and Dowling (1978), for instance, argue that the various
measures of consumer innovativeness employed in research during the
sixties and seventies are each anchored to a distinct definition of this
construct; moreover, each definition and measure indicates a particular
degree of innovativeness. Hence, each level of innovative behavior
revealed by these various measures requires explanation in successively
more abstract constructions of the personality trait "innovativeness."
At the observational level, "actualized innovativeness" is represented
by the relative time of adoption; the adoption of several innovations in
a product category (Robertson and Myers, 1969) has to be explained by
a deeper and more abstract notion of innovativeness, while in order to
account for consumer innovation across several products, we must call
upon a yet more abstract construct, "innate innovativeness." Innate
innovativeness is defined as "the degree to which an individual makes
innovation decisions independently of the communicated experience
of others," and decision-making is understood as an unobservable, a
prebehavioral event not accessible through the measurement of over
behavior. All consumers, indeed all individuals, possess innate innovativeness to some degree, though the extent to which they do so is
inferable only from its manifestation in innovative behavior.

A broadly compatible theory is presented by Hirschman (1980)
Within the framework of Dennett's three kinds of intentional psychology both are most closely akin to what he calls intentional systems
theory. They are essentially competence theories in that they spell out
logically what minimal demands would have to be made upon a
system for it to be capable of generating the behavior patterns observed
by the innovation theorist. The specify in intentional terms the kind of
"motive force" that would be required of such a system but, as competence theories, they have no need to go beyond this by specifying
the nature of the detailed decision processes – their internal structure
and the functions to which this necessarily gives rise – required to
produce the overt behavior patterns. These are inward-looking models
concerned with the semantics of decision-making. There is another
reason why they are closest to what Dennett refers to as intentional
systems theory. Although in some respects this is an unfair criticism in
view of the heroic attempt these theories made to introduce situational

variables into the study of consumer innovativeness, they do not attempt to show how this is to be accomplished in a systematic manner and, as a result, do not get sufficiently beyond the trait-behavior conception. Hence, despite their authors' assuming the name "contingency theory" for these approaches and their landmark proposal that research on consumer innovativeness move beyond the simple trait-behavior model that had dominated it up until their time, their models as they stand seem to me to place more emphasis on the kinds of trait that it would be necessary to posit in order to account for observed behavior patterns than to identify the kinds of situational interventions that would cause the innovativeness–action continuum to be facilitated or frustrated.

This sort of model-building is an important achievement insofar as it eventuates in intentional systems theories that rise well above the level of folk psychology in which much innovativeness research was content to recline prior to their appearance. Moreover, it has moved beyond the radical behaviorist approach fro which the elapsed time of adoption would be a sufficient definition of innovativeness, to posit in a far more sophisticated manner that a range of innovative behaviors must be explained. However, perhaps as a result of this movement away from descriptive behaviorism, such theories lack – and this is an attempt to locate them in terms of the framework presented earlier rather than a criticism – the extensional behavioral science which would have brought them into the category of intentional behaviorism. The inclusion of such a science, radical behaviorism for instance, would draw attention to the external antecedents and consequences of consumer choice, the contingencies of reinforcement (notably as we have seen the *pattern* of utilitarian reinforcement and informational reinforcement), rather than (of itself) to conceptual traits of personality. It would draw attention to the fact that complex innovative behavior does not just appear: it is shaped by as successive approximations to the terminal response of new product (brand, retail outlet, idea, practice) adoption are differentially reinforced. It is this element especially that helps pinpoint these contingency theories as belonging to intentional systems theory.

Accounting for imitation

Although intentional behaviorism is essentially a competence theory, its specification of the minimal requirements of a human system that would enable it to carry out the innovative acts observed of it rests fundamentally on an operant analysis of the molar behavior of the system and the environmental contingencies that are correlated with its behavior. The intentional behaviorist interpretation follows the requirements of an intentional systems theory by seeking a basic blueprint for the intrapersonal mechanisms that would be necessary to account for the consumer's behaving differentially in the face of the changing patterns of reinforcement that come into play as the sequence of new product inauguration, product development, product proliferation, and product ubiquity unfolds. The predominant source of intentional explanation is the molar patterns of consumer choice that come into being as a result of the changing contingencies of reinforcement imposed by the marketing activities of firms. But there is a major influence on consumer innovation that stems at the most only indirectly from corporate sources: the social interaction that promotes imitation be it in the form of observation of others' behavior or through word-of-mouth. Radical behaviorism has found it notoriously difficult to come to terms with the problems raised by imitation. Although radical behaviorists have drawn attention to the repetition of stimuli for different individuals each of whom is separately influenced directly by the environment, and the reinforcement of imitative behavior which leads to its propagation, only a theory at the level of the intentional system can account for some apparent imperatives of an account of this phenomenon.

Intentional specification of imitation

Bandura (1986, pp. 74–80) points out that most complex behavior is learned by modeling rather than by experienced reinforcement. He is highly critical of operant attempts at interpreting observational learning within the framework of the three-term contingency, which portray the process as one in which the modeled stimulus (S^D) is followed by an overt matching response (R) which produces a reinforcing stimulus (S^R). The elements of the three-term contingency are often missing from actual instances of observational learning. When the observer performs the matching response in a setting other than that in which it has been modeled, when neither the model's behavior nor that of the observer is reinforced, and when the modeled behavior is performed by the observer after the passage of time (which may be several months), the operant paradigm is unable to explain the behavior. "Under this set of conditions, which represents the pervasive form of observational learning, two of the factors ($R \rightarrow S^R$) in the three-element paradigm are absent during acquisition, and the third factor (S^D, the modeling cue) is absent from the situation in which the observationally-learned behavior was first performed" (Bandura, 1986, p. 74). Observational learning of this kind also requires some mechanism to aid integration of vast amounts of information. Acquisition of novel behavior particularly requires such integration of modeled information. Bandura maintains that learning through modeling requires four processes: attentional, retentional, reproductive, and motivational. Certainly, observational learning is a process that must be comprehended at the personal level of analysis. Neither sub-personal nor super-personal can cope with it.

Learning that involves rule acquisition and following must also require these four procedures in some way or other. The individual acquiring rules from others must pay attention to the behavior of others, verbal or non-verbal. Somehow this has to be retained, compared for instance with earlier-gained knowledge and experience. Then it must somehow be translated into overt behavior when the situational immediacy that makes the behavior in question possible or even likely. For Bandura, all of this argues for cognitive representation and processing and it becomes all the more urgent to develop this line of reasoning if understanding rather than prediction and control is the primary goal of scientific endeavor.

Memetics

Bandura's analysis, as far as I have presented it, does not deal with the cognitive mechanisms that are involved in (or can be theoretically posited as involved in) decision-making associated with initiation and imitation (see also, inter alia, Heyes, 2001, 2003; Heyes, Bird, Johnson and Haggard, 2005). Exactly in line with what a competence theory is intended to achieve, it only outlines the basic requirements of such a process of imitative learning through modeling. But there is more to be said about the intentional representation of imitation and this arises from consideration of the concept of memes and memetics.

"Meme" is the term used first by Dawkins (1976) to refer to units of cultural selection that prosper or fail in an evolutionary process akin to the natural selection in which genes prosper or fail. Genes are strands of DNA that are transmitted biologically in the course of physical reproduction, memes through their being modeled by writers, speakers, dancers, players, fashion icons, and so on. Memes are the ideas, practices, skills and so on that are socially broadcast from one person to another. According to Dawkins, memes prosper or fail entirely independently of genetic transmission. The flavor of his innovation is caught by the following brief quotations from *The Selfish Gene*

(Dawkins, 1976): "Cultural transmission is analogous to genetic transmission in that, although basically conservative, it can give rise to a
form of evolution.... Language seems to 'evolve' by non-genetic means,
and at a rate which is orders of magnitude faster than genetic evolution" (p. 187); "[F]or an understanding of the evolution of modern
man, we must begin by throwing out the gene as the sole basis of our
ideas on evolution.... The gene will enter my thesis as an analogy,
nothing more" (p. 191); he speaks, moreover, of "the law that all life
evolves by the differential survival of replicating entities," and goes on,
"We need a name for the new replicator, a noun that conveys the idea
of a unit of cultural transmission, or a unit of *imitation*" (p. 192).
Hence, the meme.

Several similarities and differences are to be found between memes
and genes (Janicki and Krebs, 1998). Memes are similar to genes insofar
as they are both replicators which can make inaccurate copies of themselves leading to variations in the information conveyed (mutations);
they are both subject to selection by the competitive environment
since they are differentially replicated (from other memes or genes,
respectively) and may therefore become more or less adapted to local
conditions. Both are in competition with their respective alternatives
(alleles) so that some endure longer than others; like genes, memes can
be mutually reinforcing and thus form "co-adaptive meme complexes"
or memeplexes. However, while biological evolution involves a single
interactor (i.e., vehicle or survival matching), the organisms that transmit the replicators (genes), cultural evolution involves numerous inter-
actors such as books, CDs, television programs and so on. Memes are
usually said to compete for brain space but it would be more in line
with the development of intentional behaviorism to say that they
occupy minds in rivalrous ways. Whereas genetic evolution takes place
vertically, from generation to generation, memetic evolution occurs
vertically (e.g., to offspring), horizontally (to siblings), and diagonally
(from uncles to nieces). Finally, whereas biological evolution is a slow
process, the speed of memetic diffusion can differ according to the
information bearing rate of the environment.

Memes belong at the level of IST and play exactly the same function
as do abstracta in intentional behaviorism: they are entirely theoretical
entities that "save" a purely extensional theory by accounting for
behavioral continuity, the personal level of experience and explanation, and the delineation of the scope of behavioral interpretation. The
indexical criteria that make their ascription legitimate are (a) evolutionarily consistent neurophysiological events *and* (b) patterns of

contingency shaped molar behavior, but in intentional behaviorism and super-personal cognitive psychology memes are identified with neither. In Dennett's sub-personal cognitive psychology it would be legitimate to identify them with neuronal activity; in an entirely extensional behavioral science, with the patterns of behavior; but neither of those approaches is what we are talking about at the IST/intentional behaviorism level. Neurological phenomena and patterns of behavior have tables and chairs reality; memes are real in another way – our theories cannot work without them any more than physical theories can do without centers of gravity and parallelograms of forces – we may say that these things have theoretical reality. They are of course always amenable to being replaced by entities that have tables and chairs reality but, as long as they fulfill a function at the theoretical level that these entities cannot, they are safe. They are like the idea of the gene at the time of Darwin. Nowadays, however, genes have table and chair reality while memes have only theoretical reality. The identification of memes with neuronal substrates and behavioral super-strates is a necessary part of the process of intentional behaviorist interpretation, but memes are not coterminous with either of these. They are theoretical terms that refer to mental representations (Distin, 2005). Dennett (1995), Dawkins (1982), Blackmore (1999), Aunger (2002), among others, make the same error in referring to the meme concept as Dennett makes in his treatment of IST and sub-personal cognitive psychology – namely, the mereological fallacy that is inherent in the application of the intentional stance to sub-personal entities. Nevertheless, if memes are described in terms of intentional propositions, they may play a useful theoretical role in intentional behaviorism (cf. Avital and Jablonka, 2000; Jablonka and Lamb, 2006; Wilkins, 2005).

Super-personal cognitive psychology

While the intentional ascriptions made in the course of intentional behaviorism may save the extensional behavioral theory, they are always open to the criticism that they are insufficiently anchored in an evolutionarily consistent account of behavior. This is not to disparage the necessity of using such notions inherent innovativeness in the course of competence theory-building; it is merely to point out that such an exercise takes us only so far toward the explanation of consumer choice as it is performed. The next step is the development of a super-personal cognitive psychology of innovative behavior. However, the usual cognitive depiction of adopter decision-making has more in common with the level of competence specification than that of performance.

Cognitive style

Although the major focus of the BPM research program is the testing to destruction of behavior analysis as a means of comprehending consumer choice, this of itself necessitates a parallel research program, one concerned with the competing aims of cognitive and affective psychology. The focus of much of this research, which has always accompanied the behaviorist element of the research program, has been consumers' cognitive styles and involvement. In particular, this has addressed how these cognitive and affective influences impinge on the behavior of consumer initiators, those who are the first to adopt new products, brands, retail outlets, ideas and practices, and that of consumer imitators, those who wait until the innovation in question has been legitimated by initiators before they adopt it. The results of this research are especially germane to the theoretical directions taken in this volume.

"Cognitive style" refers to the manner in which individuals make decisions and solve problems, the way in which they do so, and reflects the distinctive personal approaches that consumer bring to the process of decision-making: problem awareness, search, evaluation, decision and post-decisional activities. Psychometric measures enable everyone to be placed somewhere on a continuum between two extreme styles of decision-making: extreme adaptors prefer to make decision in an orderly and precise manner, and they confine their problem solving endeavors to the frame of reference in which the problem has arisen; the extreme innovator prefers to think tangentially, challenges rules and procedures and is uninhibited about breaking with established methods and advocating novel perspectives and solutions (Kirton, 1976). Confirmatory factor analysis (Bagozzi and Foxall, 1995, 1996) supports earlier work (reviewed in Kirton, 2006) showing that the adaption-innovation variable comprises three subscales: a tendency to favor generating a "sufficiency" of new ideas in addressing a problem rather than proliferating potential solutions (a characteristic that increases with innovativeness), a tendency to seek narrow efficiency in solving problems (increasing with adaptiveness), and a tendency toward rule-conformity (also adaptive).

Interest in using this theory in consumer research derives from the fact that the dimensions of personality shown to be weakly characteristic of *market initiators*, the earliest adopters of new brands and products are also characteristic of innovators (Kirton, 2003). A series of empirical investigations has shown that adaption–innovation is related to amount of initial purchasing and consumption. These patterns of cognitive style are related to the number of innovations adopted in diverse areas of consumption such as the purchase of new food brands and products, the adoption of new computer software and hardware, purchase and consumption of financial services, extend to computer usage. The pattern of relationship between style and adoption or consumption is not always as predicted in the marketing literature: although innovators are generally to the fore in the adoption of novelty in the novel usage of acquired items, adaptors sometimes fulfill these roles, especially when they are highly involved with the product class or in the behavioral domain in which it is employed. However, even when highly involved adaptors are responsible for the greatest degree of product trial or adoption (usually in the case of food products), other, less-involved adaptors are responsible for the smallest number of adoptions, with innovators responsible for the intermediate levels of adoptions and possibly for the greatest part of the overall market for the innovation in question. There is a strong tendency for innovators to try new items and to reconfigure existing items into new usage patterns and toward new applications on a scale that generally outstrips that of adaptors. This research program has employed several global and domain-specific measures of innovativeness, alternative measures of involvement, and a variety of behavioral indices as well as both quantitative and qualitative methodologies. In each case, the "style/involvement model" of consumer innovativeness has been supported. (Bagozzi and Foxall, 1996; Foxall, 1994a, b, 1995, 2003; Foxall and Bhate S., 1991, 1993a, b, 1999; Foxall and Goldsmith, 1988; Foxall and Haskins, 1986, 1987; Foxall and Pallister, 1998; Foxall and Szmigin, 1999; Foxall, Leek and Maddock, 1998; Leek, Maddock and Foxall, 2000; Pallister and Foxall, 1998; Pallister, Foxall and Wang, in press; Szmigin and Foxall, 1998, 1999; Wang, Pallister and Foxall, 2006a, b, c). The key factor that should be emphasized in the current context, however, is the persistent finding of an association between the innovative cognitive style and the amount of innovative behavior in which the individual is likely to engage.

Cognitive style, by which we refer specifically to adaption-innovation, is more concerned with the content of cognition than with its structure/process. It is a series of decision rules applicable to particular types of situation which guide cognitive processing and render it applicable to the problem at hand. One can see how both adaptive and innovative cognitive styles would have conveyed advantages in particular circumstances in the course of an evolutionary past; both the cautious behavior based on tried and tested methods and predictable results that are the preference of the extreme adaptor and the risk-taking, rule-defying venturesomeness of the extreme innovator have their place in an ancestral environment dominated by uncertainty and surprise, and favoring opportunism, whether one's own or that of a competitor. There is, moreover, room for all gradations of individual difference which reflect some combination of these styles rather than an extreme adherence to one or other. Some of the circumstances that call forth a particular style or combination of styles are the local environmental contexts of a society whose imperatives are distinct from those of the Pleistocene when these capabilities presumably evolved: the "facilitator," for instance, centrally between the extremes of adaptive and innovative cognitive styles, is evoked by cultural environments that require a balanced perspective on the needs of a bureaucratic situation and the capacity to interpret both the demands of the task to the entire executive team and the behaviors of each extreme style to those who characteristically evince the other.

The adaption-innovation continuum of cognitive styles is, moreover, consistent with a learning history that emphasizes and selects appropriate behavioral traits, and thus with the principle of selection by consequences. Simonton (2003, p. 314) notes that creative individuals tend to have backgrounds that enhance their "capacity to generate numerous and diverse variations," a leading characteristic of innovators. Creatives have a greater chance than others of having had developmental experiences that favor this style: "unconventional family backgrounds... [subjection] to multiple and diverse role models and mentors... diversifying and atypical educational experiences professional training." The acquisition and maintenance of the behavioral tendencies inherent in adaption-innovation with respect to idea generation, efficiency, and rule conformity, must, as Kirton (2006) points out, presumably include their intermittent reinforcement, and this requires appropriate early social and educational environments.

That the environment differentially "calls forth" adaptive and innovative cognitive styles and/or learning history is shown by the fact that creativity tends to be localized rather than universal (Simonton, 2003). Studies of organizational climate indicate that specific managerial imperatives make adaptive or innovative cognitive styles more attractive to the organization; individuals whose styles fit the requirements of the firm (whether for- or not-for-profit) tend to thrive while those whose styles do not may suffer unless they can "cope" while waiting for the climate to change. Simonton draws attention to the economic, political, cultural and societal circumstances which allow us to extend this contingency-based perspective beyond the organization to entire social systems.

The cognitive processes, upon which creativity is founded are also characteristics of the innovator are consistent with natural selection: the capacities to think divergently and to generate numerous and diverse variations most of which are impracticable. All of these are a matter of style rather than level, of intellectual manner rather than intellectual ability; once evolved, they largely influence the processes of cognition irrespective of the social and physical environments existing at the time, though these environments will of course shape the precise ways in which they are manifested. As Simonton points out, the generation of innovative solutions is in accord with a Darwinian perspective: Kirton innovators are more likely to consider diversity, to maintain diverse solutions in their problem-solving repertoires since they evince a high degree of tolerance of ambiguity. They, therefore, embrace more unworkable solutions and, since the number of high quality solutions varies directly with the total number of solutions proposed, thereby generate in the process more workable ones than do adaptors.

In natural selection, individuals who reproduce most produce more offspring that die early. Similarly, innovators produce many more ideas than adaptors but most of their ideas do not come to fruition. Simonton (2003, p. 315) notes that creatives have more successes but also more failures than the less prolific. The more variations produced, the more will survive (be selected by the environment). Quality varies directly with quantity. Simonton notes also that the rate of creative successes is constant in the individual's career: this is consistent with a Darwinian perspective which predicts that since the process of variation is blind, feasible and infeasible ideas will be randomly generated over the individual's lifespan.

But so simple an application of Darwinian principles to our subject matter misses the ingenuity of Kirton's theory which emphasizes the adaptive cognitive style as well as the innovative. Since adaption-innovation follows a normal distribution in all of the general population samples thus far examined (Kirton, 2006), half of these populations fall below the mean, half are, in a crude sense, adaptors. How did this cognitive style and associated behavioral traits survive unless it, too, is evolutionarily consistent? While at some level the genetic bases of adaption and innovation must be in conflict, there are environments which require the adaptive cognitive style of ensuring that workable selections among variation are refined and maintained with a social group, that resources are husbanded with precision and economy, and that workable rules are adhered to. Many of the environments of the Pleistocene era will have demanded the execution of both cognitive styles simultaneously as represented by the separate roles of males and females in hunting and protecting on one hand and child rearing and feeding on the other. It is therefore entirely evolutionarily consistent that the general population samples indicate that females score significantly (though not greatly) more adaptively than do males. It is noteworthy to observe that the areas of consumption in which adaptors are more prolific purchasers (namely foods and in particular, "healthy" foods) are those for which females would traditionally have been responsible, while the areas in which innovators are more likely to be initiators (technology, overall resource deployment) are traditionally male preserves. This observation, which can be no more than speculative, is nevertheless in accord with the reasoning that underlays evolutionary psychology.

There is also a kind of inclusive fitness (Exhibit 11.1) involved here insofar as adaptors and innovators are, in the process of maintaining the social system, protecting one another's genes as well as their own. It is surely a matter of cultural evolution with implications for biological evolution? Memes, culturgens, etc.

Biological bases of novelty seeking

Can the components of adaption-innovation be related to neural substrates that can in turn be linked to genetic development? Let us take these two putative relationships one at a time. The personality type having the highest correlation with adaption-innovation is introversion-extraversion, and although this is not synonymous with Kirton's construct it is clearly an important driver of adaption-innovation. Depue and Collins (1999) point out that extraversion has two components: interpersonal engagement (which includes affiliation, and agency) and impulsivity. Affiliation manifests in close interpersonal bonds and being warm and affectionate. Agency is a motivational disposition that includes dominance, ambition, mastery, efficacy, and achievement; it reflects social dominance, the enjoyment of leadership roles, assertiveness, exhibitionism, and a subjective sense of potency in accomplishing goals. Extraversion is a higher-order trait; the component lower-order

---

Exhibit 11.1   Inclusive Fitness

Explanations of behavior in terms of evolutionary logic inevitably refer to factors that promote "survival," from which it is easily inferred that the individual or species is the target. Modern evolutionary thinking emphasizes instead that it is the survival of the gene that is paramount. The survival of individual is a means to an end: that of ensuring the continuation of its genes. The individual is no more than a vehicle for the gene. "Fitness" refers to the genotype's reproductive success, i.e. the number of offspring an individual produces who survive to reproductive age compared with the average of the population. Genetic information that is preserved in the process of natural selection can survive for many generations, potentially for ever. Since an individual's genes are carried also by its close relatives, its behavior may aim at their survival, even at some personal sacrifice of fitness, and hence at the preservation of its own genes (Dawkins, 1986, 2006). Hamilton (1964a,b) proposed that behavior designed to promote not the fitness of the individual but the "inclusive fitness" of close relatives is probable if "the cost C to the altruist is exceeded by the benefit B to the recipient devalued (multiplied) by the 'coefficient of relationship' r (the proportion of genes shared, identical by descent, between them" (Dawkins, 2006, p. xxi). In the case of a full sibling, parent or offspring, $r = 0.5$; for half-sibling, grandchild, niece or nephew, 0.25.

---

traits include social dominance, positive emotional feelings, sociability, achievement, and motor activity. As Depue and Collins point out Gray (1973) earlier proposed that personality traits reflect motivation systems that evolved to increase adaptation to classes of stimulus associated with positive and negative reinforcement. Individual differences in personality therefore reflect variation in the sensitivity to such stimuli, and overall personality represents the relative strength of sensitivities to various stimulus classes. Impulsive people are more sensitive to reward than punishment, approaching rewarding situations even when punishers make restraint more appropriate. Sensitivity ultimately means reactivity of the neurobiology associated with a motivational system.

Kirton (2006, pp. 94–5) points out that the possibility that adaption-innovation has a genetic component arises from the observation that release of the monoamine neuromodulators dopamine and norepi-nephrine results in behaviors that respectively bear a resemblance to extreme innovation and extreme adaption. Excess dopamine produc-tion is associated with novelty seeking behaviors, while an excess of norepinephrine is related to reward-dependence. (van der Molen, 1994; Cloninger, 1986, 1987). The genome project has identified one of the genes on chromosome 11, D4DR, with risk-taking (akin to novelty seeking); this protein is a dopamine receptor (Ridley, 1999).

Novelty seeking is related to the regulation of dopamine which is a chemical mediator for emotions including pleasure. The gene impli-cated in this process is D4DR which is located on chromosome 11. Novelty seekers have a longer version of this gene compared to more reserved individuals. (These "versions" of the gene are more accurately terms alleles. We have already encountered the concept of the allele but it is now necessary to define it a little more clearly. An allele is (at a first approximation suitable for present purposes) one of a number of variants of a gene that may occupy a particular place on a chromo-some. Each allele produces a different version of the phenotypic outcome of the gene: e.g., blue eyes rather than brown. In the gene-centered view of evolution such as that of Dawkins (1976), the real competition on which evolution depends is between alleles.) D4DR is not the only dopamine related gene that is involved in novelty seeking and environment also plays a part but this is the first gene reported as having this effect. D4DR is expressed in limbic areas involved in emotion and cognition; in animal experiments dopamine has been found to mediate exploratory behavior; the rewarding effects of cocaine and amphetamines are related to dopamine release' novelty seeking is low in dopamine-deficient patients with Parkinson's. The D4 receptor polymorphism has been described as accounting for only a small percentage of the variance in novelty seeking, suggesting that other genes are also involved (Ebstein, Novick, Umansky, Priel, Osher, Blaine, Bennett, Nemenove, Katz and Belmaker, 1997). The association between D4DR and novelty seeking appears independent of racial dif-ferences (Ono et al., 1994). Ricketts et al. found no association between this gene and novelty seeking.

Cloninger proposed that individual differences in novelty seeking are mediated by genetic variability in dopamine transmission. Ebstein et al. (1997) report a connexion between D4 and novelty seeking. They used the TPQ (tridimensional personality questionnaire), the novelty seeking scale of which distinguishes higher-scoring individuals (who exhibit impulsiveness, fickleness, exploratoriness, excitableness, quick temperedness, and extravagance) from lower scorers (who exhibit more reflectiveness, rigidity, loyalty, stoicism, slow temperedness and frugality). These authors "show that higher than average Novelty Seeking test scores in a group of 124 unrelated Israeli subjects are significantly associated with a particular exonic polymorphism, the 7 repeat allele in the locus for the D4 dopamine receptor gene (D4DR)."

Of course, it is essential to point out that any posited connexion between genes, their expression in the production of particular neurotransmitters, effects on behavior are necessarily tentative and anything proposed now will seem simplistic in even the near future as research implicates additional genetic influences on all of these and as the interactive links between heredity and environment as they affect behavior are better understood. The same caveats that were entered in the course of the discussion of addictive behavior in Chapter 9 must be accorded great weight in the current context. As Kreek, Nielsen, Butelman and LaForge (2005, p. 1450) point out, "Many medical disorders have some genetic component, but most... involve complex genetic contributions based on multiple variants of multiple genes and different combinations of these variants in different people. For some of the most studied diseases, such as certain cancers, the specific genetic contributions and genetic variants have been identified and verified by multiple studies. However, the identified variants, in their entirety, comprise only a small proportion of the estimated genetic contribution. Studying the genetics of complex psychiatric or behavioral disorders such as addiction poses additional challenges. These include precise phenotypic characteristics of individuals and the characterization of ethnic/cultural backgrounds (as different backgrounds yield differences in allelic frequencies). These challenges also must be faced in the study of other complex genetic disorders." Drug use is related to components of personality including impulsivity, risk taking, and novelty seeking. These factors contribute not only to the initial use (trial) of drugs but to their regular use (repeat buying/consumption). "Each of these personality dimensions may have, in part, its own genetic basis" (p. 1450). Psychometric studies implicate in particular impulsivity, risk taking and novelty seeking in addiction.

Jablonka and Lamb (2006) take pains to point out the nature of any genetic basis of character traits and do so in terms that are particularly germane to the present discussion. Commenting on the sensationalism that often accompanies discovery of such genetic relationships in the press, they point out that, "If you look at the actual scientific papers rather than the newspaper stories about these wonderful genes, you find that what has been discovered is a correlation between the presence of a particular DNA sequence and the presence of the character. Usually, it is not at all clear that the DNA sequence is *causally* related to the character, and it is almost always clear that 'the gene' is neither a sufficient nor a necessary condition for the character's development." (p. 59). The mere correlation, so disturbing for those who would portray all disease as monogenic (rather than the approximately two per cent that actually are) as well taking a similarly simplistic view of the genetic origins of personality and behavioral traits in general, is not a problem for super-personal cognitive psychology. We do not assert that strong genetic links must exist; rather, we raise the empirical question of whether any genetic links can be found that support the ascription of intentionality at the personal level, and correlation, however it must be qualified, is not only adequate to this task but fits well with the ideas of causation and explanation that are offered. I should like to quote at length these authors' comments on the specific genetic link we are considering, since its reception in the popular and semi-popular prints has shown considerable exaggeration.

> Let's take a closer look at one of these traits. Not long ago, an amazed public was informed by the media that the gene for "adventurousness" or, as the scientists preferred to call it, "novelty seeking," had been isolated. A person's decision to do something exciting like becoming a fighter pilot or a revolutionary, or alternatively to be an orderly and conscientious librarian or accountant, is, the journalists told us, determined to a large extent by which alleles of one particular gene they have. However, if we turn to the original scientific papers, we find that the power of this gene is rather less than was proclaimed by the popular media. We discover that some people who have the allele that is correlated with adventurousness are in fact very cautious and conventional, whereas some of those who lack it are nevertheless impulsive, thrill-seeking risk takers. All that can be said is that those who have the allele have a somewhat greater chance of being adventurous. In fact, only 4 percent of the difference among people with respect to their adventurous behavior can be attributed to the particular gene that was investigated; 96 percent of the difference is unexplained by the purported "novelty-seeking" allele. Event the 4 percent that go so much media attention is somewhat problematical, because it is not always easy to classify a person as adventurous or not adventurous. People can be adventurous in some aspects of life, but very conventional in others.

Moreover, in their analysis, the researchers apparently did not take into account birth order, a factor which others have found to be a major influence on the development of adventurousness. Children who are born second, third, or later in the family are more adventurous than first-born or only children are. Clearly, this has nothing to do with inheriting a particular allele – it would be a gross violation of Mendelian laws if an allele was more common in first-borns than in other children (Jablonka and Lamb, 2006, pp. 59–60).

The final truth, it such is ever available, must wait upon much more research and thinking. Despite the caveats entered by Jablonka and Lamb, the possibility of a closer relationship among biological and environmental influences and innovativeness remains tantalizingly close. Keltikangas-Järvinen, Räikkönen, Ekelund and Peltonen (2004) report a significant interaction between D4DR alleles and child-rearing environment: when the environment "was more hostile (emotionally distant, low tolerance of the child's normal activity, and strict discipline), the participants carrying any two- or five-repeat alleles of the D4DR gene had a significantly greater risk of exhibiting NS [novelty seeking] scores that were above the 10th percentile on a population of 2149 adult Finnish women and men. The genotype had no effect on NS when the childhood environment was more favorable" (p. 308). Of course, although its authors urge caution and call for further investigation, this may be one of the studies to which Jablonka and Lamb are referring. But, for the purpose of establishing a framework of exposition for the explanation of consumer choice, even a weak correlation is enough; the fact that the effect of any one gene is moderated by the relevant gene background (other genetic influences) and environmental and behavioral factors fits perfectly with the view of an integrated behavioral science that is being put forward here. Only the most dyed-in-the-wool genetic determinist, evincing a position that is entirely alien to super-personal cognitive psychology, would ignore these considerations.

Summing-up

The most interesting outcome of the empirical program is the coexistence of adaptors and innovators at the earliest phase of the adoption cycle: the personality traits and decision styles that are commonly assumed uniquely to characterize consumer initiators are not exclusively those of Kirton's innovators. Moreover, in terms of the amounts of some new items purchased, adaptors – at least those who are especially engaged with or involved in the product category – buy the most. This pattern was found repeatedly for food products and brands. In addition, the more-involved adaptors have shown particular behavior patterns for new (to them, if not always to the market) products ranging from financial products such as pension schemes and mortgages, through credit card usage, to computer hardware purchases. This flies in the face of the standard wisdom found not only in the marketing literature but equally in those of biology and psychology insofar as they concern themselves with innovativeness. The explanation presumably resides in the underlying genotypes and neurophysiologies of adaptors and innovators, and in the evolutionary history of our ancestors in environments that make conflicting adaptive demands on these two intellectual types. At all events, the empirical program we have undertaken indicates that the relationship is not straightforward.

These elements also serve to unify the spectrum of consumer behaviors with which this chapter and the last have been concerned, from the routine to the novel, and on to the extreme. Individual differences in hormonal and neurotransmitter levels undoubtedly correlate with the more extreme consumer behaviors such as gambling and drug-taking; neuroanatomy is also implicated in any explanation of this behavior. Similar impulsions toward novelty-seeking and risk taking are also apparent in the behavior of the consumer initiator at least when highly involved, though the "anomaly" of the relatively small numbers of highly involved adaptors who are among the first to purchase the highest quantities of new items or to initiate novel uses for existing products must also be taken into account. Further analysis in terms of evolutionary psychology is also called for, since the precise environmental conditions to which adaptors and innovators are likely to have become adapted can be more precisely specified than has been possible in this survey. What, however, can be said of everyday routine consumer choice in these terms? Ross et al. (2005) propose that the everyday consumer who is not tempted into situations where hyperbolic discounting would take over his or her life has "made a decision" not to go there. This is a useful shorthand for what happens, though like Rachlin's addict who "decides" to change his behavior pattern, it takes us into the realm of intentional behaviorism. But no further. A more comprehensive account might call upon super-personal cognitive psychology. We might wish to inquire of the consumer's cognitive style, for instance, among other elements of cognitive content and function. This does not mean that everyday consumption is characterized by a single cognitive style, however. We must not fall into the trap of assuming that novelty-seeking behavior inevitably involves innovators while more mundane buying is the province of adaptors. The approximately normal distribution of cognitive styles in all societies in which general population samples have been obtained as well as our own researches belie such simplifications.

12
What Kind of Explanation?

Skinner's behaviorism is not, as I have heard some philosophers and psychologists assert, simply false. Skinner is certainly right that there are epistemological pitfalls to mentalistic psychology, and he is right that humans are (to some extent) operantly conditionable. He is even right that the concept of operant behavior sheds some interesting light on how psychology might deal with the conundrums about novelty and purpose. Furthermore, he has many interesting and important things to say about schedules of reinforcement and the differential effects of positive reinforcement and punishment. Nevertheless, Skinner's conception of psychology is limited, and he almost invariably gets himself into philosophical trouble whenever he makes global proclamations about metaphysics, epistemology, politics, or the nature of psychological explanation. Thus, whereas Skinner is right to be concerned about the metaphysical and methodological foundations of psychology he tends to throw the baby out with the bathwater and make psychology epistemologically safe at the price of making it epistemologically impoverished (for example, by removing cognitive processes from psychology's domain of inquiry.) ... On the other hand, *I am not sure if we would now know with such confidence that psychological explanation must be intentional and cognitive had we not met with Skinner's bold programmatic claims to the contrary.* (Flanagan, 1991, pp. 84–5; italics added).

Earlier chapters have presented a critique of Skinnerian psychology but it has also been argued that a comprehensive psychology of consumer choice cannot do without the extensional approach to behavioral science that it provides. We might not wish to be "Skinnerians" in any narrow sense, but we recognize that we would not be where we are without operant theory. But while it is a necessary part of explaining complex human behavior, it is not sufficient. There are aspects of intentional and cognitive psychology as well as aspects of biology that are as important as behavior analysis (Hardcastle, 1999; Rosenberg, 2005; Wilson, 1998).

Beyond radical behaviorism

The defining characteristic of radical behaviorism is its avoidance of intentional explanation, the confinement of its explanatory terms to those permitted by a scrupulously extensional approach to behavioral science (Foxall, 2004). The consumer behavior analysis research program raises the question whether such a science can account for consumer choice. Radical behaviorism succeeds in its goal of predicting and controlling behavior, at least in the closed setting of the experimental space. But any attempt to extend its explanation of behavior beyond this lacks means of accounting for behavioral continuity and the personal level of analysis. In its interpretations of behavior in open settings, it additionally lacks a viable means of delimiting the scope of its explanations by identifying definitively the responses and stimuli that compose its accounts. Since the required gaps in the explanation cannot be filled by appeal to more basic behavioral operations, physiology, verbal behavior, or rule-governance (Smith, 1994; Foxall, 2004), the sole remaining theoretical means available is the use of intentionality. But the behaviorist's alarm bells ring loud and clear at this suggestion since the profligate attribution of mentalistic terminology and the wanton generation of putative cognitive mechanisms is precisely what we have been led to avoid at all costs. This does not, however, remove the need of intentional usage if we wish to take explanation in behavioral science beyond the requirements of prediction and control. Dennett (1969) suggests a means by which content ascription may be legitimately executed on the basis of afferent–efferent linkages that are evolutionarily consistent.

This approach, which employs sub-personal extensional neuroscience as the basis of ascribing intentions at the personal level, proves useful but inadequate, at least in the realm of consumer choice, and the methodology must be expanded to include evolutionarily consistent patterns of environmental-behavioral relationships as a means of ascribing content (cf. Blakemore, Winston and Frith, 2004; Ochsner, 2004; Adolphs, 2003).

The resulting framework, intentional behaviorism, is, like Dennett's more limited scheme, a-ontological. While Dennett progresses beyond his initial method to derive a sub-personal cognitive psychology which makes ontological assumptions about the causation of behavior and the nature of psychology, it is equally feasible to propose a super-personal cognitive psychology that employs the patterns of behavior encountered at the super-personal level of operant functioning in order to ascribe cognitive processes at the personal level. The methodologies of both intentional behaviorism and super-personal cognitive psychology require the input of a definitively extensional behavioral science. When we examine the behavioral sciences that have, inter alia, attempted to deal with economic choice – namely teleological behaviorism and picoeconomics – we find that they, unlike radical behaviorism, do not provide an extensional basis for the philosophies of psychology that Dennett proposed or inspired: rather, they have already assumed the role of post-operant psychologies in that they have embraced intentional and/or cognitive explanation. For, wherever we use the language of intentionality, we are employing intentional explanation. This is a purely linguistic convention and carries with it no ontological implications. And, wherever we use the language of information processing, we are employing cognitive explanation. This is not merely a linguistic convention but imposes the ontological assumptions that must accompany cognitive causation. The paper has explored the roles of radical behaviorism, teleological behaviorism, and picoeconomics in the explanation of consumer choice and concludes that each lends itself uniquely to the project.

While radical behaviorism is an extensional behavioral science that provides a descriptive account of consumer choice by relating it systematically to its environmental correlates, it cannot of itself deliver a comprehensive explanation of complex behavior for three reasons. Only by incorporating the terminology of intentionality can behavioral theory account satisfactorily for the continuity of behavior, the personal level of analysis, and the delimitation of behavioral interpretation. Rachlin's teleological behaviorism can be construed as fulfilling these "imperatives of intentionality" because it exploits the philosophy of science I have called intentional behaviorism. Ainslie's picoeconomics goes beyond the ascription of intentionality by examining the kinds of mental processing required to account for intertemporal reversals of consumer preference. It is identified, therefore, with "super-personal cognitive psychology," a framework which proposes that certain processes of intrapersonal bargaining are necessary to cope with the conflict posed by delayed versus immediate rewards. Between them, these systems represent the theoretical apogee of modern behavioral economics.

Recent empirical findings in consumer behavior analysis demonstrate the relevance of behavioral economics to consumer's brand and product choices, the role of informational (symbolic) as well as utilitarian (functional) reinforcement, and the scope of the current behavior setting in shaping consumers' verbal and non-verbal responses to consumption opportunities, and the necessity of incorporating situational variables into psychological models of attitudinal-behavioral consistency (Foxall, 2005). In addition, this research program has generated behaviorist interpretations of consumers' purchase and saving behaviors, "green" consumer behavior, and the adoption and diffusion of innovations (Foxall, 1996). Teleological behaviorism, on the understanding accorded it in this paper, is particularly apposite to explaining the maintenance of brand purchase patterns, as well as the disruption that from time to time occur in such behavioral sequences, and the influence of functional variables on choice. Both teleological behaviorism and picoeconomics can provide plausible accounts of the problem of attitudinal-behavioral discrepancy. Picoeconomics appears particularly appropriate, however, to the explanation of the preference reversals encountered in consumer behaviors such as spending versus saving, and environmental conservation.

The framework of analysis presented in this book suggests an explanation of consumer choice in natural settings that goes beyond the purely descriptive purview of radical behaviorism. Despite the continuing relevance of an extensional behavioral science to the analysis of consumer choice, we now have, thanks to recent developments in behavioral economic theory, an overarching paradigm for the study of human behavior in contexts that extend well beyond the operant laboratory.

If radical behaviorism is to contribute to the explanation of the patterns of consumer behavior we have observed, it requires additional conceptualization that makes its analyses germane to the economic sphere. These are the variables that comprise the Behavioral Perspective Model (BPM), matching analysis, and behavioral economics. Insofar as our goal has been the prediction (and at least an understanding of the environmental factors that control consumer choice, radical behaviorism accounts adequately for consumer behavior (a) in relatively closed settings, (b) remaining within the scope of an extensional behavioral science, but requiring the conceptual extensions represented by the BPM, matching analysis, and behavioral economics. To some extent, these additions merely accommodate the underlying philosophy of psychology to the actualities of economic behavior, permitting not only an interpretation of complex behavior (that which is not amenable to direct experimental analysis) but an empirical analysis of that behavior which, while not yet experimental, adheres to the canons of scientific practice.

However, even by incorporating matching and behavioral economics, we have made something of a conceptual leap. For these analyses are concerned with molar rather than molecular behavior, and Rachlin (1994) argues that whereas molecular behavior involves causation that occurs prior to the enactment of behavior, the causes of molar behavior lie in the yet-to-be enacted (or realized) consequential behaviors: it is teleological. Rachlin's teleological behaviorism is, therefore, the second major contribution to the analysis of economic behavior that we need to consider. In doing so, I have argued that teleological behaviorism belongs in the intentional behaviorism camp rather than that of extensional behavioral science.

Beyond teleological behaviorism on a broad continuum of economic behavioral sciences is Ainslie's picoeconomics which considers not just the patterns of behavioral choices enacted by individuals but the "successive interaction of strategic motivational states within the individual." This is territory that goes well beyond the extensional behavioral science that radical behaviorism strives to be, and further in fact than does the competence theory intentional behaviorism in which intentional terms are used as theoretical necessities with no ontological status. Picoeconomics, I have contended, is akin to superpersonal cognitive psychology.

An important element of Dennettian philosophy of psychology has been retained throughout the exercise: the ascription of intentionality must be evolutionarily consistent and, wherever possible, whatever additional sources of evolutionary thought (such as operant conditioning and evolutionary psychology) are embraced, such ascription must be based upon evolutionarily consistent afferent-efferent linkages at the sub-personal level. This consideration remains paramount even though intentional behaviorism and super-personal cognitive psychology have moved in other ways beyond Dennett's formulations for intentional psychology. Such linkages cannot be replaced the results of fMRI scans, interesting as these may be in establishing the neurophysiological substrates of behavior. Dennett's use of the afferent–efferent relationship is far more subtle than this and is based on a distinctly separate mode of reasoning. As Kagan (2006) points out, fMRI results reflect input to a brain site rather than output from the neurons involved; brain activity in areas not well supplied with blood during the period of the scan will not be detected; most events activate several brain sites any of which may or may not be relevant to the behavior under scrutiny (see also, inter alia, Greenfield, 2001; Uttal, 2001). The finding that brand awareness of which cola drink one is sampling in a taste test is linked with specific brain responses (McClure, Li, Tomlin, Cypert, Montague and Montague, 2004) notwithstanding, there is reason to be suspicious of some of the simplicities inherent in "neuro-marketing." As far as the theoretical reasoning of the contextual psychologies examined in this book are concerned, Dennett's (1969) formulation remains supreme. The incorporation of the results of fMRI scanning into the present volume is part of the establishment of links between operant behavior and the neurophysiology of reward rather than a substitute for Dennett's criterion for the ascription of intentional content on the basis of sub-personal relationships between the inputs to an organism's sensory nervous system and corresponding motor outputs.

The first task in developing the full potential of the theory of consumer behavior developed in *Understanding Consumer Choice* (Foxall, 2005) has been to elucidate consumer choice is to clarify the methodological stance on which it rests. In particular, this clarification refers to the number of levels and stances included in the theory and their nature and implications. For, once (1) the distinction between the intentional and the non-intentional has been established as linguistic rather than essentialistic, and (2) the language of intentionality is established as applying exclusively to the personal level while extensional language applies solely to the sub-personal (and ultimately also to the super-personal) level, it follows that the personal and sub-personal (super-personal) levels can never be linguistically united. It cannot be done. If the linguistic criterion is given up what will we put in its place that avoids dualism? The refinement of the model involves the inclusion of evolutionary psychology in the establishment of the biological basis of operant conditioning and its neurological linkages. The demonstration of this has been the task of *Explaining Consumer Choice.*

Although the frameworks developed in earlier chapters may add to the explanation of consumer choice in broad terms, we are left with some points of uncertainty. One of these concerns the causation of behavior: should it be attributed to the contingencies that have shaped it or to the beliefs and desires that enter into its explanation? To a learning history or to cognition? At the level of explanation it does not much matter how we apportion these influences: part of my task has been to show that both must enter into a complete understanding of the empirical phenomena. But a key component of marketing is the attempt to change behavior. On what should it rely to accomplish this task?

The essence of intentional behaviorism has been to accord mental phenomena what might be termed a passive causal role: they are necessary to account for some necessary behavioral phenomena (such as the personal level and the continuity of behavior across situations). The remaining question is whether and how they might be said to take on an active causal role, entering directly into the determination of choice. This question has fallen into the domain of super-personal cognitive psychology. The short answer is that there is no way in which theoretical entities can play this role at an empirical level. Their ontology is such that they are materially precluded from exerting causal influence. This is not to say that they may at some point be linked to material forces that can be ascribed causal validity; parallelograms of force, for instance, may well achieve this status. In the meantime, they are devices that save the theory rather than become a part of it on a part to experimentally manipulable influences such as behavioral contingencies. (This is why it is necessary to do experiments.) The question for marketing of what to change, the contingencies or the beliefs, is answered by the fact that ultimately only the contingencies will produce the intentions to which a complete explanation of behavior must anyway appeal.

This bears on the statement of Baum and Heath (1992, p. 1316), cited earlier, to the effect that where a learning history is not empirically available it is better to assume that one does and to speculate in as informed a way about its nature. This, they argue, is more in line with scientific method than assuming mental phenomena to be necessary to the explanation of behavior. One could argue equally that in the absence of direct empirical knowledge it (of learning history) it is more in line with scientific method to admit that only a broader kind of verbal statement is possible with respect to the explanation of behavior and to employ intentional language to denote this.

Intentional explanation

The approach to explanation that arises from these considerations is as follows. Explanations are purely linguistic affairs. How we explain depends on what our explanations render intellectually intelligible to us. Different forms (structures) of locution imply different kinds of explanation. Explanations need to be consistent with observations but there is always more than one explanation of the available empirical evidence. Although this approach is consistent with pragmatism as a means of comparing explanations, it cannot rest on prediction and control as its criteria of success. Nor yet upon parsimony. For the intelligibility of a theory, as well as its persuasability, depend upon its capacity to deal with the continuity of behavior and this in turn requires that it attribute intentionality at the personal level. Any other criterion, physiological or behavioral, whether or not it be construed as necessary to the causation of the behavior in question, is not its explanation. It is, from the point of view of explanation, no more than a correlate of the behavior to be explained. Only the intentions ascribed at the personal level on the basis of these respectively sub-personal and super-personal criteria are the explanation of the behavior, though since they are purely linguistic in nature, they are not its causes.

This is the position of intentional behaviorism. We can advance further in the direction of a performance theory, however, by proposing a super-personal cognitive psychology in which the mental functions required to execute/produced collaterally with the overt behaviors we are intent on explaining are specified. They are specified, moreover, on the basis of (i) the neural substrates of that behavior (verbal and non-verbal) insofar as they can be argued to be consistent with natural selection, and (ii) the demonstrated contingency-shaping of the molar behavior patterns under review, insofar as these are argued consistent with cultural evolution. The evolutionary psychology of Tooby and Cosmides has been the means of exposition adopted here with its emphasis on the modular functionality of mental capacities in relation to human ancestral histories. But it is too early for alternative approaches to cultural evolution to be ruled out.

From the perspective of the epistemology of explanation adopted here, super-personal cognitive psychology might be most appropriately termed a neo-competence theory: the idea of a performance theory might be better reserved for more specific and, most important, empirically-testable cognitive theories such as the adaption-innovation hypothesis. As has been argued, these terms are relative. Moreover, heterophenomenology, pursued in the manner advocated here, emerges as an essential component in the explanation of consumer choice. But the essence of the contribution to explanation made here inheres in the modifications the foregoing enjoins upon the basic extensional behavioral science of consumer choice portrayed by the BPM. Can it any longer be thought of as an extension of the three-term contingency or is its explanatory scope in need of extension? Is intentional reasoning inherent in its formulation? What is its relation to evolutionary psychology?

Given the goal of the BPM research program (Foxall, 1994b) and in light of the considerations raised in the course of this volume, two conclusions can now be drawn. The empirical program of consumer behavior analysis conducted over a dozen years in several countries indicates that an affirmative answer can be given to the possibility of constructing such a model and using it to predict and identify the factors necessary to influence consumer choice. As to the epistemological status of the model, its theoretical and methodological implications, the picture is positive but more complicated. The model was originally conceived in relation to determining the relevance of radical behaviorism to consumer behavior: hence, the terms *behavioral perspective* in its title; it fully recognized that there could be other perspectives on consumer choice: sociological, economic, cognitive, Freudian, and so on. The empirical evidence to which reference has been made confirms that the BPM can provide a radical behaviorist account of consumer behavior. However, the argument of this book suggests that this is only one heuristic overlay which can be placed over the data. It is equally possible to use the BPM to propose an intentional behaviorist interpretation of the phenomena; and, beyond that, a super-personal cognitive psychological account.

We can interpret each component of the BPM in terms of an intentionalistic overlay. The current behavior setting and learning history are both highly theoretical entities in that neither can be concretely defined in any particular instance of purchase of consumption. The current behavior setting consists properly of *neutral* stimuli: they are only activated into discriminative stimuli or establishing (motivating) operations when the light of the consumer's learning history is shone upon them. And learning history, as we have seen, is a ghost in the machine, a convenient explanatory fiction that we can presume exists (on the basis of experiments with animals subjects where if can be known) but which is not empirically available to the interpreter of complex human behavior which cannot be examined directly in the laboratory. Only when current behavior setting and learning history interact to generate the "consumer situation" does any motivating tendency that can enter into an explanation of consumer behavior arise. And this interaction, what we have called the *consumer situation*, is necessarily an intentional expression. For it points to, is about, something other than itself. It signals the outcome of a particular consumer response in terms of the utilitarian reinforcement, informational reinforcement, and aversive consequences it is likely to produce. It is open to description in terms of the actor's desires and beliefs, devices that perform the central explanatory roles we have drawn attention to such as continuity of behavior. Of course, they do not have to be described in this way: the extensional behavioral science so clearly required for explanation of complex human behavior is served well by their original meanings. But that does not preclude the extension of the model to embrace intentional behaviorist interpretations of consumer choice.

Learning history itself must in this framework be understood in the intentionalistic terms of what the individual has learned: the consumer has learned *that* these brands confer certain benefits, *that* these stores are more expensive than those, *that* being the first to purchase a new product may mean taking unacceptable risks. But what is it about the interaction of the consumer behavior setting and the learning history that produces motivation? This interaction enshrines the formula for intentional explanation summarized by Rosenberg (1988, p. 25) as "Given any person, *x*, if *x* wants *d* and *x* believes that *a* is a means to attain *d*, under the circumstances, then *x* does *a*." A learning history that consists in the consumer's having learned certain intentional propositions with respect to its desires and beliefs about what consumer behaviors generate what satisfaction; it is the interaction of this learning history with the neutral stimuli that compose the current behavior setting, imbuing them with meaning so that they become discriminative stimuli which *indicate* that certain behaviors will meet with certain consequences that produces motivation to act. Compare the radical behaviorist device of adding a further discriminative stimulus in the form of an establishing or motivating operation. This is perfectly legitimate as an extensional means of coping with motivation but it cannot serve to answer the question that arises immediately on our embarking on an explanatory account: what provides the connexion between past exposure to reinforcing stimuli and the capacity of current stimuli to engender response discrimination? How, in other words, are we to account for the continuity of behavior? The same considerations apply also to the phenomena of stimulus and response generalization: how come the same stimulus evokes a different response on different occasions? Why should the same response occur in the presence of a novel stimulus? Skinner merely describes what is happening when he refers to the class of responses so produced as an operant, to the range of stimuli responsible as a class of discriminative stimuli. Explanation requires more and only intentional idioms provide the necessary explanation. The *consumer situation* which is defined as the interaction between learning history and current behavior setting can itself be described in extensional terms on the basis of observation alone; but its power to motivate requires an explanation that inheres in the realm of intentionality.

When the focus of explanation turns to the specification of the cognitive functions involved with the patterns of behavior that are the subject of interpretation, it becomes necessary to attribute appropriate intentional variables at the personal level based on observations and understandings of behavior patterns occurring at the super-personal level of environmental–behavioral relationships: operant behavior again but this time firmly linked with an evolutionary logic that accounts for culture. We have seen that some cognitive-level concepts such as the cognitive style adaption–innovation fit the requirement of evolutionary consistency and that of genetic correlation, although strict caveats have been entered with respect to the standing of any particular gene. The epistemological status of these variables is no different from that accorded the content ascribed in the process of intentional behaviorism: no ontological consequences follow from positing the cognitive variables in question.

Evolutionary explanation

There arises next the necessity of relating the variables of the BPM to the imperatives of evolutionary psychology. It is easy enough to find a basis for utilitarian reinforcement in evolutionary logic since it inheres in part in the primary reinforcement which is necessary for survival and the enhancement of inclusive fitness. It also inheres in secondary reinforcement which does the same. Informational reinforcement is equally amenable to this justification insofar as it leads to status and dominance within the group, brings resources that enhance fitness. It inheres directly in behavioral consequences that increase social status and dominance, and it the possibility has been raised that it results in higher self-esteem for the individual (Foxall, 1997a). This is consistent with thinking in evolutionary psychology which has recently emphasized self-esteem as a status tracking mechanism. Barkow (1989, p. 190) argues in a way that is surprisingly consonant with this surmise that "the evaluation that results in self-esteem is symbolic in nature, involving the application of criteria for the allocation of prestige" (quoted by

Buss, 2004, p. 364). Buss himself says "If there was ever a reasonable candidate for a universal human motive, status striving would be at or near the top of the list" (2004, pp. 244–5). Dominance hierarchies avoid fights to the death. Animals that are near the top have disproportionate access to resources that promote both survival and reproduction.

Much consumer behavior is open to interpretation in these terms (e.g., Saad and Gill, 2000, 2003). While evolutionary psychology is a maturing subdiscipline, however, its readily available explanations retain the facility of just-so stories unless we are highly critical of their meaning. The question is how far such interpretation renders consumer choice more intelligible than its alternatives. So mammoth a task cannot be undertaken in this concluding chapter but some indication of how well the framework of exposition developed in earlier chapters elucidates both initiating and imitative consumer behavior on one hand and everyday consumer behavior on the other can be gleaned. Let us examine each of the types of contextual psychology described earlier in terms of their underlying claims to elucidate consumer behavior and then discuss the nature of the explanation so derived in relation to what we know of both behavioral economics and consumer choice in a marketing context.

The promise of intentional behaviorism as a methodology of explanation requires for its fulfillment the demonstration that we can establish first an extensional behavioral science approach in which behavior can be related systematically to environmental contingencies. This has been done in terms of the operant account of diffusion. It is equally necessary to establish that the problems of such an account – with respect to the continuity of behavior, the personal level, and if necessary the delimitation of a behavioral interpretation, can be overcome by the incorporation of intentional terms. This has been done in terms (a) of Midgley and Dowling's trait-situation-behavior model, and (b) a particular understanding of memetics. What does this imply for intentional behaviorism?

Intentional behaviorism is behavioral in that behavior is the dependent variable: our aim is always to know what accounts for the consumer's adopting the product at a particular time; it is behaviorist in that environmental contingencies (utilitarian reinforcement and informational reinforcement) are the independent variables and a level of explanation is sought in terms of the functional relationships between dependent and independent variables. Discriminative stimuli and establishing operations such as advertising and the availability of finances also form part of the consumer behavior setting which explain

the timing of behavior. The dependent variable takes two forms, however: the behavior of the earliest adopters is by definition initiation (it
takes place relatively independently of the communicated experience
of others) while that of later adopters is necessarily imitative. We have
to account for the different patterns of behavioral causation here, not
simply the relative elapsed time since the launch of the innovation.
The dependent variable is, moreover, a pattern or sequence of molar
behavior that can be ascribed to the continued action of contingent
reinforcement. This is a type of behavior that is more difficult to
sustain – at least more difficult to observe – in the case of the diffusion
of innovations since the products in question are, like consumer
durables, purchased relatively infrequently by most consumers. By contrast, everyday consumer choice is frequently repeated as is addictive
consumer behavior including gambling. If the immediate motivation
for such behaviors is the release of dopamine or other neurotransmit-
ter(s), then the purchase of newness is not the only means by which
novelty seeking and risk taking manifest in the life of the individual
consumer. Rather, it is likely to be one activity among several which
result in this source of reward.

The intentionalistic component of this level of analysis stems from
the need to fill the gaps in behavior theory are by the ascription of
content: the abstract notion of inherent innovativeness accounts for
the continuity of behavior over situations of possible innovative adoption, and since it is conceived as a variable its can be said to account
for a smaller or greater degree of initiating choice. The danger here is
that such a mechanism, if seen as causative of the behavior in question, more of less innovative adoption, becomes a crutch for more
definitive investigation at either the theoretical or empirical level. It is
not accorded this status in intentional behaviorism where its sole role
is to make clear that the extensional language of radical behaviorism
cannot account adequately for behavioral continuity or the personal
level of analysis, and often cannot delimit the range of behavioral consequences that enter into its interpretations. The inability of behavioral
scientists to account for such elements of sound theory in other than
intentionalistic language, which we have noted particularly in the case
of teleological behaviorism, points to the different dimension of explanation that is the basis of intentional behaviorism.

The intentional component of super-personal cognitive psychology
extends beyond this by seeking to specify the mental operations that
would be consistent with the observed molar patterns of behavior on
the basis of which intentionality is ascribed at the personal level. The

discussion of cognitive evolutionary psychology has drawn particular attention first to the role of pleasure, arousal, and dominance (the fundamental units of emotion identified by Mehrabian and Russell and employed to effect in consumer behavior analyses of responses to consumption environments, and second to the influence of cognitive style on the adoption of innovations. These are variables that take the explanation of consumer choice to a deeper level than does intentional behaviorism alone. No longer are we simply positing intentional content in order to mark where a purely behavioral theory has proven inadequate; the task now is to advance a cognitive theory of behavior by understanding the modules of mind that would be consistent with the molar patterns observed. Once again, there is no suggestion that these elements of mental functioning are causal in the sense that they are instrumental in shaping behavior, but there is a vital function for this level of investigation in the context of a behavioral theory of choice. Behavior theory (especially that derived form radical behaviorism) displays an important theoretical inadequacy in its treatment of verbal behavior that is not amenable to experimental analysis. On one hand, it makes central use of the notion such as private events, the thoughts and feelings held to be covert though non-mental responses which are the result of environmental contingencies but which early radical behaviorism insisted were not causal entities in their own right. However, Skinner (1988a, b, c) refers to them somewhat enigmatically as "non-initiating causes" of behavior, an admission that muddies the water of a purely behaviorist account. On another, modern behavior theory founded upon empirical analyses of the verbal behavior of the listener (e.g., Hayes, 1989) accords a vital explanatory role to the rule-governance of behavior. The possibility that individuals can devise their own rules on the basis of an examination of the contingencies of reinforcement available to them (Horne and Lowe, 1993) also arises and has already been noted. This suggests that verbal behavior cannot be limited to the status of contingent consequence but has of itself an initiating (causal) role in the determination of behavior. There is not reason why covert verbal behavior should not exercise this influence as effectively as overt, and why the processes of formulating self-rules through observation of the contingencies should not be described as cognitive. The task of super-personal cognitive psychology is to show what intellectual processes would be necessarily consistent with the resulting over behavior. Rather than avoiding such considerations, falling back at the last moment of an analysis of the influence of covert language on respondents' behavior in experimental situations by reminding themselves and their readers that they are radical behaviorists and unable therefore to think beyond a simple contingency-shaped theory of action, behavior analysts should follow through their initial analyses by making the deliberations that super-personal cognitive psychology invites.

Both intentional behaviorism and super-personal cognitive psychology require the corroboration that the demonstration of links between (a) operant behavior and the reward circuitry of the brain and (b) human evolutionary history and the form of extended operant behaviors can bestow. The possibility that analysis of consumers' initiating and imitative behaviors can be linked in both directions with evolutionarily consistent accounts has been raised and some evidence has been adduced in each case. It seems inevitable that the development of a comprehensive theory of consumer choice will depends upon the demonstration of these linkages and that the biological sciences can be used to good effect in supporting this quest. However, it is important to recognize that as yet only the possibility has been raised and that firm evidence must still be assiduously pursued. The genetic basis of novelty seeking and extraversion which are at the heart of Kirton's innovative cognitive style are promising but far from certain. Genes other than D4DR are implicated (no single gene is ever responsible for so complex a behavior pattern as that of either the innovator or the adaptor). The required link will presumably be found in this realm but it would be over-ambitious to imagine that it has yet been confirmed. Similarly, although the logic of evolutionary psychology is compelling, the tendency of adaptionist thinking to resemble just-so stories cannot be denied. The need for a firming up of the arguments based on this field in providing a credible evolutionary justification for the contextual psychologies explored here cannot be denied. But while I enter these caveats I have every faith that the general framework of exposition proposed here will serve economic psychology well and that progress lies in the advocated direction.

How does this reasoning help explicate everyday consumer choice? Here it is comparatively easy to establish the molar patterns of behavior that can be systematically related to a reinforcing environment. Moreover, the pattern of reinforcement emerges from our analyses as a potent component of an operant explanation of choice. This is supported not only by the studies of matching and the differential elasticities of demand evinced by groups of consumers whose major sources of reinforcement for purchasing are represented by differing combinations of utilitarian reinforcement and informational reinforcement; it is further corroborated by studies of consumers' verbal-affective responses to stimuli representing consumption environments defined in terms of relative utilitarian and informational reinforcement, and varying degrees of impulsion to act in specific ways in response to the scope of the consumer behavior setting; and it is reflected in the interpretations of both complex consumer and marketing managerial behaviors in terms of the same BPM variables. This facilitates many of the tasks of intentional behaviorism and super-personal cognitive psychology, the notably establishment of behavior-content and behavior-cognition links. These lie at the heart of intentional behaviorism and super-personal cognitive psychology respectively and the ascription of intentionality and cognition on this basis is fully justified in itself and in turn this makes the contextual psychologies we have proposed the surer. However, what support is there for the corroborating links between these observed patterns of behavior and on the one hand the evolutionarily consistent neurophysiological processes that Dennett initially proposed as the basis of ascription, and on the other the cognitive developments that can be plausibly attributed to our ancestral history?

Although linkages between both neuroscience and evolutionary psychology and extreme consumer behaviors including the adoption of innovations have been suggested, the demonstration of a possible link between either of these and everyday consumer behavior has not been addressed. We are clearly however in the realm of evolutionary psychology here, a discipline which is itself in flux (e.g., Barendregt and van Hezewijk, 2005; Downes, 2005; Lloyd, 1999; Toates, 2005). The key is competition for resources which enhance an individual's chances of survival and inclusive fitness, and this involves behavior that increases access to utilitarian reinforcement and, because it is a means of securing utilitarian reinforcement, to informational reinforcement. In particular, in evolutionary time, we are talking here about economic (scarce) resources that increase the ability to rear offspring to the point of their being able to lead independent reproductive lives. The central dogma of evolutionary psychology – "females follow the resources and males follow the females" – is consistent with the view that males may not be interested in pursuing resources for their own sake (except as they enable them to continue exiting) but that, on account of the disproportionate investment they may in child-rearing, females are centrally interested in males who are more likely to supply them. The indication of a male's capacity to do so are shown by his status within the group, his position within a dominance hierarchy. This is consistent with the understanding that virtually all commodities, products, brands represent both utilitarian and informational reinforcers in varying degree; even where one source of reinforcement is emphasized in a product offering, the other accompanies it and/or is strongly symbolized by it. Saving and investment, for instance (CC5), are motivated principally in the short term by considerations of accumulating funds through capital appreciation and/or the addition of interest, but in the longer term by the possibility of acquiring products and services (utilitarian reinforcement) or the power that further guarantees the ability to obtain and allocate scarce economic resources.

Incentive salience theory

The crucial test of both intentional behaviorism and super-personal cognitive psychology lies in the possibility of linking sub-, super-, and personal levels of explanation not simply in the realm of philosophical discourse but empirically. Impetus for this is provided by the tricomponential approach to reward advanced by Berridge and Robinson (2003). I first summarize the position of these authors and then elaborate upon it in connexion with the related considerations that arise from the BPM.

Berridge and Robinson analyze reward in terms not only of learning (in which the individual relates stimuli and the consequences of action), but additionally as a hedonic/affective element (involving pleasure, "liking," and what we have termed utilitarian reinforcement), and a motivational element (which in terms of the extensional BPM would stem from motivating operations of the 4-term contingency and in Berridge and Robinson's terms from "wanting" and incentive salience. In terms that will be familiar to the consumer behavior analyst, they note that learning may be behavioral/associative leading procedurally to habits or cognitive leading declaratively to conscious memories. Learning may involve the establishment of stimulus-stimulus (S-S), stimulus-response (S-R) or response-consequence (R-S^R) associations, which are all mediated by subcortical and cortical substrates, and/or cognitively-based act-outcome representations which are mediated overwhelmingly by cortical substrates. Liking is usually equated with subjective pleasure but Berridge and Robinson use the term "liking" (in quotes) to refer to objectively specified affect that may not be conscious, "Liking" is associated with opioid transmission on to GABAergic neurons in the nucleus accumbens. (See also Winkielman, Berridge and Wilbarger, 2005). "Wanting" or incentive salience, the motivational element in reward, is not the equivalent of "liking." Contrary to the popular view, dopamine is does not generate pleasure or other affective response: in fact, dopamine is neither necessary not sufficient for "liking." Manipulation of the dopamine system does, however, change motivated behavior by increasing instrumental responses and the consumption of rewards, though it has not effect on taste (liking measured as affective facial expression). Hence, incentive salience is a motivational rather than an affective component of reward. Incentive motivation transforms neutral stimuli into compelling incentives.

A more detailed account allows the interactions among "wanting," learning, and "liking" to be explored. First, conditioned stimuli may act as what Berridge and Robinson call "motivational magnets." As a result of being attributed with incentive salience, stimuli come to elicit appetitive and possibly consummatory approach behaviors. In Pavlovian conditioning, conditioned stimuli (CSs) elicit approach conditioned responses (CRs). In a procedure known as autoshaping, pigeons deal behaviorally with the CSs for food and drink as they would with the food and drink stimuli (the unconditioned stimuli or UCSs) themselves. They discriminate their behavior accordingly, making eating pecks in the former case and drinking pecks in the latter, Berridge and Robinson liken this to the behavior of an addict who searches the floor for white crystals even though he or she knows that many of them are of sugar. The Pavlovian CSs in this instances are a the subject of "wanting" as they become motivational magnets that attract appropriate behavioral responses; the incentive salience attributed to them is itself a conditioned stimulus element. Incentive salience of this kind is closely connected with the activity of mesolimbic dopamine systems and the basolateral amygdala and nucleus accumbens appear to be implicated in the associative guidance it provides.

Second is the phenomenon of cue-triggered rewards. CSs may instigate motivation for their unconditioned rewards, for instance when cues associated with drugs elicit either craving for the drug and/or its ingestion. It is possible, Berridge and Robinson argue, that in this process the CSs cause mesolimbic systems to attribute incentive salience to associated neural representations of their reward UCS (and the associated responses). The outcome is "cue-triggered 'wanting' of that reward. Manipulations f the dopamine and related mesolimbic circuits seems especially to produce this result. It might also be engendered in humans, however, by strong cognitive representations of reward which activate these circuits even when the CSs are not present.

Third is response reinforcement. Instrumental (operant) responses are strengthened as a result of their contingent relationship with reward UCSs. Conditioned reinforcers (the reward CSs provided in Pavlovian conditioning) can also act to strengthen novel instrumental behaviors. The temporal ordering of events reverses that found in the Pavlovian paradigm mentioned earlier in which the response occurs prior to the rewarding stimulus that strengthens or reinforces it. But in the conditioned incentive effects paradigm that Berridge proposes, the reward precedes the "wanting" response and may therefore be said to trigger it. These two forms of response conditioning, primary and secondary, are procedurally similar but are associated with different neural circuitry. "Mesolimbic incentive salience" is accorded the property of causing "wanting" for CSs and their UCS representations, and Berridge and Robinson (2003, p. 511) remark on the possibility that the influence of dopamine on response reinforcement "might largely reflect this contribution of incentive salience." They also argue that incentive salience cannot by itself mediate the response contingency in response reinforcement (presumably because it is an environmentally determined element in the three-term contingency). Such mediation requires additional psychological processes and their brain systems such as instrumental S-R habit learning and instrumental cognitive representations of act-outcome ("cognitive incentives").

Finally come cognitive incentives, defined by Berridge and Robinson as an entity that is known or imagined ("cognitive incentive representation"), expected to be pleasant ("hedonic expectation"), subjectively desired and intended to be obtained ("explicit cognitive representation of wanting"), and possibly also known to be obtainable through specific actions that cause its occurrence ("understanding of act-outcome causality"). In short, people explicitly expect at a cognitive level to like what they want and can attain by their own behavior. In order for cognitive incentives to be activated the individual must use memory of the hedonic value of a reward and generate cognitive expectancies of its hedonic reward in the future. "One essence of rational cognition is its inferential exploitation of lawful consistencies in the world and, typically, future value is best inferred from past value" (Berridge and Robinson, 2003, p. 512.) In addition, the individual must be able to call upon his or her understanding of what actions cause what outcomes, and select the appropriate action (that which will produce the best reward) from among several possibilities. The next stage is to identify the neural substrates for cognitive incentives that can be discriminated form those associated with other components of motivation.

The acquisition of cognitive incentives in the course of natural selection confers the capacity to develop goal-directed behavioral strategies over and above capabilities conferred by acquisition of associative responding. (See also Nesse and Berridge, 1997). This does not mean that cognitive incentive mechanisms replace the "liking" and "wanting" that compose more basic learning, each of which functions uniquely. Indeed, cognitive incentive expectations occur simultaneously with Pavlovian incentive salience ("wanting"), albeit at different levels and may be exposed by different experimental tests. They generally perform together to motivate behavior in the same direction, though their directions may diverge if, for instance, future values suddenly become different from past values through a change in physiological drive state. While cognitive incentive processes are relatively immune to manipulations of the mesolimbic dopamine systems that modify Pavlovian guided "wanting," they depend heavily on neocortical structures, including orbitofrontal and insular cortical regions.

The framework of exposition developed in earlier chapters is both strengthened by this account of the linkages among the sub-, super-, and personal levels of explanation, and in turn elucidates the incentive motivation framework put forward by Berridge and Robinson. Support is apparent from the confirmation by Berridge and Robinson's that the essential elements in a framework for explaining complex human behavior are those included in intentional behaviorism and super-personal cognitive psychology. Behavior is explicable, that is, in terms of the identification of evolutionarily consistent neuronal changes at the sub-personal level and contingent rewards at the super-personal level of an extensional behavioral science. Incentive motivation theory also suggests how the components of these systems may be linked at both the neurophysiological and conceptual levels, and hints at the role of evolutionary processes in linking each with the other by reiterating what is to be explained at the cognitive level, namely goal-directed processes that cannot be wholly accounted for by associational learning. Incentive motivation research can also be understood as a search for variables that account for the continuity of behavior, a quest that moves on from the consideration of associational linkages based on environmental influences on behavior to their neurological correlates, and from there to cognitive mechanisms. What is most interesting about this intellectual movement, however, is the use of concepts such as "liking" and "wanting" and the attribution of "incentive salience." For these can be easily understood as intentional terms

Table 12.1 Dennett's Evolutionary Creatures

Type of Creature	Nature of Selection
"Darwinian"	One phenotype among a variety is selected by the environment. The underlying genotype so favored multiplies.
"Skinnerian"	One operant response among several is selected by the environment through reinforcement. The "blindly"-behaving creature is more likely to emit the reinforced response next time similar circumstances arise.
"Popperian"	An intra-creature environment previews prospective responses and selects one. The first time the creature encounters the setting, it acts "insightfully".
"Gregorian"	The inner environment is enhanced by knowledge of the designed elements of the external environment. Knowledge of such tools increases the capacity to act intelligently by constructing "ever more subtle move-generators and move-testers" (Dennett 1995, p. 377).

that are ascribed at the personal level on the basis of the findings of extensional sciences operating at other levels. They appear not to have direct empirical availability but to be inferred from stimulus, response, and reward functions. The four items entering into the definition of cognitive incentives, for instance, are immediately evocative of Rosenberg's "L," the fundamental portrayal of intentional explanation. The transition from an intentional to a cognitive mode of explanation is, moreover, signaled by evolutionary considerations, the arrival on the scene of incentive salience. This is reminiscent of Dennett's (1995) types of evolutionary creature (Table 12.1) and, in particular, the transition from the "Skinnerian" to "Popperian" forms and, thereafter, to the "Gregorian."

By concentrating on objective understandings of "liking" and "wanting," Berridge and Robinson may be attempting to build a non-intentionalistic explanation of behavior in which these terms are so closely allied with their neurological substrates that the subjective level is not required. Even if this is so, the considerations raised in the course of earlier chapters are sufficient to reveal the a-ontological status of these intentional terms and the role of non-extensional explanation.

Conclusion

The recurrence of certain explanatory variables – the environment of behavioral consequences, the neurophysiology of responses, the evolution of behavior patterns – and of the relationships among them supports the framework of exposition advanced here. Both intentional behaviorism and super-personal cognitive psychology go beyond behaviorism in the sense that they leave it behind as *the* definitive philosophy of psychology; but they embrace and require behavior analysis, the study of operant and respondent behaviors as elements in a broader social science. It embraces intentional language and does so simply in order to make our explanations of complex human behavior more complete. It denies ontological status to this mode of expression but recognizes that it entails a different kind of explanation from that of an extensional behavioral science such as neurophysiology or behavior analysis. Nevertheless, it treats intentional phenomena as real in the sense that they are theoretically essential. It draws upon the philosophy of intention but selectively and critically, so that the independence of sub-, super- and personal levels of analysis is rigorously maintained, while both the intentional and contextual stances enter into explanation. It explores the biological correlates of choice and incorporates the possibility of sub-personal neurophysiological explanation of consumer behavior and of the relationship between evolutionary psychology and consumer choice; but it is neither limited to nor uncritical of the examples of these sciences that have been adduced to illustrate the possibility of a more theoretically comprehensive theory of consumption. It encompasses a variety of consumer behaviors, ranging from the mundane to the special to the out-of-control, that have not hitherto been discussed within the same framework of conceptualization and analysis.

We have arrived at an intriguing point in the development of a theory of consumer choice in the context of the marketing-oriented economy. A means has been proposed for the ascription of intentionalistic content in the explanation of behavior which is based on sound scientific reasoning: that of evolutionarily consistent neurological processes at the sub-personal level and that of consistent environment–behavior relationships at the super-personal level. The deficiencies of a purely descriptivist approach to consumer choice and of an extensional behavioral science of consumer choice have been exposed at the level of explanation (though they remain valid, indeed essential, approaches to the prediction and influence of consumer choice, suggest lines of explanation, and act as standpoints from which the prevailing cognitive orthodoxy can be uniquely critiqued). Moreover, it appears that the kinds of contextual psychology I have proposed can be said to exist already in behavioral economics, and that each contributes, along with extensional behavioral science, to the explication not only of the extreme consumer behaviors marked by compulsion and addiction but to that of everyday consumer choice.

References

Adolphs, R. 2003. Cognitive neuroscience of human social behavior, *Nature Reviews: Neuroscience*, 4, 165–78.

Ainslie, G. 1992. *Picoeconomics: The Strategic Interaction of Successive Motivational States within the Person*. Cambridge: Cambridge University Press.

Ainslie, G. 2001. *Breakdown of Will*. Cambridge: Cambridge University Press.

Ainslie, G. and Gault, B. 1997. Intention isn't indivisible. *Behavioral and Brain Sciences*, 20, 365–6.

Ainslie, G. and Monterosso, J. 2004. A marketplace in the brain? *Science*, 306, 421–3.

Alhadeff, D. A. 1982. *Microeconomics and Human Behavior*. Los Angeles, CA: University of California Press.

Anscombe, G. E. M. 1957. *Intention*. Oxford: Blackwell.

Aunger, R. 2002. *The Electric Meme: A New Theory of How We Think*. New York: Free Press.

Avital, E. and Jablonka, E. 2000. *Animal Traditions: Behavioural Inheritance in Evolution*. Cambridge: Cambridge University Press.

Bach, K. 1992. Review of George Ainslie, *Picoeconomics: The Strategic Interaction of Successive Motivational States Within the Person*, pp. 440. Cambridge University Press. http://userwww.sfsu.edu/~kbach/Ainsliereview.htm

Bagozzi, R. P. and Foxall, G. R. 1995. The factor structure and generalizability of the Kirton Adaption-Innovation Inventory, *European Journal of Personality*, 9, 185–206.

Bagozzi, R. P. and Foxall, G. R. 1996. Construct validation of a measure of adaptive-innovative cognitive styles in consumption. *International Journal of Research in Marketing*, 13, 201–13.

Bandura, Albert A. 1986. *Social Foundations of Thought and Action*. Englewood Cliffs, NJ: Prentice-Hall.

Barendregt, M. and van Hezewijk, R. 2005. Adaptive and genomic explanations of human behavior: might evolutionary psychology contribute to behavioral genomics? *Biology and Philosophy*, 20, 57–78.

Barkow, J. 1989. *Darwin, Sex, and Status: Biological Approaches to Mind and Culture*. Toronto: University of Toronto Press.

Barrett, L., Dunbar, R. and Lycett, J. 2002. *Human Evolutionary Psychology*. London: Palgrave.

Baum, W. 1973. The correlation based law of effect. *Journal of the Experimental Analysis of Behavior*, 20, 237–53.

Baum, W. M. 1974. On two types of deviation from the matching law. *Journal of the Experimental Analysis of Behavior*, 22, 231–42.

Baum, W. M. 1979. Matching, undermatching and overmatching in studies of choice, *Journal of the Experimental Analysis of Behavior*, 32, 269–81.

Baum, W. 2002. From molecular to molar: A paradigm shift in behavior analysis, *Journal of the Experimental Analysis of Behavior*, 78, 95–116.

Baum, W. 2004. Molar and molecular views of choice, *Behavioural Processes*, 66. 349–59.

Baum. W. M. and Nevin, J. A. 1981. Maximization theory: Some empirical problems. *Behavioral and Brain Sciences*, 389–90.

Baum, W. M. and Heath, J. L. 1992. Behavioral explanations and intentional explanations in psychology. *Am. Psych.* 47, 1312–17.

Bennett, M. R. and Hacker, P. M. S. 2003. *Philosophical Foundations of Neuroscience.* Oxford: Blackwell.

Berridge, K. C. 2000. Reward learning: Reinforcement, incentives, and expectations. In Medin, D. L. (ed.) *The psychology of learning and motivation,* 49, 223–78. San Diego: Academic Press.

Berridge, K. C. 2004. Motivation concepts in behavioral neuroscience. *Physiology and Behavior,* 81, 179–209.

Berridge, K. C. and Robinson, T. E. 1998. What is the role of dopamine in reward: hedonic impact, reward learning, or incentive salience? *Brain Research Reviews,* 28, 309–69.

Berridge, K. C. and Robinson, T. E. 2003. Parsing reward. *TRENDS in Neuroscience,* 26, 507–12.

Bindra, D. 1978. How adaptive behavior is produced: A perceptual–motivation alternative to response reinforcement. *Psychological Review,* 81, 199–213.

Blackmore, S. 1999. *The Meme Machine.* Oxford: Oxford University Press.

Blakemore, S-J., Winston, J. and Frith, U. 2004. Social cognitive neuroscience: where are we heading? *TENDS in Cognitive Neuroscience,* 8, 216–22.

Boden, M. 1972. *Purposive Explanation in Psychology.* Brighton: Harvester.

Bolles, R. C. 1972. Reinforcement, expectancy, and learning. *Psychological Review,* 79, 394–409.

Bouton, M. E. and Franselow, M. S. (eds) 1997. *Learning, motivation, and cognition: The functional behaviorism of Robert C. Bolles.* Washington, DC: American Psychological Association.

Bratman, M. E. 1987. *Intention, plans, and practical reason.* Cambridge, MA: Harvard University Press.

Brentano, F. 1874. *Psychology from an Empirical Standpoint.* Leipsig: Meiner.

Buller, D. J. and Hardcastle, V. G. 2000. Evolutionary psychology, meet developmental neurobiology: against promiscuous modularity, *Brain and Mind,* 1, 307–25.

Bunge, M. 1967. *Scientific Explanation.* Berlin: Springer Verlag.

Buss, D. M. 1995. Evolutionary psychology: a new paradigm for psychological science, *Psychological Inquiry,* 6, 1–30.

Buss, D. M. 2004. *Evolutionary Psychology: The New Science of the Mind.* Boston, MA: Pearson.

Buss, D. M. 2005. (ed.) *The Handbook of Evolutionary Psychology.* Hoboken, NJ: Wiley.

Camerer, C. F., Loewenstein, G. and Prelec, D. 2004. Neuroeconomics: why economics needs brains, *Scandinavian Journal of Economics,* 106, 555–79.

Cardinal, R. N., Parkinson, J. A., Hall, J. and Everitt, B. J. 2002. Emotion and motivation: the role of the amygdala, central striatum, and prefrontal cortex, *Neuroscience and Biobehavioral Reviews,* 26, 321–52.

Catania, A. C. 1992. *Learning.* Third edition. Englewood Cliffs, NJ: Prentice-Hall.

Catania, A. C., Matthews, B. A. and Shimoff, E. 1982. Instructed versus shaped human verbal behavior: interactions with nonverbal responding. *Journal of the Experimental Analysis of Behavior*, 38, 233–48.

Chisholm, R. 1957. *Perceiving: A Philosophical Study*. Ithaca, NY: Cornell University Press.

Cloninger, C. R. 1986. A unified biosocial theory of personality and its role in the development of anxiety states. *Psychiatric Development*, 3, 167–226.

Cloninger, C. R. 1987. A systematic method for clinical description and classification of personality variants. *Archives of General Psychology*, 44, 573–88.

Commission of Inquiry into Fetal Sentience 1996. *Human Sentience before Birth. [Rawlinson Report]*. London: HMSO.

Crawford, C. and Krebs, D. (eds) 1997. *Handbook of Evolutionary Psychology: Ideas, Issues and Applications*. Hillsdale, IL: Erlbaum.

Cummins, D. D. 1998. Social norms and other minds: The evolutionary roots of higher cognition. In Cummins, D. D. and Allen, C. A. (eds) *The Evolution of Mind*, pp. 30–50. New York: Oxford University Press.

Davidson, D. 1980. *Essays on Actions and Events*. Oxford: Clarendon Press.

Davies, M. 2000. Persons and their underpinning, *Philosophical Explorations*, 3, 42–60.

Davies, J., Foxall, G. R. and Pallister, J. G. 2002. Beyond the intention–behaviour mythology: an integrated model of recycling. *Marketing Theory*, 2, 29–113.

Davison, M. and McCarthy, D. (eds) 1988. *The matching law: A research review*. Hillsdale, NJ: Erlbaum.

Dawkins, R. 1976. *The Selfish Gene*. Oxford: Oxford University Press.

Dawkins, R. 1982. *The Extended Phenotype: The Long Reach of the Gene*. Oxford: Oxford University Press.

Dawkins, R. 1986. *The Selfish Gene*. Second edition. Oxford: Oxford University Press.

Dawkins, R. 1988. Replicators, consequences, and displacement activities. In Catania, A. C. and Harnad, S. (eds) *Selection of Behavior*. NY: Cambridge University Press.

Dawkins, R. 2006. Kin selection and reciprocal altruism. In Macdonald, D. W. (ed.) *The Encyclopedia of Mammals*. New edition. Oxford: Oxford University Press.

de Villiers, P. A. and Herrnstein, R. J. 1976. Toward a law of response strength, *Psychological Bulletin*, 83, 1131–53.

Dennett, D. C. 1969. *Content and consciousness*. London: Routledge.

Dennett, D. C. 1978. *Brainstorms*. Montgomery, VT: Bradford.

Dennett, D. C. 1981. Three kinds of intentional psychology. In Healy, R. (ed.) *Reduction, time and reality*. Cambridge: Cambridge University Press. (Reproduced in Dennett, 1987a).

Dennett, D. C. 1982. How to study human consciousness empirically, or nothing comes to mind. *Synthese*, 59, 159–80.

Dennett, D. C. 1983. Intentional systems in cognitive ethology: The "Panglossian paradigm" defended. *The Behavioral and Brain Sciences*, 6, 343–90.

Dennett, D. C. 1987. *The intentional stance*. Cambridge, MA: MIT Press.

Dennett, D. C. 1991a. Real patterns. *Journal of Psychology*, 88, 27–51.

Dennett, D. C. 1991b. *Consciousness Explained*. New York: Little, Brown and Co.

Dennett, D. C. 1994. Dennett, Daniel C. In Guttenplan, S. (ed.) *A companion to the philosophy of mind*, pp. 236–44. Oxford: Blackwell.

Dennett, D. C. 1995. *Darwin's Dangerous Idea: Evolution and the Meanings of Life*. New York: Simon and Shuster.

Dennett, D. C. 1996. *Kinds of Minds: Toward an Understanding of Consciousness*. London: Weidenfeld and Nicolson.

Dennett, D. C. 1998. *Brainchildren: Essays on Designing Minds*. Cambridge, MA: MIT Press.

Dennett, D. C. 2003. *Freedom Evolves*. London: Allen Lane.

Dennett, D. C. and Haugeland, J. C. 1987. Intentionality. In Gregory, R. L. (ed.) *The Oxford Companion to the Mind*, pp. 383–6. Oxford: Oxford University Press.

Depue, R. A. and Collins, P. F. 1999. Neurobiology of the structure of personality: Dopamine, facilitation of incentive motivation, and extraversion. *Behavioral and Brain Sciences*, 22, 491–569.

Derbyshire, S. W. G. 1999. Locating the beginnings of pain. *Bioethics*, 13, 1–17.

Derbyshire, S. W. G. 2003. Fetal "pain" – A look at the evidence. *APS* [American Pain Society] *Bulletin*, 13, 4.

Derbyshire, S. W. G. 2006. Can fetuses feel pain? *British Medical Journal*, 332, 909–12.

Derbyshire, S. W. G. and Furedi, A. 1996. Fetal pain is a misnomer. *British Medical Journal*, 313, 795.

de Villiers, Peter A. and Herrnstein, R. J. 1976. Toward a law of response strength. *Psychological Bulletin*, 83(6), 1131–53.

Dickinson, A. 1997. Bolles's psychological syllogism. In Bouton, M. E. and Franselow, M. S. (eds) (1997). *Learning, motivation, and cognition: The functional behaviorism of Robert C. Bolles*, pp. 345–67. Washington, DC: American Psychological Association.

Dilman, I. 1988. *Mind, Brain and Behaviour: Discussions of B. F. Skinner and J. R. Searle*. London: Routledge.

Distin, K. 2005. *The Selfish Meme*. Cambridge: Cambridge University Press.

Donahoe, J. W., Palmer, D. C. and Burgos, J. E. 1997. The S-R issue: Its status in behavior analysis and in Donahoe and Palmer's *Learning and complex behavior*. *Journal of the Experimental Analysis of Behavior*, 67, 193–211.

Downes, S. M. 2005. Integrating the multiple causes of human behavior, *Biology and Philosophy*, 20, 177–90.

Duchaine, B., Cosmides, L. and Tooby, J. 2001. Evolutionary psychology and the brain, *Current Opinion in Neurobiology*, 11, 225–30.

Dunbar, R. I. M. 2004. *The Human Story*. London: Faber and Faber.

Dunbar, R. and Barrett, l. 2007. *Oxford Handbook of Evolutionary Psychology*. Oxford: Oxford University Press.

Ebstein, R. P., Novick, O., Umansky, R., Priel, B., Osher, Y., Blaine, D. Bennett, E. R., Nemenove, L., Katz, M. and Belmaker, R. H. 1997. Dopamine D4 receptor (D4DR) exon III polymorphism associated with the human personality trait of novelty seeking, *Nature Genetics*, 12, 78–80.

Ehrenberg, A. S. C. 1972/1988. *Repeat Buying*. North Holland, Amsterdam. (Reprinted 1988, London: Griffin).

Elton, M. 2000. Consciousness: only at the personal level. *Philosophical Explorations*, 3, 25–40.

Elton, M. 2003. *Daniel Dennett: Reconciling Science and Our Self-Conception.* Cambridge: Polity.

Fagerstrøm, A., Foxall, G. R. and Arntzen, E. 2006. Implications of motivating operations for the functional analysis of consumer behavior. Submitted paper.

Fantino, E. 1995. The future is uncertain: Eat dessert first. *Behavioral and Brain Sciences*, 18, 125–6.

Feyerabend, P. 1975. *Against method.* London: NLB.

Flanagan, O. 1991. *The Science of the Mind.* 2nd edition. Cambridge, MA: MIT Press.

Flor, H., Knost, B. and Birbaumer, N. 2002 The role of operant conditioning in chronic pain: an experimental investigation, *Pain*, 95, 111–18.

Faber, M. and Proops, L. 1991. Evolution in biology, physics and economics: a conceptual analysis. In Saviotti, P. and Metcalfe, J. S. (eds) *Evolutionary Theories of Economic and Technological Change.* Chur, Switzerland: Harwood.

Foxall, G. R. 1983. *Consumer Choice.* London: Macmillan; New York: St. Martin's Press.

Foxall, G. R. 1987. Radical behaviorism and consumer research, *International Journal of Research in Marketing*, 4, 111–29.

Foxall, G. R. 1990/2004. *Consumer Psychology in Behavioral Perspective.* London and New York: Routledge/Beard Books, Fredericks, MD.

Foxall, G. R. 1992a. The Behavioral Perspective Model of purchase and consumption: from consumer theory to marketing practice, *Journal of the Academy of Marketing Science*, 20, 189–98. (Chapter 10 in this volume).

Foxall, G. R. 1992b. The consumer situation: an integrated model for research in marketing, *Journal of Marketing Management*, 8, 383–404. (Chapter 11 in this volume).

Foxall, G. R. 1992c. A behaviorist perspective on purchase and consumption, *European Advances in Consumer Research*, 1, 501–6.

Foxall, G. R. 1993a. Situated consumer behavior: a behavioral interpretation of purchase and Consumption. In Costa, J. A. and Belk, R. W. (eds) *Research in Consumer Behavior*, 5, 113–52. Greenwich, CT.: JAI Press. (Chapter 9 in this volume).

Foxall, G. R. 1993b. *The Behavioral Perspective Model of Purchase and Consumption: Refinement, Extension and Evaluation*, Working Paper, Research Centre for Consumer Behavior, University of Birmingham. (See Chapter 13 in this volume).

Foxall, G. R. 1994a. Consumer initiators: adaptors and innovators. *British Journal of Management*, 5, S3–S12.

Foxall, G. R. 1994b. Behavior analysis and consumer psychology. *Journal of Economic Psychology*, 15, 1994, 5–91.

Foxall, G. R. 1994c. Consumer choice as an evolutionary process: an operant interpretation of adopter categories. *Advances in Consumer Research*, 21, 1994, 312–17.

Foxall G. R. 1995a. Cognitive styles of consumer initiators. *Technovation*, 15, 269–88.

Foxall, G. R. 1995b. Science and interpretation in consumer research: a radical behaviourist perspective. *European Journal of Marketing*, 29(9), 3–99.

Foxall, G. R. 1996. *Consumers in Context: The BPM Research Program.* London and New York: Routledge.

Foxall, G. R. 1997a. Explaining consumer behaviour: from social cognition to environmental control. In Cooper, C. L. and Robertson, I. T. (eds) *International review of industrial and organizational psychology*, 12, 229–87. Chichester: Wiley.

Foxall, G. R. 1997b. *Marketing psychology: The paradigm in the wings*. London: Macmillan.

Foxall, G. R. 1997c. Affective responses to consumer situations. *International Review of Retail, Distribution and Consumer Research*, 7, 191–225.

Foxall, G. R. 1998. Radical behaviorist interpretation: Generating and Evaluating an account of consumer behavior. *The Behavior Analyst*, 21, 321–54.

Foxall, G. R. 1999. The contextual stance. *Philosophical Psychology*, 12, 25–46.

Foxall, G. R. 2002a. *Consumer Behavior Analysis: Critical Perspectives*. London and New York: Routledge.

Foxall, G. R. 2002b. Marketing's attitude problem – and how to solve it. *Journal of Customer Behaviour*, 1, 19–48.

Foxall G. R. 2003. Consumer decision making: process, level and style. In Baker, M. J. (ed.) *The Marketing Book*. Fifth edition. London: Butterworth-Heinemann.

Foxall, G. R. 2004. *Context and Cognition: Interpreting Complex Behavior*. Reno, NV: Context Press.

Foxall, G. R. 2005. *Understanding Consumer Choice*. New York: Palgrave Macmillan.

Foxall, G. R. 2006. Intentional behaviorism. [submitted paper]

Foxall, G. R. 2008. *Consumer Innovativeness: A Cognitive-Behavioral Synthesis*. London and New York: Palgrave Macmillan.

Foxall, G. R. in preparation. Biological bases of consumer innovation.

Foxall, G. R. and Bhate, S. 1991. Cognitive style, personal involvement and situation as determinants of computer use. *Technovation*, 11, 183–99.

Foxall, G. R and Bhate, S. 1993a. Cognitive styles and personal involvement of market initiators for "healthy" food brands: Implications for adoption theory. *Journal of Economic Psychology*, 14, 33–56.

Foxall, G. R. and Bhate, S. 1993b. Cognitive style and use-innovativeness for applications software in home computing: Implications for new product strategy. *Technovation*, 13, 311–25.

Foxall, G. R. and Bhate, S. 1999. Computer use-innovativeness: cognition and context. *International Journal of Technology Management*, 17, 157–72.

Foxall, G. R. and Goldsmith, R. E. 1988. Personality and consumer research: Another look. *Journal of the Market Research Society*, 30, 111–25.

Foxall, G. R. and Greenley, G. E. 1998. The affective structure of consumer situations. *Environment and Behavior*, 30, 781–98.

Foxall, G. R. and Greenley, G. E. 1999. Consumers' emotional responses to service environments, *Journal of Business Research*, 46, 149–58.

Foxall, G. R. and Greenley, G. E. 2000. Predicting and explaining responses to consumer environments: An empirical test and theoretical extension of the Behavioural Perspective Model. *The Service Industries Journal*, 20, 39–63.

Foxall, G. and Haskins, C. G. 1986. Cognitive style and consumer innovativeness: An empirical test of Kirton's adaptation-innovation theory in the context of food purchasing. *European Journal of Marketing*, 20, 63–80.

Foxall, G. R. and Haskins, C. G. 1987. Cognitive style and discontinuous consumption: The case of "healthy eating". *Food Marketing*, 3(2), 19–35.

Foxall, G. R. and James, V. K. 2001. Behavior analysis of consumer brand choice: a preliminary analysis. *European Journal of Behavior Analysis*, 2, 209–20.

Foxall, G. R. and James, V. 2003. The behavioral ecology of brand choice: how and what do consumers maximize? *Psychology and Marketing*, 20, 811–36.

Foxall, G. R. and Pallister, J. G. 1998. Measuring purchase decision involvement for financial services: comparison of the Zaichkowsky and Mittal scales. *International Journal of Bank Marketing*, 16, 180–94.

Foxall, G. R. and Schrezenmaier, T. C. 2003. The behavioral economics of consumer brand choice: Establishing a methodology. *Journal of Economic Psychology*, 23, 675–95.

Foxall, G. R. and Szmigin, I. 1999. Adaption-innovation and domain-specific innovativeness. *Psychological Reports*, 84, 1029.

Foxall, G. R. and Yani-de-Soriano, M. Y. 2005. Situational influences on consumers' attitudes and behavior. *Journal of Business Research*, 58, 518–25.

Foxall, G. R., Goldsmith, R. E. and Brown, S. 1998. *Consumer Psychology for Marketing*. London and New York: Thomson.

Foxall, G. R., Leek, S. and Maddock, S. 1998. Cognitive Antecedents of Consumers' Willingness to Purchase Fish Rich in Polyunsaturated Fatty Acids (PUFA). *Appetite*, 31, 391–402.

Foxall, G. R., Oliveira-Castro, J. M. and Schrezenmaier, T. C. 2004. The behavioral economics of consumer brand choice: Patterns of reinforcement and utility maximization. *Behavioural Processes*, 65, 235–60.

Foxall, G. R., James, V. K., Chang, S. W. and Oliveira-Castro, J. M. 2006. What is a brand? [Submitted paper]

Foxall, G. R., Oliveira-Castro, J. M., James, V. K., Yani-de-Soriano, M. M. and Sigurdsson, V. 2006. Consumer Behavior Analysis and Social Marketing: The Case of Environmental Conservation, *Behavior and Social Issues*, 15, 1–24.

Foxall, G. R., Oliveira-Castro, J. M., James, V. K. and Schrezenmaier, T. C. 2007. *Brand Choice in Behavioral Perspective*. London and New York: Palgrave Macmillan.

Friedman, M. 1953. *Essays in Positive Economics*. Chicago: University of Chicago Press.

Gardner, S. 2000. Psychoanalysis and the personal/sub-personal distinction, *Philosophical Explorations*, 3, 96–119.

Geertz, C. 1973. *The Interpretation of Cultures*. New York: Basic Books.

Glimcher, P. W. 2004. *Decisions, Uncertainty, and the Brain: The Science of Neuroeconomics*. Cambridge, MA: MIT Press.

Glimcher, P.W. and Rustichini, A. 2004. Neuroeconomics: The consilience of brain and decision, *Science*, 306, 447–52.

Glover, F. V. and Fisk, N. M. 1999. Fetal pain: implications for research and practice. *British Journal of Obstetrics and Gynaecology*, 106, 881–6.

Goldsmith, R. E. and Foxall, G. R. 2003. The measurement of innovativeness. In Shavinina, L. (ed.) *The International Handbook of Innovation*, pp. 321–30. Oxford: Pergamon.

Gray, J. A. 1973. Causal theories of personality and how to test them. In Royce, J. R. (ed.) *Multivariate Analysis and Psychological Theory*. New York: Academic Press.

Green, L. and Freed, D. E. 1993. The substitutability of reinforcers, *Journal of the Experimental Analysis of Behavior*, 60, 141–58.

Greenfield, S. 2001. *The Secret Life of the Brain*. London: Penguin Books.

Gunderson, K. 1972. Content and consciousness and the mind-body problem. *Journal of Philosophy*, 69, 591–604.

Gurtman, M. B. 1992. Trust, distrust, and interpersonal problems: A circumplex analysis. *Journal of Personality and Social Psychology*, 62, 989–1002.

Hamilton, W. D. 1964a. The genetical evolution of social behavior: I. *Journal of Theoretical Biology*, 7, 1–16.

Hamilton, W. D. 1964b. The genetical evolution of social behavior: II. *Journal of Theoretical Biology*, 7, 17–52.

Hardcastle, V. G. (ed.) 1999 *Where Biology Meets Psychology: Philosophical Essays*. Cambridge, MA: MIT Press.

Hayes, S. C. and Cone, J. D. 1977. Reducing residential electrical energy use: Payments, information, and feedback. *Journal of Applied Behavior Analysis*, 10, 425–35.

Hayes, S. C. (ed.) 1989. *Rule-Governed Behavior: Cognition, Contingencies, and Instructional Control*. New York: Plenum.

Hayes, S. C., Zettle, R. D. and Rosenfarb, I. 1989. Rule-following. In Hayes, S. C. (ed.) *Rule-governed behavior: Cognition, contingencies, and instructional control*, pp. 191–220. New York: Plenum.

Herrnstein, R. J. 1961. Relative and absolute strength of response as a function of frequency of reinforcement, *J. Exp. Anal. Behav.* 4, 267–72.

Herrnstein, R. J. 1970. On the law of effect, *Journal of the Experimental Analysis of Behavior*, 13, 243–66.

Herrnstein, R. J. 1979. Derivatives of matching, *Psychological Review*, 86, 486–95.

Herrnstein, R. J. 1981. Self-control as response strength. In Bradshaw, C. M., Szabadi, E. and Lowe, C. F. (eds) *Recent Developments in the Quantification of Steady-State Operant Behavior*, pp. 3–20. Amsterdam: Elsevier/North Holland Biomedical Press.

Herrnstein, R. J. 1997. *The Matching Law: Papers in Psychology and Economics*. (Edited by H. Rachlin and D. I. Laibson). New York: Russell Sage Foundation; Cambridge, MA: Harvard University Press.

Herrnstein, R. J. and Prelec, D. 1991. Melioration: A theory of distributed choice. *Journal of Economic Perspectives*, 5, 137–56.

Herrnstein, R. J. and Prelec, D. 1992. A theory of addiction. In Lowenstein, G. and Elster, J. (eds) *Choice over Time*, pp. 331–61. New York: Russell Sage Press.

Herrnstein, R. J. and Vaughan, W. 1980. Melioration and behavioral allocation. In Staddon, J. E. R. (ed.) *Limits to Action: The Allocation of Individual Behavior*, pp. 143–76. New York: Academic Press.

Heyes, C. 2000. Evolutionary psychology in the round. In Heyes, C. and Huber, L. (eds) *The Evolution of Cognition*, pp. 3–22. Cambridge, MA: MIT Press.

Heyes, C. M. 2001. Causes and consequences of imitation, *TRENDS in Cognitive Sciences*, 5, 253–61.

Heyes, C. M. 2003. Four routes of cognitive evolution *Psychological Review*, 110, 713–27.

Heyes, C. M., Bird, G., Johnson, H. and Haggard, P. 2005. Experience modulates automatic imitation, *Cognitive Brain Research*, 22, 233–40.

Heyman, G. M. 1996. Elasticity of demand for alcohol in humans and rats. In Leonard Green and John H. Kagel (eds) *Advances in Behavioral Economics. Vol 3. Substance Use and Abuse*, pp. 107–32. Norwood, NJ: Ablex.

Hinde, R. A. 1970. *Animal Behaviour: A Synthesis of Ethology and Comparative Psychology*. London: McGraw-Hill.

Hirschman, E. C. 1980. Innovativeness, novelty-seeking, and consumer creativity. *Journal of Consumer Research, 7*, 283–95.

Horne, P. J. and Lowe, F. C. 1993. Determinants of human performance on concurrent schedules. *Journal of the Experimental Analysis of Behavior, 59*, 29–60.

Hornsby, J. 2000. Personal and sub-personal: a defence of Dennett's early distinction, *Philosophical Explorations, 3*, 6–24.

Hursh S. R. 1978. The economics of daily consumption controlling food- and water-reinforced responding. *Journal of the Experimental Analysis of Behavior, 29*, 475–91.

Jablonka, E. and Lamb, M. J. 2006. *Evolution in Four Dimensions: Genetic, Epigenetic, Behavioral, and Symbolic Variations in the History of Life*. Cambridge, MA: MIT Press.

Janicki, M. G. and Krebs, D. L. 1998. Evolutionary approaches to culture. In Crawford, C. and Krebs, D. L. (eds) *Handbook of Evolutionary Psychology: Ideas, Issues, and Applications*, pp. 163–207. Mahawa, NJ: Lawrence Erlbaum.

Juarrero, A. 1999. *Dynamics in Action: Intentional Behavior as a Complex System*. Cambridge, MA: MIT Press.

Kagan, J. 2006. *An Argument for Mind*. New Haven: Yale University Press.

Kagel, J. H. 1988. Economics according to the rats (and pigeons too): what have we learned and what can we hope to learn? In Roth, A. E. (ed.) *Laboratory Experimentation in Economics: Six Points of View*, pp. 155–92. Cambridge: Cambridge University Press.

Kagel, J. H., Battalio, R. C. and Green, L. 1995. *Economic Choice Theory: An Experimental Analysis of Animal Behavior*. Cambridge: Cambridge University Press.

Kane, R. 1995. Patterns, Acts and Self-control: Rachlin's Theory. *Behavioral and Brain Sciences, 18*, 131–2.

Katona, G. 1975. *Behavioral Economics*. New York: Elsevier Scientific.

Keltikangas-Järvinen, L., Räikkönen, K., Ekelund, J. and Peltonen, L. 2004. Nature and nurture in novelty seeking, *Molecular Psychiatry, 9*, 308–11.

Kendrick, D. T., Sadalla, E. K. and O'Keefe, R. C. 1998. Evolutionary cognitive psychology: The missing heart of modern cognitive science. In Crawford, C. and Krebs, D. L. (eds) *Handbook of Evolutionary Psychology: Ideas, Issues, and Applications*, pp. 485–514. Mahawa, NJ: Lawrence Erlbaum.

Kirton, M. J. 1976. Adaptors and innovators: A description and measure. *Journal of Applied Psychology, 61*, 622–9.

Kirton, M. J. 2006. *Adaption-Innovation: In the Context of Diversity and Change*. London: Routledge.

Kreek, M. J., Nielsen, D. A., Butelman, E. R. and LaForge, K. S. 2005. Genetic influences on impulsivity, risk taking, stress responsivity and vulnerability to drug abuse and addiction, *Nature Neuroscience, 8*, 1450–7.

Lee, V. L. 1988. *Beyond behaviorism*. London: Erlbaum.

Leek, S., Maddock, S. and Foxall, G. R. 2000. Situational determinants of fish consumption, *British Food Journal, 102*, 18–39.

Lindqvist, A. 1981. *Household Saving – Behavioral Measurement of Household Saving Behavior.* Doctoral thesis. Stockholm: Stockholm School of Economics.

Lloyd, E. A. 1999. Evolutionary psychology: the burdens of proof, *Biology and Philosophy*, 14, 211–33.

Mach, E. 1893/1974. *The Science of Mechanics: A Critical and Historical Account of its Development.* 6th edn., Trans. T. J. McCormack. LaSalle, IL: Open Court.

Mach, E. 1896/1959. *The Analysis of Sensations: And the Relation of the Physical to the Psychical*, Trans. C. M. Williams. New York: Dover.

Mach, E. 1905/1976. *Knowledge and Error: Sketches on the Psychology of Enquiry*, Trans. T. J. McCormack and P. Foulkes. Boston, MA: Reidel.

Malcolm, N. 1977. Behaviorism as a philosophy of psychology. In Malcolm, N. *Thought and Knowledge*, pp. 85–103. Ithaca, NY: Cornell University Press. First published in T. W. Wann (ed.) (1964). *Behaviorism and Phenomenology: Contrasting Bases for Modern Psychology*, pp. 141–62. Chicago: University of Chicago Press.

McClure, S. M., Laibson, D. I., Loewenstein, G. and Cohen, J. D. 2004. Separate neural systems value immediate and delayed monetary rewards. *Science*, 306, October 15, 503–7.

McClure, S. M., Li, J., Tomlin, D., Cypert, K. S., Montague, L. M. and Montague, P. R. 2004. Neural correlates of behavioural performance for culturally familiar drinks, *Neuron*, 44, 379–87.

McCullagh, P. 1997. Do fetuses feel pain? *British Medical Journal*, 314, 312.

McDowell, J. 1994. *Mind and World.* Cambridge, MA: Harvard University Press.

McGinn, C. 1989a. *Mental Content.* Oxford: Blackwell.

McGinn, C. 1989b. Can we solve the mind-body problem? *Mind*, 98, 349–66.

McGinn, C. 1991. *The Problem of Consciousness.* Oxford: Blackwell.

Mehrabian, A. and Russell, J. A. 1974. *An Approach to Environmental Psychology.* Cambridge, MA: MIT Press.

Michael, J. 1982. Distinguishing between discriminative and motivational functions of stimuli. *Journal of the Experimental Analysis of Behavior*, 37, 149–55.

Michael, J. 1993. Establishing operations. *The Behavior Analyst*, 16, 191–206.

Midgley, D. F. 1977. *Innovation and New Product Marketing.* London: Croom Helm.

Midgley, D. F. and Dowling, G. R. 1978. Innovativeness: the concept and its measurement, *Journal of Consumer Research*, 4, 228–38.

Milgram, S. 1974. *Obedience to Authority.*

Moore, J. 1999. The basic principles of behaviorism. In Thyler, B. (ed.) *The philosophical legacy of behaviorism*, pp. 41–68. Dordrecht: Kluwer Academic Publishers.

Nesse, R. M. and Berridge, K. C. 1997. Psychoactive drug use in evolutionary perspective, *Science*, 278, 63–6.

Nestler, E. J. 2000. Genes and addiction. *Nature Genetics*, 26, 277–81.

Ochsner, K. N. 2004. *Current Opinion in Neurobiology*, 14, 254–8.

Oliveira-Castro, J. M., Ferreira, D. C. S., Foxall, G. R. and Schrezenmaier, T. C. 2005. Dynamics of repeat buying for packaged food products, *Journal of Marketing Management*, 21, 37–61.

Oliveira-Castro, J. M., Foxall, G. R. and Schrezenmaier, T. C. 2005. Patterns of consumer response to retail price differentials. *Service Industries Journal*, 25, 309–27.

Oliveira-Castro, J. M., Foxall, G. R. and Schrezenmaier, T. C. 2006. Consumer brand choice: individual and group analyses of demand elasticity. *Journal of the Experimental Analysis of Behavior*, 85, 147–66.

Ono, K. 1994 'Verbal control of superstitious behavior: superstitions as false rules'. In Hayes, S. C., Hayes, L. J., Sato, M. and Ono, K. (eds) *Behavior Analysis of Language and Cognition*, pp. 181–96. Reno, NV.: Context Press.

Pallister, J. G. and Foxall, G. R. 1998. Psychometric properties of the Hurt-Joseph-Cook scales for the measurement of innovativeness. *Technovation*, 18, 1998.

Pallister, J. G., Foxall, G. R. and Wang, H-C., in press. Consumer Innovativeness and Product Involvement as Determinants of Purchases of Financial Services, *Technovation*.

Pinker, S. 2002. *The Blank Slate: The Modern Denial of Human Nature*. London: Penguin Books.

Quine, W. V. O. 1960. *Word and Object*. Cambridge, MA: MIT Press.

Rachlin, H. 1989. *Judgment, Decision, and Choice: A Cognitive/behavioral Synthesis*. San Francisco, CA: Freeman.

Rachlin, H. 1994. *Behavior and Mind: The Roots of Modern Psychology*. New York: Oxford University Press.

Rachlin, H. 1995. Self-control: Beyond commitment. *Behavioral and Brain Sciences*, 18, 109–59.

Rachlin, H. 1997. Author's response to Ainslie and Gault. *Behavioral and Brain Sciences*, 20, 367–8.

Rachlin, H. 2000a. *The Science of Self Control*. Cambridge, MA: Harvard University Press.

Rachlin, H. 2000b. Teleological behaviorism. In O'Donohue, W. and Kitchener, R. (eds) *Handbook of behaviorism*, pp. 195–215. San Diego: Academic Press.

Rachlin, R., Battalio, R. C., Kagel, J. H. and Green, L. 1981. Maximization theory in behavioral psychology. *Behavioral and Brain Sciences*, 4, 371–417.

Reber, A. S. 1985. *The Penguin Dictionary of Psychology*. London: Penguin Books.

Rey, G. 1993. Sensational sentences. In Davies, M. and Humphreys, G. (ed.) *Consciousness*. Oxford: Blackwell.

Ridley, M. 1999. *Genome: The Autobiography of a Species in 23 Chapters*. London: Fourth Estate.

Robinson, T. E. and Berridge, K. C. 2003. Addiction. *Annual Review of Psychology*, 54, 25–53.

Rogers, E. M. 2003. *Diffusion of Innovations*. Fifth edition. New York: Free Press.

Romero, S., Foxall, G. R., Schrezenmaier, T. C. and Oliveira-Castro, J. 2006. Deviations from matching in consumer choice. *European Journal of Behavior Analysis*, 7, 15–39.

Rosenberg, A. 1988. *Philosophy of Social Science*. Oxford: Clarendon Press.

Rosenberg, A. 2005. Lessons from biology for philosophy of the human sciences, *Philosophy of the Social Sciences*, 35, 3–19.

Ross, D. 2005. *Economic Theory and Cognitive Science: Microexplanation*. Cambridge, MA: MIT Press.

Ross, D., Spurrett, D. and Vuchinich, R. 2005. *The Behavioral Economics and Neuroeconomics of Disordered Gambling: A Policy-Focused Survey of Research*. Cape Town: University of Cape Town.

Ryle, G. 1949. *The Concept of Mind*. London: Hutchinson.

Saad, G. and Gill, T. 2000. Applications of evolutionary psychology in marketing. *Psychology and Marketing*, 17, 1005–34.

Saad, G. and Gill, T. 2003. An evolutionary psychology perspective on gift giving among young adults. *Psychology and Marketing*, 20, 765–84.

Saunders, P. J. 1997. We should give them the benefit of the doubt. *British Medical Journal*, 312, 314.

Schnaitter, R. 1999. Some criticisms of behaviorism. In Thyer, B. A. (ed.) *The Philosophical Legacy of Behaviorism*, pp. 209–49. Dordrecht: Kluwer.

Searle, J. 1983. *Intentionality: An Essay in the Philosophy of Mind*. Cambridge: Cambridge University Press.

Searle, J. 2001. *Rationality in Action*. Cambridge, MA: The MIT Press.

Searle, J. R. 2004. *Mind: A Brief Introduction*. Oxford: Oxford University Press.

Shapiro, L. A. 1999. Presence of mind. In Hardcastle, V. G. (ed.) *Where Biology Meets Psychology: Philosophical Essays*, pp. 83–98. Cambridge, MA: MIT Press.

Sidman, M. 1994. *Equivalence Relations and Behavior: A Research Story*. Boston, MA: Authors Cooperative.

Simon, H. 1959. Theories of decision making in economics and behavioral science, *American Economic Review*, 49, 223–83.

Simon, H. 1979. *Models of Thought*, Volumes 1 and 2. New Haven, CT: Yale University Press.

Simonton, D. K. 2003. Human creativity: Two Darwinian analyses. In Reader, S. M. and Laland, K. N. (eds) *Animal Innovation*, pp. 309–25. Oxford: Oxford University Press.

Skinner, B. F. 1938. *The Behavior of Organisms*. New York: Century.

Skinner, B. F. 1945. The operational analysis of psychological terms. *Psychological Review*, 52, 270–7.

Skinner, B. F. 1953. *Science and Human Behavior*. New York: Macmillan.

Skinner, B. F. 1957. *Verbal Behavior*. New York: Appleton-Century-Crofts.

Skinner, B. F. 1974. *About Behaviorism*. New York: Knopf.

Skinner, B. F. 1981. Selection by consequences, *Science*, 213, 31 July, 501–4.

Skinner, B. F. 1988a. Reply to Schnaitter. In Catania, A. C. and Harnad, S. (eds) *The selection of behavior. The operant behaviorism of B. F. Skinner: Comments and consequences*, p. 354. New York: Cambridge University Press.

Skinner, B. F. 1988b. Reply to Mackenzie. In Catania, A. C. and Harnad, S. (eds) *The selection of behavior. The operant behaviorism of B. F. Skinner: Comments and consequences*, pp. 113–14. New York: Cambridge University Press.

Skinner, B. F. 1988c. Reply to Stalker and Ziff. In Catania, A. C. and Harnad, S. (eds) *The selection of behavior. The operant behaviorism of B. F. Skinner: Comments and consequences*, pp. 207–8. New York: Cambridge University Press.

Skinner, B. F. 1988d. Reply to Zuriff. In Catania, A. C. and Harnad, S. (eds) *The selection of behavior. The operant behaviorism of B. F. Skinner: Comments and consequences*, p. 217. New York: Cambridge University Press.

Smith, L. D. 1986. *Behaviorism and logical positivism: A reassessment of the alliance*. Stanford, CA: Stanford University Press.

Smith, T. L. 1994. *Behavior and Its Causes: Philosophical Foundations of Operant Psychology*. Dordrecht: Kluwer.

Sober, E. and Wilson, D. S. 1998. *Unto Others: The Evolution and Psychology of Unselfish Behavior*. Cambridge, MA: Harvard University Press.

Staddon, J. E. R. 1973. On the notion of cause with applications to behaviorism. *Behaviorism*, 1, 25–64.

Soriano, M. Y. and Foxall, G. R. 2001. Validation of a Spanish translation of Mehrabian and Russell's emotional scales, *Journal of Consumer Behaviour*, 2, 23–36.

Soriano, M. Y. and Foxall, G. R. 2002. Emotional responses to consumers' environments: An empirical examination of the Behavioural Perspective Model in a Latin American context. *Journal of Consumer Behaviour*, 2, 138–54.

Strawson, G. 1994. *Mental Reality*. Cambridge, MA: MIT Press.

Szmigin, I. and Foxall, G. 1998. Three forms of innovation resistance: The case of retail payment methods. *Technovation*, 18, 459–68.

Szmigin, I. and Foxall, G. R. 1999. Styles of cashless consumption. *International Review of Retail, Distribution and Consumer Research*, 9, 349–65.

Tapper, K. 2005. Motivating operations in appetite research, *Appetite*, 45, 93–107.

Taylor, C. 1964. *The Explanation of Behaviour*. London: Routledge and Kegan Paul.

Toates, F. 1986. *Motivational Systems*. Cambridge: Cambridge University Press.

Toates, F. 2005. Evolutionary psychology: towards a more integrative model, *Biology and Philosophy*, 20, 305–28.

Tooby, J. and Cosmides, L. 1992. The psychological foundations of culture. In Barkow, J. H., Cosmides, L. and Tooby, J. (eds) *The Adapted Mind: Evolutionary Psychology and the Generation of Culture*, pp. 19–136. New York: Oxford University Press.

Uttal, W. R. 2001. *The New Phrenology: The Limits of Localizing Cognitive Processes in the Brain*. Cambridge, MA: MIT Press.

Van der Molen, P. P. 1994. Adaption-innovation and changes in social structure: On the anatomy of catastrophe. In Kirton, M. J. (ed.) *Adaptors and Innovators: Styles of Creativity*. London: Croom Helm.

Van Parijs, P. 1981. *Evolutionary Explanation in the Social Sciences: An Emerging Paradigm*. Totowa, NJ: Rowman and Littlefield.

Virués-Ortega, J. 2006. The cast against B. F. Skinner 45 years later: An encounter with N. Chomsky. *The Behavior Analyst*, 29, 243–51.

Wahlund, R. and K.-E. Wärneryd, 1987. Aggregate saving and the saving behavior of saver groups, *Skandinaviska Enskilda Banken Quarterly Review*, 3, 52–64.

Wang, H-C., Pallister, J. G. and Foxall, G. R. 2006a. Innovativeness and Involvement as Determinants of Website Loyalty: I. A Test of the Style/Involvement Model in the Context of Internet Buying, *Technovation*, 26, 1357–65.

Wang, H-C., Pallister, J. G. and Foxall, G. R. 2006b. Innovativeness and Involvement as Determinants of Website Loyalty: II. Determinants of Consumer Loyalty in B2C e-Commerce, *Technovation*, 26, 1366–73.

Wang, H-C., Pallister, J. G. and Foxall, G. R. 2006c. Innovativeness and Involvement as Determinants of Website Loyalty: III. Theoretical and Managerial Contributions, *Technovation*, 26, 1374–83.

Wärneryd, K.-E. 1989a. On the psychology of saving: an essay on economic behavior, *Journal of Economic Psychology*, 10, 515–41.

Wärneryd, K.-E. 1989b. Improving psychological theory through studies of economic behavior: the case of saving, *Applied Psychology: An International Review*, 38, 213–36.

Webb, S. 1994. Witnessed behavior and Dennett's intentional stance. *Philosophical Topics, 22,* 457–70.

White, G. M. 1980. Conceptual universals in interpersonal language. *American Anthropologist,* 82, 759–81.

Wiggins, J. S. and Broughton, R. 1985. The interpersonal circle: A Structural model for integration of personality research. In Hogan, R. and Jones, W. H. (eds) *Perspectives in Personality,* Vol. 1, pp. 1–48. Greenwich, CT: JAI Press.

Wilkins, J. S. 2005. Is "meme" a new "idea"? Reflections on Aunger, *Biology and Philosophy,* 20, 585–98.

Wilson, E. O. 1998. *Consilience.* New York: Knopf.

Winger, G., Woods, J. H., Galuska, C. M. and Wade-Galuska, T. 2005. Behavioral perspectives on the neuroscience of drug addiction. *Journal of the Experimental Analysis of Behavior,* 84, 667–81.

Winkielman, P., Berridge, K. C. and Wilbarger, J. L. 2005. Emotion, behavior, and conscious experience. In Barrett, L. F., Niedenthal, P. M. and Winkielman, P. (eds) *Emotion and Consciousness,* pp. 335–62. New York: The Guilford Press.

Wittgenstein, L. 1953. *Philosophical Investigations.* (Ed. Anscombe, G. E. M. and Rhees, R., trans. Anscombe, G. E. M.). Oxford: Blackwell.

Yani-de-Soriano, M. Y. and Foxall, G. R. 2002. Emotional Responses to consumers' environments: An empirical examination of the behavioural perspective model in a Latin American context. *Journal of Consumer Behaviour,* 2, 138–54.

Yani-de-Soriano, M. and Foxall, G. R. 2006. The emotional power of place: The fall and rise of dominance in retail research, *Journal of Retailing and Consumer Services,* in press.

Zettle, R. D. and Hayes, S. C. 1982. Rule-governed behavior: a potential framework for cognitive-behavioral therapy. In Kendall, P. C. (ed.) *Advances in Cognitive-Behavioral Research and Therapy,* pp. 73–117. New York: Academic Press.

Zuriff, G. R. 1979. Ten inner causes. *Behaviorism, 7,* 1–8.

Index